Fifth Workshop on Syntax, Semantics and Structure in Statistical Translation 2011

(SSST-5)

Held at ACL HLT 2011

Portland, Oregon, USA
23 June 2011

Editors:

Dekai Wu
Marianna Apidianaki
Marine Carpuat
Lucia Specia

ISBN: 978-1-61839-257-2

Printed from e-media with permission by:

Curran Associates, Inc.
57 Morehouse Lane
Red Hook, NY 12571

Some format issues inherent in the e-media version may also appear in this print version.

Printed by Curran Associates, Inc. (2011)

Association for Computational Linguistics
209 N. Eighth Street
Stroudsburg, Pennsylvania 18360

Phone: 1-570-476-8006
Fax: 1-570-476-0860

acl@aclweb.org

Additional copies of this publication are available from:

Curran Associates, Inc.
57 Morehouse Lane
Red Hook, NY 12571 USA
Phone: 845-758-0400
Fax: 845-758-2634
Email: curran@proceedings.com
Web: www.proceedings.com

Introduction

The Fifth Workshop on Syntax, Semantics and Structure in Statistical Translation (SSST-5) was held on 23 June 2011 following the ACL HLT 2011 conference in Portland, Oregon. Like the first four SSST workshops in 2007, 2008, 2009, and 2010, it aimed to bring together researchers from different communities working in the rapidly growing field of structured statistical models of natural language translation.

During these past five years, statistical machine translation research has seen a movement toward not only tree-structured and syntactic models incorporating stochastic synchronous/transduction grammars, but also increasingly semantic models. There is no doubt that issues of deep syntax and shallow semantics are closely linked, and this encouraging trend has been reflected at recent SSST workshops. Semantic SMT research now includes context-dependent WSD (word sense disambiguation) for SMT (Carpuat and Wu 2007, 2008; Chan, Ng and Chiang 2007; Giménez and Màrquez 2007); SRL (semantic role labeling) for SMT (Wu and Fung 2009); and SRL for MT evaluation (Lo and Wu 2010, 2011).

In order to emphasize structure and representation at semantic and not only syntactic levels, "Semantics" has been explicitly added to the name of this year's Workshop (the acronym remains SSST), and is a special workshop theme.

We selected 15 papers for this year's workshop. Many either directly fall under the special theme of Semantics in SMT, or span the area between deep syntax and shallow semantics, illustrating the variety of semantic representations and models that are relevant to current statistical MT.

SRL predicate-argument structure clearly emerges as a useful representation for many aspects of SMT and MT evaluation. Wu and Palmer show that it is possible to automatically learn accurate cross-lingual SRL mappings between Chinese and English SRL annotated bitext. Input-side SRL is used to define reordering rules for Chinese-English word alignment (Meyers, Kosaka, Liao and Xue), and to improve pairwise translation hypothesis ranking (Pighin and Màrquez). Output-side SRL informs rule extraction in hierarchichal phrase-based SMT (Gao and Vogel), and provides structure for meaningfully comparing translation hypotheses and references in MT evaluation (Lo and Wu).

WSD also emerges as a prominent research direction with semantically richer SMT models designed to address ambiguity in translation lexical choice. Banchs and Costa-jussa use Latent Semantic Indexing to build a context-dependent phrase-based SMT model. Jiang, Du and Way integrate input paraphrases into SMT via confusion networks. Lefever and Hoste show that dedicated classifiers learned on parallel corpora outperform phrase-based SMT on a cross-lingual WSD task. SMT can also be seen as a tool to enrich semantic resources: McCrae, Espinoza, Ponsoda, Aguado-de-Cea and Cimiano propose several strategies for automatically translating ontologies and taxonomies, leveraging their rich semantic structure to compensate for the weakness of standard text translation methods.

A rich range of syntactic and tree-based approaches for learning translation rules is also seen. Attardi, Chanev and Miceli Barone learn reordering rules for a decoding approach drivenby a input-side dependency parser to guide reordering. Hanneman and Lavie describe a method for inducing nonterminals in synchronous/transduction grammars, by clustering nonterminal-pairs across input and output languages. Na and Lee propose a method for encoding alternative binarizations of a single input-side dependency tree into a forest by merging vertices before extracting translation rules. Hanneman,

Burroughs and Lavie extract synchronous/transduction grammar rules combining input-side and output-side parse tree information with the highly lexicalized approach of hierarchical phrase-based methods. Input-side parse features are incorporated within a maximum-entropy reordering approach by Xiang, Ge and Ittycheriah. On the formal side, Saers and Wu show how to simplify calculation of rule expectations for expectation-maximization training of transduction grammars as well as monolingual grammars, by reifying rules directly into the hypergraph representation of a deductive system so that a rule becomes an extra child rather than meta-information of a hyperedge.

Thanks once again this year are due to our authors and our Program Committee for making the SSST workshop another success.

Dekai Wu, Marianna Apidianaki, Marine Carpuat, and Lucia Specia

Acknowledgements

This work was supported in part by the Defense Advanced Research Projects Agency (DARPA) under GALE Contract Nos. HR0011-06-C-0022, subcontract BBN Technologies and HR0011-06-C-0023, subcontract SRI International, and by the Hong Kong Research Grants Council (RGC) research grant GRF621008 (Dekai Wu); Alpage INRIA (Marianna Apidianaki); the National Research Council Institute for Information Technology (Marine Carpuat); and the Defense Advanced Research Projects Agency (DARPA) under GALE Contract No. HR0011-08-C-0110, subcontract IBM (Lucia Specia). Any opinions, findings and conclusions or recommendations expressed in this material are those of the authors and do not necessarily reflect the views of the Defense Advanced Research Projects Agency.

Organizers:

Dekai WU, Hong Kong University of Science and Technology (HKUST), Hong Kong

Co-chairs for special theme on Semantics in SMT:

Marianna APIDIANAKI, Alpage, INRIA and University Paris 7, France
Marine CARPUAT, National Research Council (NRC), Canada
Lucia SPECIA, University of Wolverhampton, UK

Program Committee:

Eneko AGIRRE, University of the Basque Country, Spain
Colin CHERRY, National Research Council (NRC), Canada
Marc DYMETMAN, Xerox Research Center Europe, France
Hieu HOANG, University of Edinburgh, UK
Philipp KOEHN, University of Edinburgh, UK
Philippe LANGLAIS, University of Montreal, Canada
Aurélien MAX, Université Paris Sud 11, France
Diana MCCARTHY, Lexical Computing, UK
Sudip Kumar NASKAR, Dublin City University, Ireland
Roberto NAVIGLI, University of Rome "La Sapienza", Italy
Hwee Tou NG, National University of Singapore, Singapore
Sebastian PADO, Universität Heidelberg, Germany
Martha PALMER, University of Colorado, USA
Ted PEDERSEN, University of Minnesota, USA
Markus SAERS, Hong Kong University of Science and Technology (HKUST), Hong Kong
Matthew SNOVER, City University of New York, USA
Nicolas STROPPA, Google, Switzerland
François YVON, Université Paris Sud 11, France

Table of Contents

Conference Program

Session 1

09:00 Opening Remarks

09:15 *Automatic Projection of Semantic Structures: an Application to Pairwise Translation Ranking*
Daniele Pighin and Lluís Màrquez

09:40 *Structured vs. Flat Semantic Role Representations for Machine Translation Evaluation*
Chi-kiu Lo and Dekai Wu

10:05 *Semantic Mapping Using Automatic Word Alignment and Semantic Role Labeling*
Shumin Wu and Martha Palmer

10:30 Coffee Break / Poster Session

Incorporating Source-Language Paraphrases into Phrase-Based SMT with Confusion Networks
Jie Jiang, Jinhua Du and Andy Way

Multi-Word Unit Dependency Forest-based Translation Rule Extraction
Hwidong Na and Jong-Hyeok Lee

An Evaluation and Possible Improvement Path for Current SMT Behavior on Ambiguous Nouns
Els Lefever and Véronique Hoste

Improving Reordering for Statistical Machine Translation with Smoothed Priors and Syntactic Features
Bing Xiang, Niyu Ge and Abraham Ittycheriah

Session 2

11:00 *Reestimation of Reified Rules in Semiring Parsing and Biparsing*
Markus Saers and Dekai Wu

11:25 *A Dependency Based Statistical Translation Model*
Giuseppe Attardi, Atanas Chanev and Antonio Valerio Miceli Barone

11:50 *Improving MT Word Alignment Using Aligned Multi-Stage Parses*
Adam Meyers, Michiko Kosaka, Shasha Liao and Nianwen Xue

12:15 Lunch

Automatic Projection of Semantic Structures: an Application to Pairwise Translation Ranking

Daniele Pighin Lluís Màrquez
TALP Research Center
Universitat Politècnica de Catalunya
{pighin,lluism}@lsi.upc.edu

Abstract

We present a model for the inclusion of semantic role annotations in the framework of confidence estimation for machine translation. The model has several interesting properties, most notably: 1) it only requires a linguistic processor on the (generally well-formed) source side of the translation; 2) it does not directly rely on properties of the translation model (hence, it can be applied beyond phrase-based systems). These features make it potentially appealing for system ranking, translation re-ranking and user feedback evaluation. Preliminary experiments in pairwise hypothesis ranking on five confidence estimation benchmarks show that the model has the potential to capture salient aspects of translation quality.

1 Introduction

The ability to automatically assess the quality of translation hypotheses is a key requirement towards the development of accurate and dependable translation models. While it is largely agreed that proper transfer of predicate-argument structures from source to target is a very strong indicator of translation quality, especially in relation to adequacy (Lo and Wu, 2010a; 2010b), the incorporation of this kind of information in the Statistical Machine Translation (SMT) evaluation pipeline is still limited to few and isolated cases, e.g., (Giménez and Màrquez, 2010).

In this paper, we propose a general model for the incorporation of predicate-level semantic annotations in the framework of Confidence Estimation (CE) for machine translation, with a specific focus on the sub-problem of pairwise hypothesis ranking. The model is based on the following underlying assumption: by observing how automatic alignments project semantic annotations from source to target in a parallel corpus, it is possible to isolate features that are characteristic of good translations, such as movements of specific arguments for some classes of predicates. The presence (or absence) of these features in automatic translations can then be used as an indicator of their quality. It is important to stress that we are *not* claiming that the projections preserve the meaning of the original annotation. Still, it should be possible to observe regularities that can be helpful to rank alternative translation hypotheses.

The general workflow (which can easily be extended to cope with different annotation layers, such as sequences of meaningful phrase boundaries, named entities or sequences of chunks or POS tags) is exemplified in Figure 1. During training (on the left), the system receives a parallel corpus of source sentences and the corresponding reference translations. Source sentences are annotated with a linguistic processor. The annotations are projected using training alignments, obtaining *gold* projections that we can use to learn a model that captures correct annotation movements, i.e., observed in reference translations. At test time, we want to assess the quality of a translation hypothesis given a source sentence. As shown on the right side of Figure 1, the first part of the process is the same as during training: the source sentence is annotated, and the annotation is projected onto the translation hypothesis via automatic alignments. The model is then used

Proceedings of SSST-5, Fifth Workshop on Syntax, Semantics and Structure in Statistical Translation, pages 1–9,
ACL HLT 2011, Portland, Oregon, USA, June 2011.

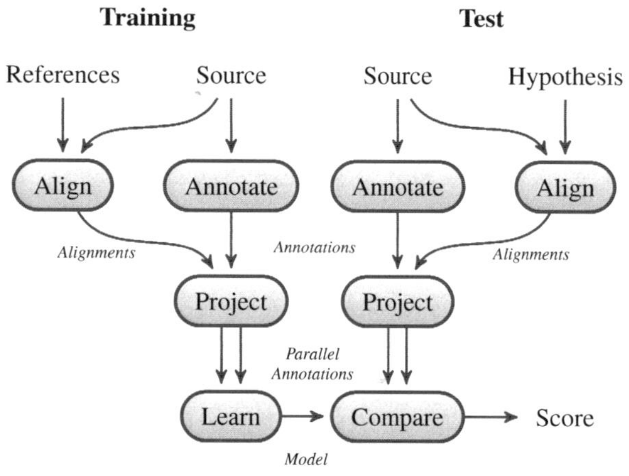

Figure 1: Architectural overview.

to compare the observed projection against the *expected* projection given the source annotation. The distance between the two projections (observed and expected) can then be used as a measure of the quality of the hypothesis.

As it only considers one-sided annotations, our framework does not require the availability of comparable linguistic processors and linguistic annotations, tagsets, etc., on both sides of the translation process. In this way, it overcomes one of the main obstacles to the adoption of linguistic analysis for MT confidence estimation. Furthermore, the fact that source data is generally well-formed lowers the requirements on the linguistic processor in terms of robustness to noisy data, making it possible to employ a wider range of linguistic processors.

Within this framework, in this paper we describe our attempt to bridge Semantic Role Labeling (SRL) and CE by modeling proposition-level semantics for pairwise translation ranking. The extent to which this kind of annotations are transferred from source to target has indeed a very high correlation with respect to human quality assessments (Lo and Wu, 2010a; 2010b). The measure that we propose is then an ideal addition to already established CE measures, e.g., (Specia et al., 2009; Blatz et al., 2004), as it attempts to explicitly model the adequacy of translation hypotheses as a function of predicate-argument structure coverage. While we are aware of the fact that the current definition of the model can be improved in many different ways, our preliminary investigation, on five English to Spanish translation benchmarks, shows promising accuracy on the difficult task of pairwise translation ranking, even for translations with very few distinguishing features.

To capture different aspects of the projection of SRL annotations we employ two instances of the abstract architecture shown in Figure 1. The first works at the *proposition level*, and models the correct movement of arguments from source to target. The second works at the *argument level*, and models the fluency and adequacy of individual arguments within each predicate-argument structure. The *models* that we learn during training are simple phrase-based translation models working on different kinds of sequences, i.e., role labels in the former case and words in the latter. To evaluate the adequacy of an automatically projected proposition or argument, we force the corresponding translation model to generate it (via constrained decoding). The reachability and confidence of each translation are features that we exploit to compare alternative translations, by combining them in a simple voting scheme.

To score systems which are not under our direct control (the typical scenario in CE benchmarks), we introduce a component that generates source-target alignments for any pair of aligned test sentences. This addition has the nice property of allowing us to handle the translation as a black-box, decoupling the evaluation from a specific system and, in theory, allowing the model to cope with phrase-based, rule-based or hierarchical systems alike, as well as with human-generated translations.

The rest of the paper is structured as follows: in Section 2 we will review a selection of related work; in Section 3 we will detail our approach; in Section 4 we will present the results of our evaluation; finally, in Section 5 we will draw our conclusions.

2 Related work

Confidence estimation is the sub-problem within MT evaluation concerned with the assessment of translation quality in the absence of reference translations. A relevant initial work on this topic is the survey by Blatz et al. (2004), in which the authors define a rich set of features based on source data, translation hypotheses, n-best lists and model characteristics to classify translations as "good" or "bad". In their observations, they conclude that the most relevant features are those based on source/target pairs and on characteristics of the translation model.

Specia et al. (2009) build on top these results by designing a feature-selection framework for confidence estimation. Translations are considered as black-boxs (i.e., no system or model-dependent features are employed), and novel features based on the number of content words, a POS language model on the target side, punctuation and number matchers in source and target translations and the percentage of uni-grams are introduced. Features are selected via Partial Least Squares (PLS) regression (Wold et al., 1984). Inductive Confidence Machines (Papadopoulos et al., 2002) are used to estimate an optimal threshold to distinguish between "good" and "bad" translations. Even though the authors show that a small set of shallow features and some supervision can produce good results on a specific benchmark, we are convinced that more linguistic features are needed for these methods to perform better across a wider spectrum of domains and applications.

Concerning the usage of SRL for SMT, Wu and Fung (2009) reported a first successful application of semantic role labels to improve translation quality. They note that improvements in translation quality are not reflected by traditional MT evaluation metrics (Doddington, 2002; Papineni et al., 2002) based on n-gram overlaps. To further investigate the topic, Lo and Wu (2010a; 2010b) involved human annotators to demonstrate that the quality of semantic role projection on translated sentences is very highly correlated with human assessments.

Giménez and Màrquez (2010) describe a framework for MT evaluation and meta-evaluation combining a rich set of n-gram-based and linguistic metrics, including several variants of a metric based on SRL. Automatic and reference translations are annotated independently, and the lexical overlap between corresponding arguments is employed as an indicator of translation quality. The authors show that syntactic and semantic information can achieve higher reliability in system ranking than purely lexical measures.

Our original contribution lies in the attempt to exploit SRL for assessing translation quality in a CE scenario, i.e., in the absence of reference translations. By accounting for whole predicate-argument sequences as well as individual arguments, our model has the potential to capture aspects which relate both to the adequacy and to the fluency of a translation. Furthermore, we outline a general framework for the inclusion of linguistic processors in CE that has the advantage of requiring resources and software tools only on the source side of the translation, where well-formed input can reasonably be expected.

3 Model

The task of semantic role labeling (SRL) consists in recognizing and automatically annotating semantic relations between a *predicate* word (not necessarily a verb) and its *arguments* in natural language texts. The resulting predicate-argument structures are commonly referred to as *propositions*, even though we will also use the more general term *annotations*.

In PropBank (Palmer et al., 2005) style annotations, which our model is based on, predicates are generally verbs and roles are divided into two classes: core roles (labeled A0, A1, ... A5), whose semantic value is defined by the predicate syntactic frame, and adjunct roles (labeled AM-*, e.g., AM-TMP or AM-LOC) [1] which are a closed set of verb-independent semantic labels accounting for predicate aspects such as temporal, locative, manner or purpose. For instance, in the sentence "The commission met to discuss the problem" we can identify two predicates, *met* and *discuss*. The corresponding annotations are "[$_{\text{A0}}$ The commission] [$_{\text{pred}}$ met] [$_{\text{AM-PRP}}$ to discuss the problem]" and "[$_{\text{A0}}$ The commission] met to [$_{\text{pred}}$ discuss] [$_{\text{A1}}$ the problem]". Here, A0 and A1 play the role of prototypical subject and object, respectively, and AM-PRP is an adjunct modifier expressing a notion of purpose.

Sentence annotations are inherently non-sequential, as shown by the previous example in which the predicate and one of the arguments of the second proposition (i.e., *discuss* and A1) are completely embedded within an argument of the first proposition (i.e., AM-PRP). Following a widely adopted simplification, the annotations in a sentence are modeled independently. Furthermore we de-

[1] The actual role labels are in the form Arg0, ... Arg1 and ArgM-*, but we prefer to adopt their shorter form.

scribe each annotation at two levels: a *proposition level*, where we model the movement of arguments from source to target; and an *argument level*, were we model the adequacy and fluency of individual argument translations. The comparison of two alternative translations takes into account all these factors but it models each of them independently, i.e., we consider how properly each propositions is rendered in each hypothesis, and how properly each argument is translated within each proposition.

3.1 Annotation and argument projection

At the proposition level, we simply represent the sequence of role-label in each proposition, ignoring their lexical content with the exception of the predicate word. Considering the previous example, the sentence would then be represented by the two sequences "A0 met AM-PRP" and "A0 * discuss A1". In the latter case, the special character "*" marks a "gap" between A0 and the predicate word. The annotation is projected onto the translation via direct word alignments obtained through a constrained machine translation process (i.e., we force the decoder to generate the desired translation). Eventual discontinuities in the projection of an argument are modeled as gaps. If two arguments insist on a shared subset of words, then their labels are combined. If the projection of an argument is a subset of the projection of the predicate word, then the argument is discarded. If the overlap is partial, then the non-overlapping part of the projection is represented.

If a word insertion occurs next to an argument or the predicate, then we include it in the final sequence. This decision is motivated by the consideration that insertions at the boundary of an argument may be a clue of different syntactic realizations of the same predicate across the two languages (Levin, 1993). For example, the English construct "*A0 give A2 A1*" could be rendered as "*doy A1 a A2*" in Spanish. Here, the insertion of the preposition "*a*" at decoding can be an important indicator of translation quality.

This level of detail is insufficient to model some important features of predicate-argument structures, such as inter-argument semantic or syntactic dependencies, but it is sufficient to capture a variety of interesting linguistic phenomena. For instance, A0-predicate inversion translating SVO into VSO languages, or the convergence of multiple source arguments into a single target argument when translating into a morphologically richer language. We should also stress again that we are not claiming that the structures that we observe on the target side are linguistically motivated, but only that they contain relevant clues to assess quality aspects of translation.

As for the representation of individual arguments, we simply represent their surface form, i.e., the sequence of words spanning each argument. So, for example, the argument representations extracted from "[$_{\text{A0}}$ The commission] [$_{\text{pred}}$ met] [$_{\text{AM-PRP}}$ to discuss the problem]" would be "*The commission*", "*met*", "*to discuss the problem*". To project each argument we align all its words with the target side. The leftmost and the rightmost aligned words define the boundaries of the argument in the target sentence. All the words in between (including eventual gaps) are considered as part of the projection of the argument. This approach is consistent with PropBank style annotations, in which arguments are contiguous word sequences, and it allows us to employ a standard translation model to evaluate the fluency of the argument projection. The rationale here is that we rely on proposition level annotations to convey the semantic structure of the sentence, while at the argument level we are more interested in evaluating the lexical appropriateness of their realization.

The projection of a proposition and its arguments for an example sentence is shown in Figure 2. Here, s is the original sentence and h_1 and h_2 are two translation hypotheses. The figure shows how the whole proposition (p) and the predicate word ($pred$) along with its arguments (*A0, A1* and *A2*) are represented after projection on the two hypotheses. As we can observe, in both cases *thank* (the predicate word) gets aligned with the word *gracias*. For h_1, the decoder aligns *I* (A0) to *doy*, leaving a gap between A0 and the predicate word. The gap gets filled by generating the word *las*. Since the gap is adjacent to at least one argument, *las* is included in the representation of p for h_1. In h_2, the projection of A0 exactly overlaps the projection of the predicate ("Gracias"), and therefore A0 is not included in n for h_2.

3.2 Comparing hypotheses

At test time, we want to use our model to compare translation pairs and recognize the most reli-

s	I thank the commissioner for the detailed reply		
h_1	Doy las gracias al comisario por la detallada respuesta		
h_2	Gracias , al señor comisario por para el respuesta		
p	A0 thank A1 A2	**pred**	thank
h_1	A0 +las gracias A1 A2	h_1	gracias
h_2	Gracias A1 A2	h_2	Gracias
A1	the commissioner	**A0**	I
h_1	al comisario	h_1	doy
h_2	al señor comisario	h_2	Gracias
A2	for the detailed reply		
h_2	por la detallada respuesta		
h_2	para el respuesta		

Figure 2: Comparison between two alternative translations h_1 and h_2 for the source sentence s.

able. Let s be the source sentence, and h_1 and h_2 be two translation hypotheses. For each proposition p in s, we assign a confidence value to its representation in h_1 and h_2, i.e., p_1 and p_2, by forcing the proposition-level translation system to generate the projection observed in the corresponding hypothesis. The reachability of p_1 (respectively, p_2) and the decoder confidence in translating p as p_1 are used as features to estimate p_1 (p_2) accuracy. Similarly, for each argument a in each proposition p we generate its automatic projection on h_1 and h_2, i.e., a_1 and a_2. We force the argument-level decoder to translate a into a_1 and a_2, and use the respective reachability and translation confidence as features accounting for their appropriateness.

The best translation hypothesis (h_1 or h_2) is then selected according to the following decision function:

$$h^* = \arg\max_{i \in \{0,1\}} \sum_k \mathrm{f}_k(h_i, h_{j \neq i}, s) \qquad (1)$$

where each feature function $\mathrm{f}_k(\cdot,\cdot,\cdot)$ defines a comparison measure between its first two arguments, and returns 1 if the first argument is greater (better) than the second, and 0 otherwise. In short, the decision function selects the hypothesis that wins the highest number of comparisons.

The feature functions that we defined account for the following factors, the last three being evaluated once for each proposition in s: (1) Number of successfully translated propositions; (2) Average translation confidence for projected propositions; (3) Number of times that a proposition in h_i has higher confidence than the corresponding proposition in $h_{i \neq j}$; (4) Number of successfully translated arguments; (5) Average translation confidence for projected arguments; (6) Number of times that an argument in h_i has higher confidence than the corresponding argument in $h_{i \neq j}$.

With reference to Figure 2, the two translation hypotheses have been scored 4 (very good) and 2 (bad) by human annotators. The score assigned by the proposition decoder to p_1 is higher than p_2, hence comparisons (2) and (3) are won by h_1. According to the arguments decoder, h_1 does a better job at representing A0 and A2; h_2 is better at rendering A1, and *pred* is a tie. Therefore, h_1 also prevails according to (6). Given the very high confidence assigned to the translation of A2 in h_1, the hypothesis also prevails in (5). In this case, (1) and (4) do not contribute to the decision as the two projections have the same coverage.

4 Evaluation

In this section, we present the results obtained by applying the proposed method to the task of ranking consistency, or pairwise ranking of alternative translations: that is, given a source sentence s, and two candidate translations h_1 and h_2, decide which one is a better translation for s. Pairwise ranking is a simplified setting for CE that is general enough to model the selection of the best translation among a finite set of alternatives. Even though it cannot measure translation quality in isolation, a reliable pairwise ranking model would be sufficient to solve many common practical CE problems, such as system ranking, user feedback filtering or hypotheses re-ranking.

4.1 Datasets

We ran our experiments on the human assessments released as part of the ACL Workshops on Machine Translations in 2007 (Callison-Burch et al., 2007), 2008 (Callison-Burch et al., 2008), 2009 (Callison-Burch et al., 2009) and 2010 (Callison-Burch et al., 2010). These datasets will be referred to as *wmtYY(t)* in the remainder, *YY* being the last two digits of the year of the workshop and $t = n$ for newswire data or $t = e$ for Europarl data. So, for example, *wmt08e* is the Europarl test set of the 2008 edition of the workshop. As our system is trained on Europarl data, newswire test sets are to be considered out-of-domain. All the experiments are relative to English to Spanish translations.

The *wmt08*, *wmt09* and *wmt10* datasets provide a ranking among systems within the range [1,5] (1 being the worst system, and 5 the best). The different datasets contain assessments for a different number of systems, namely: 11 for *wmt08(e)*, 10 for *wmt08(n)*, 9 for *wmt09* and 16 for *wmt10n*. Generally, multiple annotations are available for each annotated sentence. In all cases in which multiple assessments are available, we used the average of the assessments.

The *wmt07* dataset would be the most interesting of all, in that it provides separate assessments for the two main dimensions of translation quality, adequacy and fluency, as well as system rankings. Unluckily, the number of annotations in this dataset is very small, and after eliminating the ties the numbers are even smaller. As results on such small numbers would not be very representative, we decided not to include them in our evaluation.

We also evaluated on the dataset described in (Specia et al., 2010), which we will refer to as *specia*. As the system is based on Europarl data, it is to be considered an in-domain benchmark. The dataset includes results produced by four different systems, each translation being annotated by only one judge. Given the size of the corpus (the output of each system has been annotated on the same set of 4,000 sentences), this dataset is the most representative among those that we considered. It is also especially interesting for two other reasons: 1) systems are assigned a score ranging from 1 (*bad*) to 4 (*good as it is*) based on the number of edits required to produce a publication-ready translation. Therefore, here we have an absolute measure of translation accuracy, as opposed to relative rankings; 2) each system involved in the evaluation has very peculiar characteristics, hence they are very likely to generate quite different translations for the same input sentences.

4.2 Setup

Our model consists of four main components: an automatic semantic role labeler (to annotate source sentences); a lexical translation model (to generate the alignments required to map the annotations onto a translation hypothesis); a translation model for predicate-argument structures, to assign a score to projected annotations; and a translation model for role fillers, to assign a score to the projection of each argument.

To automatically label our training data with semantic roles we used the Swirl system[2] (Surdeanu and Turmo, 2005) with the bundled English models for syntactic and semantic parsing. On the CoNLL-2005 benchmark (Carreras and Màrquez, 2005), Swirl sports an F1-measure of 76.46. This figure drops to 75 for mixed data, and to 65.42 on out-of-domain data, which we can regard as a conservative estimate of the accuracy of the labeler on *wmt* benchmarks.

For all the translation tasks we employed the Moses phrase-based decoder[3] in a single-factor configuration. The `-constraint` command line parameter is used to force Moses to output the desired translation. For the English to Spanish lexical translation model, we used an already available model learned using all available *wmt10e* data.

To build the *proposition level* translation system, we first annotated all the English sentences from the *wmt10e* (en→es) training set with Swirl; then, we forced the lexical translation model to generate the alignments for the reference translations and projected the annotations on the target side. The process resulted in 2,493,476 parallel annotations. 5,000 annotations were held-out for model tuning. The training data was used to estimate a 5-gram language model and the translation model, which we later optimized on held-out data.

As for the *argument level* translator, we trained it on parallel word sequences spanning the same role in an annotation and its projection. Each such pair constitutes a training example for the argument translator, each argument representation being modeled independently from the others. With the same setup used for the proposition translator, we collected 4,578,480 parallel argument fillers from *wmt10e* en→es training data, holding out 20,000 pairs for model tuning.

[2] `http://www.surdeanu.name/mihai/swirl/`
[3] `http://www.statmt.org/moses/`

4.3 A note on recall

The main limitation of the model in its current implementation is its low recall. The translation model that we use to generate the alignments is mostly responsible for it. In fact, in approximately 35% of the cases the constrained translation model is not able to generate the required hypothesis. An obvious improvement would consist in using just an alignment model for this task, instead of resorting to translation, for instance following the approach adopted in (Esplà et al., 2011). It should also be noted that, while this component adds the interesting property of decoupling the measure from the system that produced the hypothesis, it is not strictly necessary in all those cases in which translation alignments are already available, e.g., for N-best re-ranking.

The second component that suffers from recall problems is the semantic role labeler, which fails in annotating sentences in approximately 6% of the remaining cases. These failures are by and large due to the lack of proper verbal predicates in the target sentence, and as such expose a limiting factor of the underlying model. In another 3% of the cases, an annotation is produced but it cannot be projected on the hypothesis, since the predicate word on the target side gets deleted during translation.

Another important consideration is that no measure for CE is conceived to be used in isolation, and our measure is no exception. In combination with others, the measure should only trigger when appropriate, i.e., when it is able to capture interesting patterns that are significant to discriminate translation quality. If it abstains, the other measures would compensate for the missing values. In this respect, we should also consider that not being able to produce a translation may be inherently considered an indicator of translation quality.

specia	Corr	Wrong	Und(%)	Acc(%)
$d = 1$	1076	656	14.26	62.12
$d = 2$	272	84	11.00	76.40
$d = 3$	30	8	13.64	78.95
$d \geq 1$	1378	748	13.72	**64.82**
$d \geq 2$	302	92	11.26	76.65
$d \geq 3$	30	8	13.64	78.95
wmt10n	Corr	Wrong	Und(%)	Acc(%)
$d = 1$	428	374	15.04	53.37
$d = 2$	232	196	18.01	54.21
$d = 3$	98	74	16.50	56.98
$d \geq 1$	784	664	16.20	**54.14**
$d \geq 2$	356	290	17.60	55.11
$d \geq 3$	124	94	16.79	56.88
wmt09n	Corr	Wrong	Und(%)	Acc(%)
$d = 1$	70	60	19.75	53.85
$d = 2$	30	40	20.45	42.86
$d = 3$	26	10	18.18	72.22
$d \geq 1$	134	116	19.87	**53.60**
$d \geq 2$	64	56	20.00	53.33
$d \geq 3$	34	16	19.35	68.00
wmt08n	Corr	Wrong	Und(%)	Acc(%)
$d = 1$	64	36	12.28	64.00
$d = 2$	26	24	19.35	52.00
$d = 3$	12	6	18.18	66.67
$d \geq 1$	104	70	14.71	**59.77**
$d \geq 2$	40	34	17.78	54.05
$d \geq 3$	14	10	14.29	58.33
wmt08e	Corr	Wrong	Und(%)	Acc(%)
$d = 1$	62	34	21.31	64.58
$d = 2$	40	30	10.26	57.14
$d = 3$	22	8	11.76	73.33
$d \geq 1$	134	80	15.75	**62.62**
$d \geq 2$	72	46	10.61	61.02
$d \geq 3$	32	16	11.11	66.67

Table 1: Results on five confidence estimation benchmarks. An *n* next to the task name (e.g. wmt08n) stands for a news (i.e. out of domain) corpus, whereas an *e* (e.g. wmt08e) stands for a Europarl (i.e. in domain) corpus. The *specia* corpus is in-domain.

4.4 Results

Table 1 lists, in each block of rows, pairwise classification accuracy results obtained on a specific benchmark. The benchmarks are sorted in order of reverse relevance, the largest benchmark (*specia*) being listed first. In each row, we show results obtained for different configurations in which the variable is the distance d between two assessment scores. So, for example, the row $d = 1$ accounts for all the comparisons in which the distance between scores is exactly one, while row $d \geq 2$ considers all the cases in which the distance is at least 2. For each test, the columns show: the number of correct (*Corr*) and wrong (*Wrong*) decisions, the percentage of undecidable cases (*Und*), i.e., the cases in which the scoring function cannot decide between the two hypotheses, and the accuracy of classification (*Acc*) measured without considering the unbreakable ties.

The accuracy for $d \geq 1$, i.e., on all the available annotations, is shown in bold.

First, we can observe that the results are above the baseline (an accuracy of 50% for evenly distributed binary classification) on all the benchmarks and for all configurations. The only outlier is *wmt09n* for $d = 2$, with an accuracy of 42.86%. Across the different datasets, results vary from promising (*specia* and *wmt08e*, where accuracy is generally above 60%) to mildly good (*wmt10n*), but across all the board the method seems to be able to provide useful clues for confidence estimation.

As expected, the accuracy of classification tends to increase as the difference between hypotheses becomes more manifest. In four cases out of six, the accuracy for $d = 3$ is above 60%, with the notable peaks on *specia*, *wmt09n* and *wmt08e* where it goes over 70% (on the first, it arrives almost at 80%). Unluckily, very few translations have very different quality (a measure of the difficulty of the task). Nevertheless, the general trend seems to support the reliability of the approach.

When we consider the results on the whole datasets (i.e., $d \geq 1$), pairwise classification accuracy ranges from 54% (for *wmt09n* and *wmt10n*, both out-of-domain), to 63-64% (for *specia* and *wmt08e*, both in-domain). Interestingly, the performance on *wmt08n*, which is also out-of-domain, is closer to in-domain benchmarks, i.e., 60%. These figures suggest that the method is consistently reliable on in-domain data, but also out-of-domain evaluation can benefit from its application. The difference in performance between *wmt08n* and the other out-of-domain benchmarks will be reason of further investigation as future work, as well as the drop in performance for $d = 2$ on three of the benchmarks.

5 Conclusions

We have presented a model to exploit the rich information encoded by predicate-argument structures for confidence estimation in machine translation. The model is based on a battery of translation systems, which we use to study the movement and the internal representation of propositions and arguments projected from source to target via automatic alignments. Our preliminary results, obtained on five different benchmarks, suggest that the approach is well grounded and that semantic annotations have the potential to be successfully employed for this task.

The model can be improved in many ways, its major weakness being its low recall as discussed in Section 4.3. Another area in which there is margin for improvement is the representation of predicate argument structures. It is reasonable to assume that different representations could yield very different results. Introducing more clues about the semantic content of the whole predicate argument structure, e.g., by including argument head words in the representation of the proposition, or considering a more fine-grained representation at the proposition level, could make it possible to assess the quality of a translation reducing the need to back-off to individual arguments. As for the representation of arguments, a first and straightforward improvement would be to train a separate model for each argument class, or to move to a factored model that would allow us to model explicitly the insertion of words or the overlap of argument words due to the projection.

Another important research direction involves the combination of this measure with already assessed metric sets for CE, e.g., (Specia et al., 2010), to understand to what extent it can contribute to improve the overall performance. In this respect, we would also like to move from a heuristic scoring function to a statistical model.

Finally, we would like to test the generality of the approach by designing other features based on the same "annotate, project, measure" framework, as we strongly believe that it is an effective yet simple way to combine several linguistic features for machine translation evaluation. For example, we would like to apply a similar framework to model the movement of chunks or POS sequences.

Acknowledgments

We would like to thank the anonymous reviewers for their valuable comments. This research has been partially funded by the Spanish Ministry of Education and Science (OpenMT-2, TIN2009-14675-C03) and the European Community's Seventh Framework Programme (FP7/2007-2013) under grant agreement numbers 247762 (FAUST project, FP7-ICT-2009-4-247762) and 247914 (MOLTO project, FP7-ICT-2009-4-247914).

References

John Blatz, Erin Fitzgerald, George Foster, Simona Gandrabur, Cyril Goutte, Alex Kulesza, Alberto Sanchis, and Nicola Ueffing. 2004. Confidence estimation for machine translation. In *Proceedings of the 20th international conference on Computational Linguistics*, COLING '04, Stroudsburg, PA, USA. ACL.

Chris Callison-Burch, Philipp Koehn, Cameron Shaw Fordyce, and Christof Monz, editors. 2007. *Proceedings of the Second Workshop on Statistical Machine Translation*. ACL, Prague, Czech Republic.

Chris Callison-Burch, Philipp Koehn, Christof Monz, Josh Schroeder, and Cameron Shaw Fordyce, editors. 2008. *Proceedings of the Third Workshop on Statistical Machine Translation*. ACL, Columbus, Ohio.

Chris Callison-Burch, Philipp Koehn, Christof Monz, and Josh Schroeder, editors. 2009. *Proceedings of the Fourth Workshop on Statistical Machine Translation*. ACL, Athens, Greece.

Chris Callison-Burch, Philipp Koehn, Christof Monz, Kay Peterson, and Omar Zaidan, editors. 2010. *Proceedings of the Joint Fifth Workshop on Statistical Machine Translation and MetricsMATR*. ACL, Uppsala, Sweden.

Xavier Carreras and Lluís Màrquez. 2005. Introduction to the CoNLL-2005 shared task: Semantic role labeling. In *Proceedings of the Ninth Conference on Computational Natural Language Learning (CoNLL-2005)*, pages 152–164, Ann Arbor, Michigan, June. Association for Computational Linguistics.

George Doddington. 2002. Automatic evaluation of machine translation quality using n-gram co-occurrence statistics. In *Proceedings of the second international conference on Human Language Technology Research*, HLT '02, pages 138–145, San Francisco, CA, USA. Morgan Kaufmann Publishers Inc.

Miquel Esplà, Felipe Sánchez-Martínez, and Mikel L. Forcada. 2011. Using word alignments to assist computer-aided translation users by marking which target-side words to change or keep unedited. In *Proceedings of the 15th Annual Conference of the European Associtation for Machine Translation*.

Jesús Giménez and Lluís Màrquez. 2010. Linguistic measures for automatic machine translation evaluation. *Machine Translation*, 24:209–240. 10.1007/s10590-011-9088-7.

Beth Levin. 1993. *English Verb Classes and Alternations*. The University of Chicago Press.

Chi-kiu Lo and Dekai Wu. 2010a. Evaluating machine translation utility via semantic role labels. In *Proceedings of the Seventh conference on International Language Resources and Evaluation (LREC'10)*, Valletta, Malta. European Language Resources Association (ELRA).

Chi-kiu Lo and Dekai Wu. 2010b. Semantic vs. syntactic vs. n-gram structure for machine translation evaluation. In *Proceedings of the 4th Workshop on Syntax and Structure in Statistical Translation*, pages 52–60, Beijing, China.

Martha Palmer, Daniel Gildea, and Paul Kingsbury. 2005. The Proposition Bank: An Annotated Corpus of Semantic Roles. *Comput. Linguist.*, 31(1):71–106.

Harris Papadopoulos, Kostas Proedrou, Volodya Vovk, and Alexander Gammerman. 2002. Inductive confidence machines for regression. In *AMAI'02*.

Kishore Papineni, Salim Roukos, Todd Ward, and Wei-Jing Zhu. 2002. BLEU: a method for automatic evaluation of machine translation. In *Proceedings of the 40th Annual Meeting on Association for Computational Linguistics*, ACL '02, pages 311–318, Stroudsburg, PA, USA. ACL.

Lucia Specia, Marco Turchi, Zhuoran Wang, John Shawe-Taylor, and Craig Saunders. 2009. Improving the confidence of machine translation quality estimates. In *Machine Translation Summit XII*, Ottawa, Canada.

Lucia Specia, Nicola Cancedda, and Marc Dymetman. 2010. A dataset for assessing machine translation evaluation metrics. In *Proceedings of the Seventh conference on International Language Resources and Evaluation (LREC'10)*, Valletta, Malta. European Language Resources Association (ELRA).

Mihai Surdeanu and Jordi Turmo. 2005. Semantic role labeling using complete syntactic analysis. In *Proceedings of the Ninth Conference on Computational Natural Language Learning (CoNLL-2005)*, pages 221–224, Ann Arbor, Michigan, June. Association for Computational Linguistics.

S. Wold, A. Ruhe, H Wold, and W.J. Dunn. 1984. The collinearity problem in linear regression. the partial least squares (pls) approach to generalized inverses. 5:735–743.

Dekai Wu and Pascale Fung. 2009. Semantic roles for SMT: a hybrid two-pass model. In *Proceedings of Human Language Technologies: The 2009 Annual Conference of the North American Chapter of the Association for Computational Linguistics, Companion Volume: Short Papers*, NAACL-Short '09, pages 13–16, Stroudsburg, PA, USA. ACL.

Structured vs. Flat Semantic Role Representations for Machine Translation Evaluation

Chi-kiu Lo and **Dekai Wu**
HKUST
Human Language Technology Center
Dept. of Computer Science and Engineering
Hong Kong University of Science and Technology
{jackielo|dekai}@cs.ust.hk

Abstract

We argue that failing to capture the degree of contribution of each semantic frame in a sentence explains puzzling results in recent work on the MEANT family of semantic MT evaluation metrics, which have disturbingly indicated that dissociating semantic roles and fillers from their predicates actually improves correlation with human adequacy judgments even though, intuitively, properly segregating event frames should more accurately reflect the preservation of meaning. Our analysis finds that both properly structured and flattened representations fail to adequately account for the contribution of each semantic frame to the overall sentence. We then show that the correlation of HMEANT, the human variant of MEANT, can be greatly improved by introducing a simple length-based weighting scheme that approximates the degree of contribution of each semantic frame to the overall sentence. The new results also show that, without flattening the structure of semantic frames, weighting the degree of each frame's contribution gives HMEANT higher correlations than the previously best-performing flattened model, as well as HTER.

1 Introduction

In this paper we provide a more concrete answer to the question: what would be a better representation, structured or flat, of the roles in semantic frames to be used in a semantic machine translation (MT) evaluation metric? We compare recent studies on the MEANT family of semantic role labeling (SRL) based MT evaluation metrics (Lo and Wu, 2010a,b, 2011a,b) by (1) contrasting their variations in semantic role representation and observing disturbing comparative results indicating that segregating the event frames in structured role representation actually *damages* correlation against human adequacy judgments and (2) showing how SRL based MT evaluation can be improved beyond the current state-of-the-art compared to previous MEANT variants as well as HTER, through the introduction of a simple weighting scheme that reflects the degree of contribution of each semantic frame to the overall sentence. The weighting scheme we propose uses a simple length-based heuristic that reflects the assumption that a semantic frame that covers more tokens contributes more to the overall sentence translation. We demonstrate empirically that when the degree of each frame's contribution to its sentence is taken into account, the properly structured role representation is more accurate and intuitive than the flattened role representation for SRL MT evaluation metrics.

For years, the task of measuring the performance of MT systems has been dominated by lexical n-gram based machine translation evaluation metrics, such as BLEU (Papineni *et al.*, 2002), NIST (Doddington, 2002), METEOR (Banerjee and Lavie, 2005), PER (Tillmann *et al.*, 1997), CDER (Leusch *et al.*, 2006) and WER (Nießen *et al.*, 2000). These metrics are excellent at ranking overall systems by averaging their scores over entire documents. However, as MT systems improve, the shortcomings of such metrics are becoming more apparent. Though containing roughly the correct words, MT output at the sentence remains often quite incomprehensible, and fails to preserve the meaning of the input. This results from the fact that n-gram based metrics are not as reliable at ranking the adequacy of translations of individual sentences, and are particularly

Proceedings of SSST-5, Fifth Workshop on Syntax, Semantics and Structure in Statistical Translation, pages 10–20,
ACL HLT 2011, Portland, Oregon, USA, June 2011. ©2011 Association for Computational Linguistics

poor at reflecting translation quality improvements involving more meaningful word sense or semantic frame decisions—which human judges have no trouble distinguishing. Callison-Burch *et al.* (2006) and Koehn and Monz (2006), for example, study situations where BLEU strongly disagrees with human judgment of translation quality.

Newer avenues of research seek substitutes for n-gram based MT evaluation metrics that are better at evaluating translation adequacy, particularly at the sentence level. One line of research emphasizes more the structural correctness of translation. Liu and Gildea (2005) propose STM, a metric based on syntactic structure, that addresses the failure of lexical similarity based metrics to evaluate translation grammaticality. However, the problem remains that a grammatical translation can achieve a high syntax-based score yet still make significant errors arising from confusion of semantic roles. On the other hand, despite the fact that non-automatic, manually evaluated metrics, such as HTER (Snover *et al.*, 2006), are more adequacy oriented exhibit much higher correlation with human adequacy judgment, their high labor cost prohibits widespread use. There has also been work on explicitly evaluating MT adequacy by aggregating over a very large set of linguistic features (Giménez and Màrquez, 2007, 2008) and textual entailment (Pado *et al.*, 2009).

2 SRL based MT evaluation metrics

A blueprint for more direct assessment of meaning preservation across translation was outlined by Lo and Wu (2010a), in which translation utility is manually evaluated with respect to the accuracy of semantic role labels. A good translation is one from which human readers may successfully understand at least the basic event structure—"who did what to whom, when, where and why" (Pradhan *et al.*, 2004)–which represents the most essential meaning of the source utterances. Adopting this principle, the MEANT family of metrics compare the semantic frames in reference translations against those that can be reconstructed from machine translation output.

Preliminary results reported in (Lo and Wu, 2010b) confirm that the blueprint model outperforms BLEU and similar n-gram oriented evaluation metrics in correlation against human adequacy judgments, but does not fare as well as HTER. The more complete study of Lo and Wu (2011a) introduces MEANT and its human variants HMEANT, which implement an extended version of blueprint methodology. Experimental results show that HMEANT correlates against human adequacy judgments as well as the more expensive HTER, even though HMEANT can be evaluated using low-cost untrained monolingual semantic role annotators while still maintaining high inter-annotator agreement (both are far superior to BLEU or other surface oriented evaluation metrics). The study also shows that replacing the human semantic role labelers with an automatic shallow semantic parser yields an approximation that is still vastly superior to BLEU while remaining about 80% as closely correlated with human adequacy judgments as HTER. Along with additional improvements to the accuracy of the MEANT family of metrics, Lo and Wu (2011b) study the impact of each individual semantic role to the metric's correlation against human adequacy judgments, as well as the time cost for humans to reconstruct the semantic frames and compare the translation accuracy of the role fillers.

In general, the MEANT family of SRL MT evaluation metrics (Lo and Wu, 2011a,b) evaluate the translation utility as follows. First, semantic role labeling is performed (either manually or automatically) on both the reference translation (**REF**) and the machine translation output (**MT**) to obtain the semantic frame structure. Then, the semantic predicates, roles and fillers reconstructed from the MT output are compared to those in the reference translations. The number of correctly and partially correctly annotated arguments of each type in each frame of the MT output are collected in this step:

$$\begin{aligned}
C_{i,j} &\equiv \text{\# correct ARG i of PRED i in MT} \\
P_{i,j} &\equiv \text{\# partially correct ARG j of PRED i in MT} \\
M_{i,j} &\equiv \text{total \# ARG j of PRED i in MT} \\
R_{i,j} &\equiv \text{total \# ARG j of PRED i in REF}
\end{aligned}$$

In the following three subsections, we describe how the translation utility is calculated using these counts in (a) the original blueprint model, (b) the first version of HMEANT and MEANT using structured role representations, and (c) the more accu-

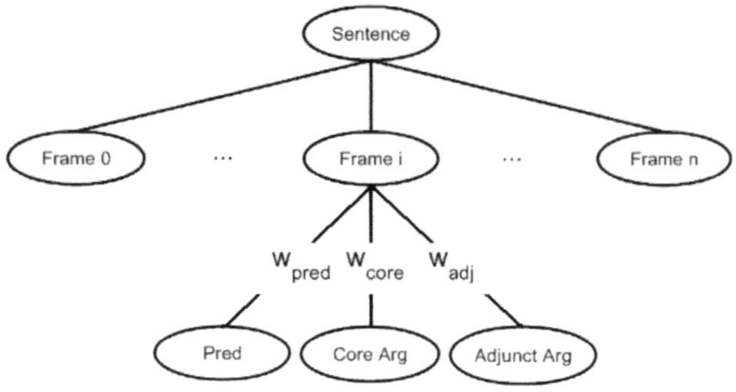

Figure 1: The structured role representation for the blueprint SRL-based MT evaluation metric as proposed in Lo and Wu (2010a,b), with arguments aggregated into core and adjunct classes.

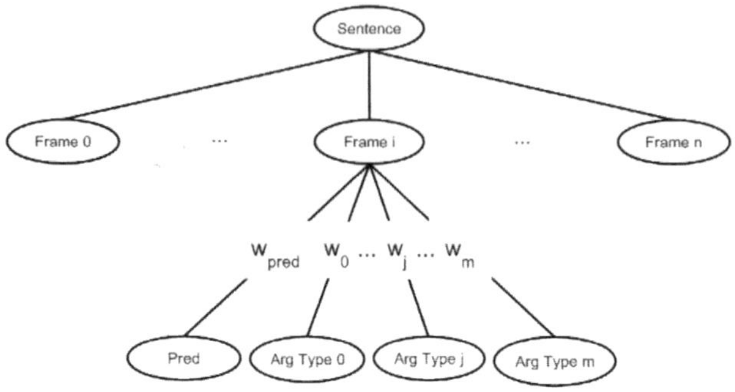

Figure 2: The structured role representation for the MEANT family of metrics as proposed in Lo and Wu (2011a).

rate flattened-role implementation of HMEANT and MEANT.

2.1 Structured core vs. adjunct role representation

Figure 1 depicts the semantic role representation in the blueprint model of SRL MT evaluation metric proposed by Lo and Wu (2010a,b). Each sentence consists of a number of frames, and each frame consists of a predicate and two classes of arguments, either core or adjunct. The frame precision/recall is the weighted sum of the number of correctly translated roles (where arguments are grouped into the core and adjunct classes) in a frame normalized by the weighted sum of the total number of all roles in that frame in the MT/REF respectively. The sentence precision/recall is the sum of the frame precision/recall for all frames averaged by the total number of frames in the MT/REF respectively. The SRL evaluation metric is then defined in terms of f-score in order to balance the sentence precision and recall. More precisely, assuming the above definitions of $C_{i,j}$, $P_{i,j}$, $M_{i,j}$ and $R_{i,j}$, the sentence precision and recall are defined as follows.

$$\text{precision} = \frac{\sum_i \frac{w_{\text{pred}} + \sum_t w_t \left(\sum_{j \in t} (C_{i,j} + w_{\text{partial}} P_{i,j})\right)}{w_{\text{pred}} + \sum_t w_t \left(\sum_{j \in t} M_{i,j}\right)}}{\#\text{ frames in MT}}$$

$$\text{recall} = \frac{\sum_i \frac{w_{\text{pred}} + \sum_t w_t \left(\sum_{j \in t} (C_{i,j} + w_{\text{partial}} P_{i,j})\right)}{w_{\text{pred}} + \sum_t w_t \left(\sum_{j \in t} R_{i,j}\right)}}{\#\text{ frames in REF}}$$

where w_{pred} is the weight for predicates, and w_t where $t \in \{\text{core}, \text{adj}\}$ is the weight for core arguments and adjunct arguments. These weights represent the degree of contribution of the predicate and different classes of arguments (either core or adjunct) to the overall meaning of the semantic frame they attach to. In addition, w_{partial} is a weight controlling the degree to which "partially correct" translations are penalized. All the weights can be automatically estimated by optimizing the correlation with human adequacy judgments.

We conjecture that the reason for the low correlation with human adequacy judgments of this model as reported in Lo and Wu (2010b) is that the abstraction of arguments actually reduces the representational power of the original predicate-argument structure in SRL. Under this representation, all the arguments in the same class, e.g. all adjunct arguments, are weighted uniformly. The assumption that all types of arguments in the same class have the same degree of contribution to their frame is obviously wrong, and the empirical results confirm that the assumption is too coarse.

2.2 Structured role representation

Figure 2 shows the structured role representation used in the MEANT family of metrics as proposed in Lo and Wu (2011a), which avoids aggregating arguments into core and adjunct classes. The design of the MEANT family of metrics addresses the incorrect assumption in the blueprint model by assuming each type of argument has a unique weight representing its degree of contribution to the overall sentence translation. Thus, the number of dimensions of the weight vector is increased to allow an independent weight to be assigned to each type of argument. Unlike the previous representation in the blueprint model, there is no aggregation of arguments into core and adjunct classes. Each sentence consists of a number of frames, and each frame consists of a predicate and a number of arguments of type j.

Under the new approach, the frame precision/recall is the weighted sum of the number of correctly translated roles in a frame normalized by the weighted sum of the total number of all roles in that frame in the MT/REF respectively. Similar to the previous blueprint representation, the sentence precision/recall is the sum of the frame precision/recall for all frames averaged by the total number of frames in the MT/REF respectively. More precisely, following the previous definitions of $C_{i,j}$, $P_{i,j}$, $M_{i,j}$, $R_{i,j}$, w_{pred} and w_{partial}, the sentence precision and recall are redefined as follows.

$$\text{precision} = \frac{\sum_i \frac{w_{\text{pred}} + \sum_j w_j (C_{i,j} + w_{\text{partial}} P_{i,j})}{w_{\text{pred}} + \sum_j w_j M_{i,j}}}{\text{\#frames in MT}}$$

$$\text{recall} = \frac{\sum_i \frac{w_{\text{pred}} + \sum_j w_j (C_{i,j} + w_{\text{partial}} P_{i,j})}{w_{\text{pred}} + \sum_j w_j R_{i,j}}}{\text{\# frames in REF}}$$

where w_{j} is the weight for the arguments of type j. These weights represent the degree of contribution of different types of arguments to the overall meaning of their semantic frame.

2.3 Flat role representation

Figure 3 depicts the flat role representation used in the more accurate variants of MEANT as proposed in Lo and Wu (2011b). This representation is motivated by the studies of the impact of individual semantic role. The highly significant difference between this flat representation and both of the previous two structured role representations is that the semantic frames in the sentence are no longer segregated.

The flat role representation desegregates the frame structure, resulting in a flat, single level structure. Therefore, there is no frame precision/recall. The sentence precision/recall is the weighted sum of the number of correctly translated roles in all frames normalized by the weighted sum of the total number of roles in all frames in the MT/REF respectively. More precisely, again assuming the previous definitions of $C_{i,j}$, $P_{i,j}$, $M_{i,j}$, $R_{i,j}$ and w_{partial}, the sentence precision and recall are redefined as follows.

$$\begin{aligned} C_{\text{pred}} &\equiv \text{total \# correctly translated predicates} \\ M_{\text{pred}} &\equiv \text{total \# predicates in MT} \\ R_{\text{pred}} &\equiv \text{total \# predicates in REF} \end{aligned}$$

$$\text{precision} = \frac{w_{\text{pred}} C_{\text{pred}} + \sum_j w_j \left(\sum_i (C_{i,j} + w_{\text{partial}} P_{i,j})\right)}{w_{\text{pred}} M_{\text{pred}} + \sum_j w_j \left(\sum_i M_{i,j}\right)}$$

$$\text{recall} = \frac{w_{\text{pred}} C_{\text{pred}} + \sum_j w_j \left(\sum_i (C_{i,j} + w_{\text{partial}} P_{i,j})\right)}{w_{\text{pred}} R_{\text{pred}} + \sum_j w_j \left(\sum_i R_{i,j}\right)}$$

Note that there is a small modification of the definition of w_{pred} and w_j. Instead of the degree of contribution to the overall meaning of the semantic frame that the roles attached to, $w_{\text{pred}}$and w_j now represent the degree of contribution of the predicate and the arguments of type j to the overall meaning of the *entire* sentence.

It is worth noting that the semantic role features in the ULC metric proposed by Giménez and Màrquez (2008) also employ a flat feature-based representation of semantic roles. However, the definition of those semantic role features adopts a different methodology for determining the role fillers' translation accuracy, which prevents a controlled consistent environment for the comparative experiments that the present work focuses on.

3 Experimental setup

The evaluation data for our experiments consists of 40 sentences randomly drawn from the DARPA GALE program Phase 2.5 newswire evaluation corpus containing Chinese input sentence, English reference translations, and the machine translation from three different state-of-the-art GALE systems. The Chinese and the English reference translation have both been annotated with gold standard PropBank (Palmer *et al.*, 2005) semantic role labels. The weights w_{pred}, w_{core}, w_{adj}, w_j and w_{partial} can be estimated by optimizing correlation against human adequacy judgments, using any of the many standard optimization search techniques. In the work of Lo and

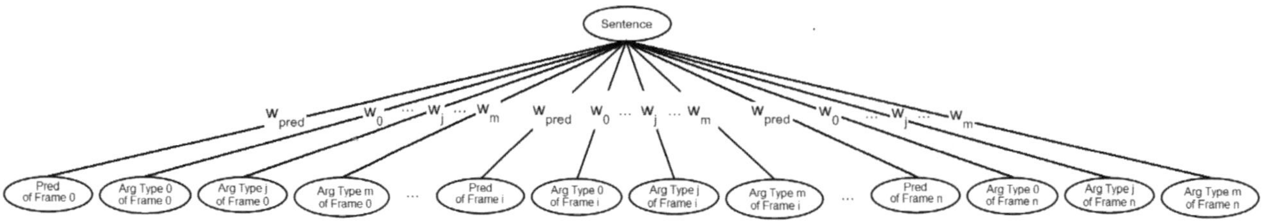

Figure 3: The flat role representation for the MEANT family of metrics as proposed in Lo and Wu (2011b) .

Wu (2011b), the correlations of all individual roles with the human adequacy judgments were found to be non-negative, therefore we found grid search to be quite adequate for estimating the weights. We use linear weighting because we would like to keep the metric's interpretation simple and intuitive.

Following the benchmark assessment in NIST MetricsMaTr 2010 (Callison-Burch *et al.*, 2010), we assess the performance of the semantic MT evaluation metric at the sentence level using the summed-diagonal-of-confusion-matrix score. The human adequacy judgments were obtained by showing all three MT outputs together with the Chinese source input to a human reader. The human reader was instructed to order the sentences from the three MT systems according to the accuracy of meaning in the translations. For the MT output, we ranked the sentences from the three MT systems according to their evaluation metric scores. By comparing the two sets of rankings, a confusion matrix is formed. The summed diagonal of confusion matrix is the percentage of the total count when a particular rank by the metric's score exactly matches the human judgments. The range of possible values of summed diagonal of confusion matrix is [0,1], where 1 means all the systems' ranks determined by the metric are identical with that of the human judgments and 0 means all the systems' ranks determined by the metric are different from that of the human judgment.

Since the summed diagonal of confusion matrix scores only assess the absolute ranking accuracy, we also report the Kendall's τ rank correlation coefficients, which measure the correlation of the proposed metric against human judgments with respect to their relative ranking of translation adequacy. A higher the value for τ indicates the more similar the ranking by the evaluation metric to the human judgment. The range of possible values of correlation coefficient is [-1,1], where 1 means the systems are ranked in the same order as the human judgment and -1 means the systems are ranked in the reverse order as the human judgment.

Table 1: Sentence-level correlations against human adequacy judgments as measured by Kendall's τ and summed diagonal of confusion matrix as used in MetricsMaTr 2010. "SRL - blueprint" is the blueprint model described in section 2.1. "HMEANT (structured)" is HMEANT using the structured role representation described in section 2.2. "HMEANT (flat)" is HMEANT using the flat role representation described in section 2.3.

Metric	Kendall	MetricsMaTr
HMEANT (flat)	**0.4685**	**0.5583**
HMEANT (structured)	0.4324	0.5083
SRL - blueprint	0.3784	0.4667

4 Round 1: Flat beats structured

Our first round of comparative results quantitatively assess whether a structured role representation (that properly preserves the semantic frame structure, which is typically hierarchically nested in compositional fashion) outperforms the simpler (but less intuitive, and certainly less linguistically satisfying) flat role representation.

As shown in table 1, disturbingly, HMEANT using flat role representations yields higher correlations against human adequacy judgments than using structured role representations, regardless of whether role types are aggregated into core and adjunct classes. The results are consistent for both Kendall's tau correlation coefficient and MetricsMaTr's summed diagonal of confusion matrix. HMEANT using a flat role representation achieved a Kendall's tau correlation coefficient and summed diagonal of confusion matrix score of 0.4685 and 0.5583 respectively, which is superior to both

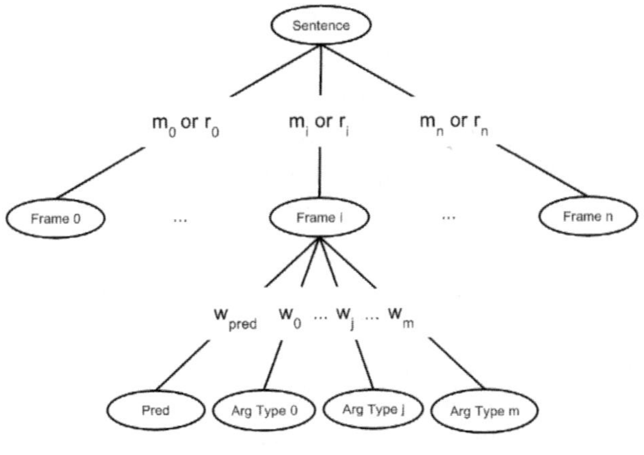

Figure 4: The new proposed structured role representation, incorporating a weighting scheme reflecting the degree of contribution of each semantic frame to the overall sentence.

HMEANT using a structured role representation (0.4324 and 0.5083 respectively) and the blueprint model (0.3784 and 0.4667 respectively).

Error analysis, in light of these surprising results, strongly suggests that the problem lies in the design which uniformly averages the frame precision/recall over all frames in a sentence when computing the sentence precision/recall. This essentially assumes that each frame in a sentence contributes equally to the overall meaning in the sentence translation. Such an assumption is trivially wrong and could well hugely degrade the advantages of using a structured role representation for semantic MT evaluation. This suggests that the structured role representation could be improved by also capturing the degree of contribution of each frame to the overall sentence translation.

5 Capturing the importance of each frame

To address the problem in the previous models, we introduce a weighting scheme to reflect the degree of contribution of each semantic frame to the overall sentence. However, unlike the contribution of each role to a frame, the contribution of each frame to the overall sentence cannot be estimated across sentences. This is because unlike semantic roles, which can be identified by their types, frames do not necessarily have easily defined types, and their construction is also different from sentence to sentence so that the positions of their predicates in the sentence are the only way to identify the frames. However, the degree of contribution of each frame does not depend on the position of the predicate in the sentence. For example, the two sentences I met Tom when I was going home and When I was walking home, I saw Tom have similar meanings. The verbs met and saw are the predicates of the key event frames which contribute more to the overall sentences, whereas going and walking are the predicates of the minor nested event frames (in locative manner roles of the key event frames) and contribute less to the overall sentences. However, the two sentences are realized with different surface constructions, and the two key frames are in different positions. Therefore, the weights learned from one sentence cannot directly be applied to the other sentence.

Instead of estimating the weight of each frame using optimization techniques, we make an assumption that *a semantic frame filled with more word tokens expresses more concepts and thus contributes more to the overall sentence.* Following this assumption, we determine the weights of each semantic frame by its span coverage in the sentence. In other words, the weight of each frame is the percentage of word tokens it covers in the sentence.

Figure 4 depicts the structured role representation with the proposed new frame weighting scheme. The significant difference between this representation and the structured role representation in the MEANT variants proposed in Lo and Wu (2011a) is that each frame is now assigned an independent weight, which is its span coverage in the MT/REF when obtaining the frame precision/recall respectively.

As in Lo and Wu (2011a), each sentence consists of a number of frames, and each frame consists of a predicate and a number of arguments of type j. Each type of argument is assigned an independent weight to represent its degree of contribution to the overall meaning of the semantic frame they attached to. The frame precision/recall is the weighted sum of the number of correctly translated roles in a frame normalized by the weighted sum of the number of all roles in that frame in the MT/REF. The sentence precision/recall is the weighted sum of the frame precision/recall for all frames normalized by the weighted sum of the total number of frames in MT/REF respectively. More precisely, again assuming the earlier definitions of $C_{i,j}$, $P_{i,j}$, $M_{i,j}$, $R_{i,j}$, w_{pred} and w_{partial} in section 2, the sentence precision and recall are redefined as follows.

$$
\begin{aligned}
m_i &\equiv \frac{\text{\# tokens filled in frame i of MT}}{\text{total \# tokens in MT}} \\
r_i &\equiv \frac{\text{\# tokens filled in frame i of REF}}{\text{total \# tokens in REF}}
\end{aligned}
$$

$$
\text{precision} = \frac{\sum_i m_i \frac{w_{\text{pred}} + \sum_j w_j (C_{i,j} + w_{\text{partial}} P_{i,j})}{w_{\text{pred}} + \sum_j w_j M_{i,j}}}{\sum_i m_i}
$$

$$
\text{recall} = \frac{\sum_i r_i \frac{w_{\text{pred}} + \sum_j w_j (C_{i,j} + w_{\text{partial}} P_{i,j})}{w_{\text{pred}} + \sum_j w_j R_{i,j}}}{\sum_i r_i}
$$

where m_{i} and r_{i} are the weights for frame i, in the MT/REF respectively. These weights estimate the degree of contribution of each frame to the overall meaning of the sentence.

6 Round 2: Structured beats flat

We now assess the performance of the new proposed structured role representation, by comparing it with the previous models under the same experimental setup as in section 4. We have also run contrastive experiments against BLEU and HTER under the same experimental conditions. In addition, to investigate the consistency of results for the automated variants of MEANT, we also include comparative experiments where shallow semantic parsing (ASSERT) replaces human semantic role labelers for each model of role representation.

Figure 5 shows an example where HMEANT with the frame weighting scheme outperforms HMEANT using other role representations in correlation against human adequacy judgments. **IN** is the Chinese source input. **REF** is the corresponding reference translation. **MT1**, **MT2** and **MT3** are the three corresponding MT output. The human adequacy judgments for this set of translation are that MT1>MT3>MT2. HMEANT with the proposed frame weighting predicts the same ranking order as the human adequacy judgment, while HMEANT with the flat role representation and HMEANT with the structured role representation without frame weighting both predict MT3>MT1>MT2. There are four semantic frames in IN while there are only three semantic frames in the REF. This is because the predicate • • •in IN is translated in REF as had which is not a predicate. However, for the same frame, both MT1 and MT2 translated ARG1 • • • • • • • •into the predicate affect, while MT3 did not translate the predicate • • •and translated the ARG1 • • • • • •into•the noun phrase adverse impact. Therefore, using the flat role representation or the previous structured role representation which assume all frames have an identical degree of contribution to the overall sentence translation, MT1's and MT2's sentence precision is greatly penalized for having one more extra frame than the reference. In contrast, applying the frame weighting scheme, the degree of contribution of each frame is adjusted by its token coverage. Therefore, the negative effect of the less important extra frames is minimized, allowing the positive effect of correctly translating more roles in more important frames to be more appropriately reflected.

Table 2 shows that HMEANT with the proposed new frame weighting scheme correlates more closely with human adequacy judgments than HMEANT using the previous alternative role representations. The results from Kendall's tau correlation coefficient and MetricsMaTr's summed diagonal of confusion matrix analysis are consistent. HMEANT using the frame-weighted structured role representation achieved a Kendall's tau correlation coefficient and summed diagonal of confusion matrix score of 0.2865 and 0.575 respectively, bettering both HMEANT using the flat role representation (0.4685 and 0.5583) and HMEANT using the previous un-frame-weighted structured role representation (0.4324 and 0.5083).

HMEANT using the improved structured role representation also outperforms other commonly used MT evaluation metrics. It correlates with human adequacy judgments more closely than HTER (0.4324 and 0.425 in Kendall's tau correlation coefficient and summed diagonal of confusion matrix, respectively). It also correlates with human adequacy judgments significantly more closely than BLEU (0.1982 and 0.425).

Turning to the variants that replace human SRL with automated SRL, table 2 shows that MEANT

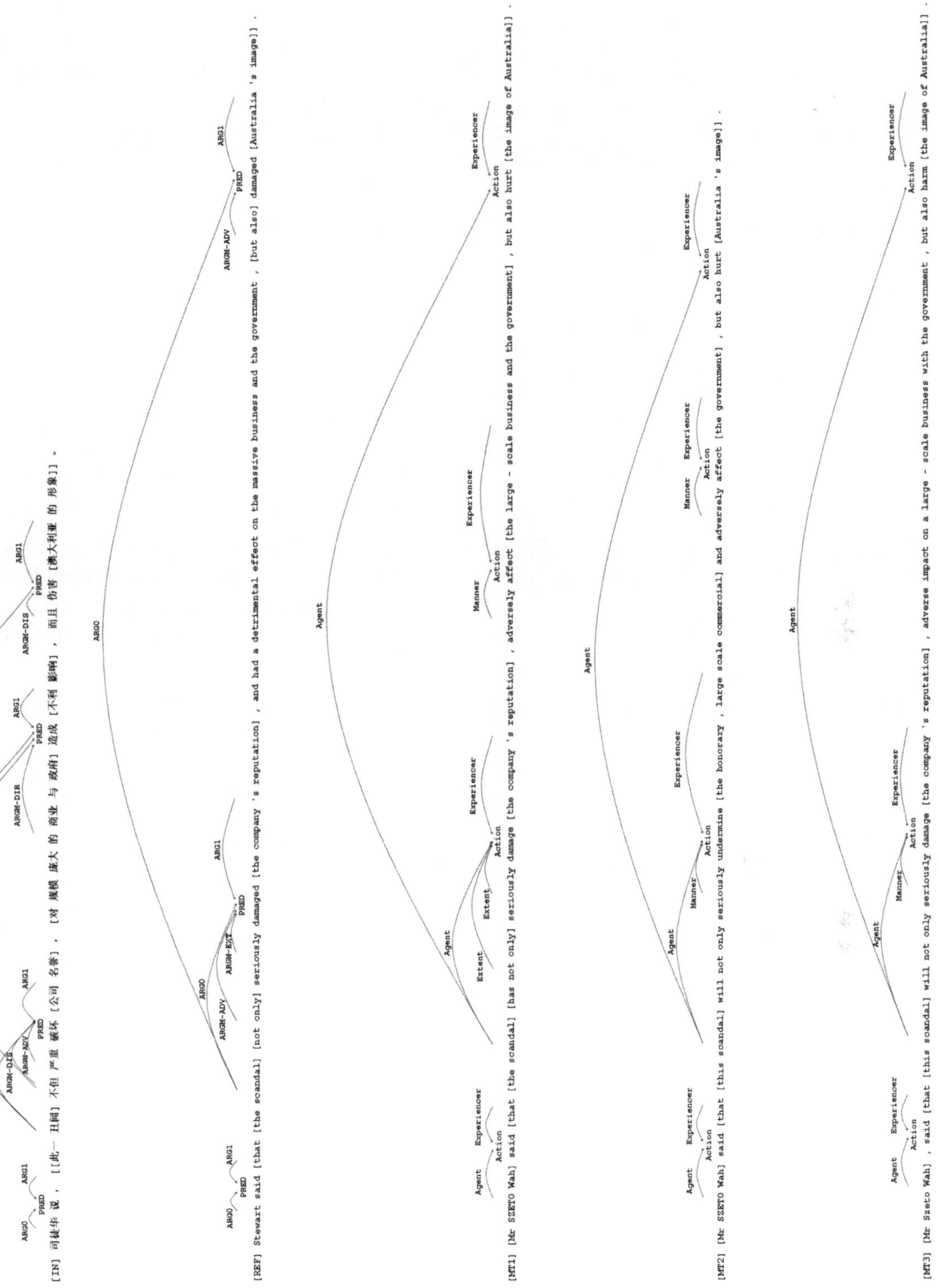

Figure 5: Example input sentence along with reference and machine translations, annotated with semantic frames in Propbank format. The MT output is annotated with semantic frames by minimally trained humans. HMEANT with the new frame-weighted structured role representation successfully ranks the MT output in an order that matches with human adequacy judgments (MT1>MT3>MT2), whereas HMEANT with a flat role representation or the previous un-frame-weighted structured role representation fails to rank MT1 and MT3 in an order that matches with human adequacy judgments. See section 6 for details.

Table 2: Sentence-level correlations against human adequacy judgments as measured by Kendall's τ and summed diagonal of confusion matrix as used in MetricsMaTr 2010. "SRL - blueprint", "HMEANT (structured)" and "HMEANT (flat)" are the same as in table 1. "MEANT (structured)" and "MEANT (flat)" use automatic rather than human SRL. "MEANT (frame)" and "HMEANT (frame)" are MEANT/HMEANT using the structured role representation with the frame weighting scheme described in section 5.

Metric	Kendall	MetricsMaTr
HMEANT (frame)	**0.4865**	**0.575**
HMEANT (flat)	0.4685	0.5583
HMEANT (structured)	0.4324	0.5083
HTER	0.4324	0.425
SRL - blueprint	0.3784	0.4667
MEANT (frame)	0.3514	0.4333
MEANT (structured)	0.3423	0.425
MEANT (flat)	0.3333	0.425
BLEU	0.1982	0.425

using the new frame-weighted structured role representation yields an approximation that is about 81% as closely correlated with human adequacy judgment as HTER, and is better than all previous MEANT variants using alternative role representations. All results consistently confirm that using a structured role representation with the new frame weighting scheme, which captures the event structure and an approximate degree of contribution of each frame to the overall sentence, outperforms using a flat role representation for SRL based MT evaluation metrics.

7 Conclusion

We have shown how the MEANT family of SRL based MT evaluation metrics is significantly improved beyond the state-of-the-art for both HTER and previous variants of MEANT, through the introduction of a simple but well-motivated weighting scheme to reflect the degree of contribution of each semantic frame to the overall sentence translation. Following the assumption that a semantic frame filled with more word tokens tends to express more concepts, the new model weight each frame by its span coverage. Consistent experimental results have been demonstrated under conditions utilizing both human and automatic SRL. Under the new frame weighted representation, properly nested structured semantic frame representations regain an empirically preferred position over the less intuitive and linguistically unsatisfying flat role representations.

One future direction of this work will be to compare MEANT against the feature based and string based representations of semantic relations in ULC. Such a comparison could yield a more complete credit/blame perspective on the representation model when operating under the condition of using automatic SRL.

Another interesting extension of this work would be to investigate the discriminative power of the MEANT family of metrics to distinguish distances in translation adequacy. In this paper we confirmed that the MEANT family of metrics are stable in correlation with human ranking judgments of translation adequacy. Further studies could focus on the correlation of the MEANT family of metrics against human scoring. We also plan to experiment on meta-evaluating MEANT on a larger scale in other genres and for other language pairs.

Acknowledgments

This material is based upon work supported in part by the Defense Advanced Research Projects Agency (DARPA) under GALE Contract Nos. HR0011-06-C-0022 and HR0011-06-C-0023 and by the Hong Kong Research Grants Council (RGC) research grants GRF621008, GRF612806, DAG03/04.EG09, RGC6256/00E, and RGC6083/99E. Any opinions, findings and conclusions or recommendations expressed in this material are those of the authors and do not necessarily reflect the views of the Defense Advanced Research Projects Agency.

References

Satanjeev Banerjee and Alon Lavie. METEOR: An Automatic Metric for MT Evaluation with Improved Correlation with Human Judgments. In *43th Annual Meeting of the Association of Computational Linguistics (ACL-05)*, pages 65–72, 2005.

Chris Callison-Burch, Miles Osborne, and Philipp Koehn. Re-evaluating the role of BLEU in Machine Translation Research. In *13th Confer-*

ence of the European Chapter of the Association for Computational Linguistics (EACL-06), pages 249–256, 2006.

Chris Callison-Burch, Philipp Koehn, Christof Monz, Kay Peterson, Mark Pryzbocki, and Omar Zaidan. Findings of the 2010 Joint Workshop on Statistical Machine Translation and Metrics for Machine Translation. In *Joint 5th Workshop on Statistical Machine Translation and MetricsMATR*, pages 17–53, Uppsala, Sweden, 15-16 July 2010.

G. Doddington. Automatic Evaluation of Machine Translation Quality using N-gram Co-occurrence Statistics. In *2nd International Conference on Human Language Technology Research (HLT-02)*, pages 138–145, San Francisco, CA, USA, 2002. Morgan Kaufmann Publishers Inc.

Jesús Giménez and Lluís Màrquez. Linguistic Features for Automatic Evaluation of Heterogenous MT Systems. In *2nd Workshop on Statistical Machine Translation*, pages 256–264, Prague, Czech Republic, June 2007. Association for Computational Linguistics.

Jesús Giménez and Lluís Màrquez. A Smorgasbord of Features for Automatic MT Evaluation. In *3rd Workshop on Statistical Machine Translation*, pages 195–198, Columbus, OH, June 2008. Association for Computational Linguistics.

Philipp Koehn and Christof Monz. Manual and Automatic Evaluation of Machine Translation between European Languages. In *Workshop on Statistical Machine Translation*, pages 102–121, 2006.

Gregor Leusch, Nicola Ueffing, and Hermann Ney. CDer: Efficient MT Evaluation Using Block Movements. In *13th Conference of the European Chapter of the Association for Computational Linguistics (EACL-06)*, 2006.

Ding Liu and Daniel Gildea. Syntactic Features for Evaluation of Machine Translation. In *ACL Workshop on Intrinsic and Extrinsic Evaluation Measures for Machine Translation and/or Summarization*, page 25, 2005.

Chi-Kiu Lo and Dekai Wu. Evaluating Machine Translation Utility via Semantic Role Labels. In *7th International Conference on Language Resources and Evaluation (LREC-2010)*, 2010.

Chi-Kiu Lo and Dekai Wu. Semantic vs. Syntactic vs. N-gram Structure for Machine Translation Evaluation. In *Proceedings of the 4th Workshop on Syntax and Structure in Statistical Translation (SSST-4)*, 2010.

Chi-Kiu Lo and Dekai Wu. MEANT: An Inexpensive, High-Accuracy, Semi-Automatic Metric for Evaluating Translation Utility based on Semantic Roles. In *Joint conference of the 49th Annual Meeting of the Association for Computational Linguistics : Human Language Technologies (ACL HLT 2011)*, 2011.

Chi-Kiu Lo and Dekai Wu. SMT vs. AI redux: How semantic frames evaluate MT more accurately. In *To appear in 22nd International Joint Conference on Artificial Intelligence*, 2011.

Sonja Nießen, Franz Josef Och, Gregor Leusch, and Hermann Ney. A Evaluation Tool for Machine Translation: Fast Evaluation for MT Research. In *2nd International Conference on Language Resources and Evaluation (LREC-2000)*, 2000.

Sebastian Pado, Michel Galley, Dan Jurafsky, and Chris Manning. Robust Machine Translation Evaluation with Entailment Features. In *Joint conference of the 47th Annual Meeting of the Association for Computational Linguistics and the 4th International Joint Conference on Natural Language Processing of the Asian Federation of Natural Language Processing (ACL-IJCNLP-09)*, 2009.

Martha Palmer, Daniel Gildea, and Paul Kingsbury. The Proposition Bank: an Annotated Corpus of Semantic Roles. *Computational Linguistics*, 31(1):71–106, 2005.

Kishore Papineni, Salim Roukos, Todd Ward, and Wei-Jing Zhu. BLEU: A Method for Automatic Evaluation of Machine Translation. In *40th Annual Meeting of the Association for Computational Linguistics (ACL-02)*, pages 311–318, 2002.

Sameer Pradhan, Wayne Ward, Kadri Hacioglu, James H. Martin, and Dan Jurafsky. Shallow Semantic Parsing Using Support Vector Machines.

In *2004 Conference on Human Language Technology and the North American Chapter of the Association for Computational Linguistics (HLT-NAACL-04)*, 2004.

Matthew Snover, Bonnie J. Dorr, Richard Schwartz, Linnea Micciulla, and John Makhoul. A Study of Translation Edit Rate with Targeted Human Annotation. In *7th Conference of the Association for Machine Translation in the Americas (AMTA-06)*, pages 223–231, 2006.

Christoph Tillmann, Stephan Vogel, Hermann Ney, Arkaitz Zubiaga, and Hassan Sawaf. Accelerated DP Based Search For Statistical Translation. In *5th European Conference on Speech Communication and Technology (EUROSPEECH-97)*, 1997.

Semantic Mapping Using Automatic Word Alignment and Semantic Role Labeling

Shumin Wu
Department of Computer Science
University of Colorado at Boulder
shumin.wu@colorado.edu

Martha Palmer
Department of Linguistics
Univeristy of Colorado at Boulder
martha.palmer@colorado.edu

Abstract

To facilitate the application of semantics in statistical machine translation, we propose a broad-coverage predicate-argument structure mapping technique using automated resources. Our approach utilizes automatic syntactic and semantic parsers to generate Chinese-English predicate-argument structures. The system produced a many-to-many argument mapping for all PropBank argument types by computing argument similarity based on automatic word alignment, achieving 80.5% F-score on numbered argument mapping and 64.6% F-score on all arguments. By measuring predicate-argument structure similarity based on the argument mapping, and formulating the predicate-argument structure mapping problem as a linear-assignment problem, the system achieved 84.9% F-score using automatic SRL, only 3.7% F-score lower than using gold standard SRL. The mapping output covered 49.6% of the annotated Chinese predicates (which contains predicate-adjectives that often have no parallel annotations in English) and 80.7% of annotated English predicates, suggesting its potential as a valuable resource for improving word alignment and reranking MT output.

1 Introduction

As the demand for semantically consistent machine translation rises (Wu and Fung, 2009a), the need for a comprehensive semantic mapping tool has become more apparent. With the current architecture of machine translation decoders, few ways of incorporating semantics in MT output include using word sense disambiguation to select the correct target translation (Carpuat and Wu, 2007) and reordering/reranking MT output based on semantic consistencies (Wu and Fung, 2009b) (Carpuat et al., 2010). While a comprehensive semantic mapping tool can supplement or improve the results of such techniques, there are many other exciting ideas we can explore: with automatic SRL, we can improve coverage (and possibly accuracy) of Chinese semantic class generation (Wu et al., 2010) by running the system on a large, unannotated parallel corpus. Using predicate-argument mappings as constraints, it may be possibly to improve SRL output by performing joint inference of SRL in source and target languages simultaneously, much like what Burkett and Klein (2008) was able to achieve with syntactic parsing.

As the foundation of many machine translation decoders (DeNeefe and Knight, 2009), word alignment has continuously played an important role in machine translation. There have been several attempts to improve word alignment, most of which have focused on tree-to-tree alignments of syntactic structures (Zhang et al., 2007; Mareček, 2009a). Our hypothesis is that the predicate-argument structure alignments can abstract away from language specific syntactic variation and provide a more robust, semantically coherent alignment across sentences.

We begin by running GIZA++ (Och and Ney, 2003), one of the most popular alignment tools, to obtain automatic word alignments between parallel English/Chinese corpora. To achieve a broader coverage of semantic mappings than just those anno-

Proceedings of SSST-5, Fifth Workshop on Syntax, Semantics and Structure in Statistical Translation, pages 21–30,
ACL HLT 2011, Portland, Oregon, USA, June 2011.

tated in parallel PropBank-ed corpora, we attempt to map automatically generated predicate-argument structures. For each Chinese and English verb predicate pairs within a parallel sentence, we examine the quality of both the predicate and argument alignment (using GIZA++ word alignment output) and devise a many-to-many argument mapping technique. From that, we pose predicate-argument mapping as a linear assignment problem (optimizing the total similarity of the mapping) and solve it with the Kuhn-Munkres method (Kuhn, 1955). With this approach, we were able to incur only a small predicate-argument F-score degradation over using manual PropBank annotation. The output also provides much more fine-grained argument mapping that can be used for downstream MT applications.

2 Related work

Our basic approach to semantic mapping is similar to the idea of semantic similarity based on triangulation between parallel corpora outlined in Resnik (2004) and Madnani et al. (2008a; 2008b), but is implemented here quite differently. It is most similar in execution to the work of (Mareček, 2009b), which improves word alignment by aligning tectogrammatical trees in a parallel English/Czech corpus. The Czech corpus is first lemmatized because of the rich morphology, and then the word alignment is "symmetrized". However, this approach does not explicitly make use of the predicate-argument structure to confirm the alignments or to suggest new ones.

Padó and Lapata (2005; 2006) used word alignment and syntax based argument similarity to project English FrameNet semantic roles to German. The approach relied on annotated semantic roles on the source side only, precluding joint inferenece of the projection using reference or automatic target side semantic roles.

Fung et al. (2007) demonstrated that there is poor semantic parallelism between Chinese-English bilingual sentences. Their technique for improving Chinese-English predicate-argument mapping ($ARG_{Chinese,i} \mapsto ARG_{English,j}$) consists of matching predicates with a bilingual lexicon, computing cosine-similarity (based on lexical translation) of arguments and tuning on an unannotated parallel corpus. The system differs from ours in that it only provided one-to-one mapping of numbered arguments and may not be able to detect predicate mapping with no lexical relations that are nevertheless semantically related. Later, Wu and Fung (2009b) used parallel semantic roles to improve MT system outputs. Given the outputs from Moses (Koehn et al., 2007), a machine translation decoder, they reordered the outputs based on the best predicate-argument mapping. The resulting system showed a 0.5 point BLEU score improvement even though the BLEU metric often discounts improvement in semantic consistency of MT output.

Choi et al. (2009) (and later Wu et al. (2010)) showed how to enhance Chinese-English verb alignments by exploring predicate-argument structure alignment using parallel PropBanks. The resulting system showed improvement over pure GIZA++ alignment. Those two systems differs from ours in that they operated on gold standard parses and semantic roles. The systems also did not provide explicit argument mapping between the aligned predicate-argument structures.

3 Resources

To perform automatic semantic mapping, we need an annotated corpus to evaluate the results. In addition, we also need a word aligner, a syntactic parser, and a semantic role labeler (as well as annotated and unannotated corpora to train each system).

3.1 Corpus

We used the portion of the Penn Chinese TreeBank with word alignment annotation as the basis for evaluating semantic mapping. The word-aligned portion, containing around 2000 parallel sentences, is exclusive to Xinhua News (and covers around 50% of the Xinhua corpus in the Chinese TreeBank). We then merged the word alignment annotation with the TreeBank and PropBank annotation of Ontonotes 4.0 (Hovy et al., 2006), which includes a wide array of data sources like broadcast news, news wire, magazine, web text, etc. A small percentage of the 2000 sentences were discarded because of tokenization differences. We dubbed the resulting 1939 parallel sentences as the triple-gold Xinhua corpus.

3.2 Word Alignment

We chose GIZA++ (Och and Ney, 2003) as our word alignment tool primarily because of its popularity, though there are other alternatives like Lacoste-Julien et al. (2006).

3.3 Phrase Structure Parsing

We chose the Berkeley Parser (Petrov and Klein, 2007) for phrase structure parsing since it has been tested on both English and Chinese corpora and can be easily retrained.

3.4 Semantic Role Labeling

For semantic role labeling (SRL), we built our own system using a fairly standard approach: SRL is posed as a multi-class classification problem requiring the identification of argument candidates for each predicate and their argument types. Typically, argument identification and argument labeling are performed in two separate stages because of time/resource constraints during training/labeling. For our system, we chose LIBLINEAR (Fan et al., 2008), a library for large linear classification problems, as the classifier. This alleviated the need to separate the identification and labeling stages: argument identification is trained simply by incorporating the "`NOT-ARG`" label into the training data.

Most the of the features used by the classifier are standard features found in many SRL systems; these include:

Predicate predicate lemma and its POS tag

Voice indicates the voice of the predicate. For English, we used the six heuristics detailed by Igo (2007), which detects both ordinary and reduced passive constructions. For Chinese, we simply detected the presence of passive indicator words (those with `SB`, `LB` POS tags) amongst the siblings of the predicate.

Phrase type phrase type of the constituent

Subcategorization phrase structure rule expanding the predicate parent

Head word the head word and its POS tag of the constituent

Parent head word whether the head word of the parent is the same as the head word of the constituent

Position whether the constituent is before or after the predicate

Path the syntactic tree path from the predicate to the constituent (as well as various path generalization methods)

First word first word and its POS tag of the constituent

Last word last word and its POS tag of the constituent

Syntactic frame the siblings of the constituent

Constituent distance the number of potential constituents with the same phrase type between the predicate and the constituent

We also created many bigrams (and a few trigrams) of the above features.

By default, LIBLINEAR uses the one-vs-all approach for multi-class classification. This does not always perform well for some easily confusable class labels. Also, as noted by Xue (2004), certain features are strong discriminators for argument identification but not for argument labeling, while the reverse is true for others. Under such conditions, mixing arguments and non-arguments within the same class may produce sub-optimal results for a binary classifier. To address these issues, we built a pairwise multi-class classifier (using simple majority voting) on top of LIBLINEAR.

The resulting English SRL system, evaluated using the CoNLL 2005 methodology, achieved a 77.3% F-score on the WSJ corpus, comparable to the leading system (Surdeanu and Turmo, 2005) using a single parser output. The Chinese SRL system, on the other hand, achieved 74.4% F-score on the triple-gold Xinhua corpus (similar but not directly comparable to Wu et al. (2006) and Xue (2008) because of differences in TreeBank/PropBank revisions as well as differences in test set).

4 Predicate-arguments mapping

4.1 Argument mapping

To produce a good predicate-argument mapping, we needed to consider 2 things: whether good argument mapping can be produced based on argument type only, and whether each argument only maps to one argument in the target language.

4.1.1 Predicate-dependent argument mapping

Theoretically, PropBank numbered arguments are supposed to be consistent across predicates: `ARG0` typically denotes the agent of the predicate and `ARG1` the theme. While this consistency may hold true for predicates in the same language, as Fung et al. (2007) noted, this is not a reliable indicator when mapping predicate-arguments between Chinese and English. For example, when comparing the PropBank frames of the English verb *arrive* and the synonymous Chinese verb 抵达, we see `ARG1` (entity in motion) for *arrive*.01 is equivalent to `ARG0` (agent) of 抵达.01 while `ARG4` (end point, destination) is equivalent to `ARG1` (destiny).

4.1.2 Many-to-many argument mapping

Just as there are shortcomings in assuming predicate independent argument mappings, assuming one-to-one argument mapping may also be overly restrictive. For example, in the following Chinese sentence:

大 通道 建设 **搞活** 了 大 西南 的 物流
big passage construction invigorated big southwest's material flow

the predicate 搞活(invigorate) has 2 arguments:

- `ARG0`: 大 通道 建设 (big passage construction)
- `ARG1`: 大 西南 的 物流 (big southwest's material flow)

In the parallel English sentence:

Construction of the main passage has ***activated*** *the flow of materials in the great southwest*

activate has 3 arguments:

- `ARG0`: *construction of the main passage*
- `ARG1`: *the flow of materials*
- `ARGM-LOC`: *in the great southwest*

In these parallel sentences, `ARG1` of 搞活 should be mapped to both `ARG1` and `ARGM-LOC` of *activate*.

While the English translation of 搞活, *invigorate*, is not a direct synonym of *activate*, they at least have some distant relationship as indicated by sharing the inherited hypernym *make* in the WordNet (Fellbaum, 1998) database. The same cannot be said for all predicate-pairs. For example, in the following parallel sentence fragments:

街上 客流 如 潮
on the street people ***flow*** *like the tide*

the Chinese predicate-argument structure for 如(like) is:

- `ARG0`: 客流 (flow of guests)
- `ARG1`: 潮 (tide)
- `ARGM-LOC`: 街上 (on the street)

while the English predicate-argument structure for *flow* is:

- `ARG1`: *people*
- `ARGM-LOC`: *on the street*
- `ARGM-MNR`: *like the tide*

Semantically, the predicate-argument pairs are equivalent. The argument mapping, however, is more complex:

- 如.`ARG0` $\Longleftrightarrow$ *flow*.`ARG1`, *flow*.`V`
- 如.`V`, 如.`ARG1` $\Longleftrightarrow$ *flow*.`ARGM-MNR`
- 如.`ARGM-LOC` $\Longleftrightarrow$ *flow*.`ARGM-LOC`

Table 1 details the argument mapping for the triple-gold Xinhua data. The mapping distribution for `ARG0` and `ARG1` is relatively deterministic (and similar to ones found by Fung et al. (2007)). Mappings involving `ARG2-5` and modifier arguments, on the other hand, are much more varied. Typically, when there is a many-to-many argument mapping, it's constrained to a one-to-two or two-to-one mapping. Much more rarely is there a case of a two-to-two or even more complex mapping.

4.2 Word alignment based argument mapping

To achieve optimal mappings between parallel predicate-argument structure, we would like to maximize the number of words in the mapped argument set (over the entire set of arguments) while minimizing the number of unaligned words in the mapped argument set.

Let $a_{c,i}$ and $a_{c,j}$ denote arguments in Chinese and English respectively, A_I as a set of arguments, $W_{c,i}$ as words in argument $a_{c,i}$, and $map_e(a_i) = W_{e,i}$ as the word alignment function that takes the source argument and produces a set of words in the target

arg type	A0	A1	A2	A3	A4	ADV	BNF	DIR	DIS	EXT	LOC	MNR	PRP	TMP	TPC	V
A0	***1610***	79	25	0	0	28	1	0	0	0	8	5	1	11	1	9
A1	432	***2665***	128	**11**	0	83	**9**	**12**	0	0	29	12	5	21	**3**	142
A2	43	*310*	**140**	8	3	55	6	9	0	**2**	20	10	1	4	1	67
A3	2	14	*21*	7	0	2	4	2	0	0	1	2	1	0	1	4
A4	1	*37*	9	3	**6**	0	0	0	0	0	1	0	1	0	0	4
ADV	33	36	9	6	0	***307***	2	5	6	0	44	**121**	6	11	2	19
CAU	1	0	0	0	0	1	0	0	0	0	0	0	*16*	0	0	1
DIR	1	13	3	2	0	1	0	3	0	0	3	0	0	0	0	*20*
DIS	2	0	0	0	0	*69*	0	0	**40**	0	2	1	3	3	0	0
EXT	0	4	0	0	0	*26*	0	0	0	0	0	0	0	0	0	2
LOC	23	*65*	13	1	0	3	1	0	0	0	**162**	0	0	5	0	4
MNR	9	9	5	0	0	*260*	0	0	0	1	3	34	0	0	0	25
MOD	1	0	0	0	0	*159*	0	0	0	0	0	0	0	0	0	84
NEG	0	0	0	0	0	*24*	0	0	0	0	0	0	0	0	0	5
PNC	3	23	11	4	0	1	6	1	0	0	1	2	***35***	2	0	8
PRD	0	0	*3*	0	0	0	0	0	0	0	0	0	0	0	0	1
TMP	14	21	2	0	0	235	0	3	0	1	8	16	0	***647***	0	6
V	25	28	22	1	0	211	1	0	1	0	2	12	0	0	0	***3278***

Table 1: Chinese argument type (column) to English argument type (row) mapping on triple-gold Xinhua corpus

language sentence. We define precision as the fraction of aligned target words in the mapped argument set:

$$P_{c,I} = \frac{|(\cup_{i \in I} map_e(a_{c,i})) \cap (\cup_{j \in J} W_{e,j})|}{|\cup_{i \in I} map_e(a_{c,i})|} \quad (1)$$

and recall as the fraction of source words in the mapped argument set:

$$R_{c,I} = \frac{\sum_{i \in I} |W_{c,i}|}{\sum_{\forall i} |W_{c,i}|} \quad (2)$$

We then choose $A_{c,I}$ that optimizes the F1-score of P_c and R_c:

$$A_{c,I} = \arg\max_{I} \frac{2 \cdot P_{c,I} \cdot R_{c,I}}{P_{c,I} + R_{c,I}} = F_{c,I} \quad (3)$$

Finally, to constrain both source and target argument set, we optimize:

$$A_{c,I}, A_{e,J} = \arg\max_{I,J} \frac{2 \cdot F_{c,I} \cdot F_{e,J}}{F_{c,I} + F_{e,J}} = F_{IJ} \quad (4)$$

To measure similarity between a single pair of source, target arguments, we define:

$$P_{ij} = \frac{|map_e(a_{c,i}) \cup W_j|}{|map_e(a_{c,i})|}, R_{ij} = \frac{|map_c(a_{e,j}) \cup W_i|}{|map_c(a_{e,j})|} \quad (5)$$

To generate the set of argument mapping pairs, we simply choose all pairs of $a_{c,i}, a_{e,j} \in A_{c,I}, A_{e,J}$ where $F_{ij} \geq \epsilon$ ($\epsilon > 0$).

Directly optimizing equation 4 requires exhaustive search of all argument set combinations between the source and target, which is NP-complete. While the typical number of arguments for each predicate is relatively small, this is nevertheless inefficient. We performed the following greedy-based approximation with quadratic complexity:

1. Compute the best (based on F-score of equation 5) pair of source-target argument mappings for each source argument (target argument may be reused)
2. Select the remaining argument pair with the highest F-score
3. Insert the pair in $A_{c,I}, A_{e,J}$ if it increases F_{IJ}, else discard
4. repeat until all argument pairs are exhausted
5. repeat 1-4 reversing the source and target direction
6. merge the output of the 2 directions

Much like GIZA++ word alignment where the output of each direction produces only one-to-many mappings, merging the output of the two directions produces many-to-many mappings.

4.3 One-to-one predicate-argument mapping

To find the best predicate-argument mapping between Chinese and English parallel sentences, we assume each predicate in a Chinese or English sentence can only map to one predicate in the target sentence. As noted by Wu et al. (2010), this assumption is mostly valid for the Xinhua news corpus, though occasionally, a predicate from one sentence may align more naturally to two predicates in the target sentence. This typically occurs with verb conjunctions. For example the Chinese phrase "观光 旅游" (sightseeing and tour) is often translated to the single English verb "travel". As noted by Xue and Palmer (2009), the Chinese PropBank annotates predicative adjectives, which tend not to have an equivalent in the English PropBank. Additionally, some verbs in one language are nominalized in the other. This results in a good portion of Chinese or English predicates in parallel sentences not having an equivalent in the other language.

With the one-to-one mapping constraint, we optimize the mapping by maximizing the sum of the F1-scores (as defined by equation 4) of the predicates and arguments in the mapping. Let P_C and P_E denote the sets of predicates in Chinese and English respectively, with $G(P_C, P_E) = \{g : P_C \mapsto P_E\}$ as the set of possible mappings between the two predicate sets, then the optimal mapping is:

$$g^* = \arg\max_{g \in G} \sum_{i,j \in g} F_{C_i,E_j} \quad (6)$$

To turn this into a classic linear assignment problem, we define $Cost(P_{C_i}, P_{E_j}) = 1 - F_{C_i,E_j}$, and (6) becomes:

$$g^* = \arg\min_{g \in G} \sum_{i,j \in g} Cost(P_{C,i}, P_{E,j}) \quad (7)$$

(7) can be solved in polynomial time with the *Kuhn-Munkres* algorithm (Kuhn (1955)).

5 Experimental setup

5.1 Reference predicate-argument mapping

To generate reference predicate-argument mappings, we ran the mapping system described in section 4.2 with a cutoff threshold of $F_{C_i,E_j} < 0.65$ (i.e., alignments with F-score below 0.65 are discarded). We reviewed a small random sample of the output and found it to have both high precision and recall, with only occasional discrepancies caused by possible word alignment errors. If one-to-one argument mapping is imposed, the reference predicate-argument mapping will lose 8.2% of the alignments. For mappings using automatic word alignment, we chose a cutoff threshold of $F_{C_i,E_j} < 0.15$. This can easily be tuned for higher precision or recall based on application needs.

5.2 Parser, SRL, GIZA++

We trained the Berkeley parser and our SRL system on Ontonotes 4.0, excluding the triple-gold Xinhua sections as well as the non-English or Chinese sourced portion of the corpus. GIZA++ was trained on 400K parallel Chinese-English sentences from various sources with the default parameters. For the word mapping functions $map_e(a_c)$, $map_c(a_e)$ in equation 5, instead of taking the word alignment intersection of the source-target and target-source directions as Padó and Lapata (2006), we used the two alignment outputs seperately (using the Chinese-English output when projecting Chinese argument to English words, and vice versa). On average (from the 400K corpus), an English sentence contains 28.5% more tokens than the parallel Chinese sentence (even greater at 36.2% for the Xinhua portion). Taking either the intersection or union will significantly affect recall or precision of the alignment.

6 Results

6.1 Semantic role labeling

We first provide some results of the SRL system on the triple-gold Xinhua corpus in table 2. Unlike the conventional wisdom which expects English SRL to outperform Chinese SRL, when running on the Chinese-sourced Xinhua parallel corpus, our SRL actually performed better on Chinese than English (74.4% vs 71.8% F-score). The Berkeley parser output also seemed to be of higher quality on Chinese; the system was able to pick out better constituent candidates in Chinese than English, as evidenced by the higher recall for oracle SRL (92.6% vs 91.1%). Comparing the quality of the output by argument type, we found the only argument type where the Chinese SRL system performed signifi-

language	type	P	R	F1
Chinese	CoNLL	77.9%	71.1%	**74.4%**
	oracle	100%	92.6%	96.1%
	word match	84.8%	74.6%	79.4%
English	CoNLL	75.6%	68.4%	**71.8%**
	oracle	100%	91.1%	95.2%
	word match	82.7%	69.4%	75.5%

Table 2: SRL results on triple-gold Xinhua corpus. "arg match" is the standard CoNLL 2005 evaluation metric, "oracle" is the oracle SRL based on automatic parser output, and "word match" is scoring based on length of argument overlap with the reference

Evaluation	gold	P	R	F1
predicate-argument	yes	88.7%	88.5%	88.6%
	no	84.6%	85.3%	**84.9%**
`A0-5` label	yes	97.8%	96.2%	97.0%
	no	87.0%	74.9%	**80.5%**
`A0-5` span	no	67.9%	57.9%	62.5%
all arg label	yes	84.0%	79.3%	81.6%
	no	70.3%	59.8%	*64.6%*
all arg span	no	61.6%	52.2%	56.5%

Table 3: Predicate-argument mapping results

cantly worse is `ARG0` (almost 10% F-score lower). This is likely caused by dropped pronouns in Chinese sentences (Yang and Xue, 2010), making it harder for both the syntactic and semantic parsers to identify the correct subject.

We also report the SRL result scored at word level instead of at argument level (79.4% F-score for Chinese and 75.5% for English). The CoNLL 2005 shared task scoring (Surdeanu and Turmo, 2005) discounts arguments that are not a perfect word span match, even if the system output is semantically close to the reference argument. While this is important in some applications of SRL, for other applications like improving word alignment with SRL, improving recall on approximate arguments may be a better trade-off than having high precision on perfectly matched arguments. We noticed that while overall improvement in SRL improves both word level and argument level performance, for otherwisely identical systems, we can slightly favor word level performance (up to 1-3% F-score) by including positive training samples that are not a perfect argument match.

6.2 Predicate-argument mapping

Table 3 details the results of Chinese-English predicate-argument mapping. Using automatic SRL and word alignment, the system achieved an 84.9% F-score, only 3.7% F-score less than using gold standard SRL annotation. When looking at only arguments, however, the differences are larger: automatic SRL based output produced an 80.5% F-score for core arguments. While this compares favorably to Fung et al. (2007)'s 72.5% (albeit with different sections of the corpus), it's 16.5% F-score lower than gold SRL based output. When including all arguments, automatic SRL based output achieved 64.6% while the gold SRL based output achieved 81.6%. This indicates that the mapping result for all arguments is limited by errors in word alignment. We also report the results of automatic SRL on both producing the correct argument mappings and word spans (62.5% for core arguments and 56.5% for all arguments). This may be relevant for applications such as joint inference between word alignment and SRL.

We also experimented with discriminative (reweighing) word alignment based on part-of-speech tags of the words to improve the mapping system but were not able to achieve better results. This may be due to the top few POS types accounting for most of the words in a language, therefore it did not prove to be a strong discriminator.

6.3 Mapping coverage

Table 4 provides predicate and word coverage details of the predicate-argument mapping, another potentially relevant statistic for applications of predicate-argument mapping. High coverage of predicates and words in the mappings may provide more relevant constraints to help reorder MT output or rerank word alignment. We expect labeling English nominalized predicate-arguments will help increase both predicate and word coverage in the mapping output.

In order to build a comprehensive probability model of Chinese-English predicate-argument mapping, we applied the mapping technique on an unannotated 400K parallel sentence corpus. Automatic

output	type	language	coverage
triple-gold	predicate	Chinese	50.0%
	predicate	English	81.3%
	word	Chinese	66.0%
	word	English	64.2%
automatic	predicate	Chinese	49.6%
	predicate	English	80.7%
	word	Chinese	57.4%
	word	English	55.4%

Table 4: Predicate-argument mapping coverage. Predicate coverage denotes the number of mapped predicates over all predicates in the corpus, word coverage denotes the number of words in the mapped predicate-arguments over all words in the corpus

language	PropBank verb framesets	appeared in corpus	appeared in mapping
Chinese	16122	8591	7109
English	5473	3689	3121

Table 5: Frameset coverage on the 400K parallel sentence corpus

SRL found 1.6 million Chinese predicate instances and 1.3 million English predicate instances. The mapping system found around 700K predicate-pairs (with $F_{C,E} < 0.3$). Table 5 shows the number of unique verbs in the corpus and contained in the mapping results within the Chinese and English PropBank verb framesets. The corpus also included some verbs that do not appear in PropBank framesets.

7 Conclusion and future work

We proposed a broad-coverage predicate-argument mapping system using automatically generated word alignment and semantic role labeling. We also provided a competitive Chinese and English SRL system using a LIBLINEAR classifier and pairwise multi-class classification approach. By exploring predicate-argument structure, the mapping system is able to generate mappings between semantically similar predicate-argument structures containing non-synonymous predicates, achieving an 84.9% F-score, only 3.7% lower than the F-score of gold-standard SRL based mappings. Utilizing word alignment information, the system was able to provide detailed many-to-many argument mappings (occurs in 8.2% of the reference mappings) for core arguments and modifier arguments, achieving an 80.5% F-score for core arguments and 64.6% F-score for all arguments.

While our experiment with discriminative word alignment based on POS tags did not show improvement, there are other word grouping/weighing metrics like n-gram based clustering, verb classification, term frequency, that may be more appropriate for semantic mapping. With the advent of a predicate-argument annotation resource for nominalization, Ontonotes 5, we plan to update our SRL system to produce nominalized predicate-arguments. This would potentially increase the predicate-argument mapping coverage in the corpus as well as increasing the accuracy of mapping (by reducing the number of unmappable predicate-arguments), making the mapping more useful for downstream applications.

We are also experimenting with a probabilistic approach to predicate-argument mapping to improve the robustness of mapping against word alignment errors. Using the output of the current system on a large corpus, we can establish models for $p(pred_e|pred_c)$, $p(arg_e|pred_c, pred_e, arg_c)$ and refine them through iterations of expectation-maximization. If this approach shows promise, the next step would be to explore integrating the mapping model directly into GIZA++ for joint inference of word alignment and predicate-argument mapping. Other statistical translation specific applications we would like to explore include extensions of MT output reordering (Wu and Fung, 2009b) and reranking using predicate-argument mapping, as well as predicate-argument projection onto the target language as an evaluation metric for MT output.

Acknowledgement

We gratefully acknowledge the support of the National Science Foundation Grants CISE- CRI-0551615, and a grant from the Defense Advanced Research Projects Agency (DARPA/IPTO) under the GALE program, DARPA/CMO Contract No. HR0011-06-C-0022, subcontract from BBN, Inc. Any opinions, findings, and conclusions or recommendations expressed in this material are those of the authors and do not necessarily reflect the views of the National Science Foundation.

References

David Burkett and Dan Klein. 2008. Two languages are better than one (for syntactic parsing). In *Proceedings of the Conference on Empirical Methods in Natural Language Processing*, EMNLP '08, pages 877–886, Stroudsburg, PA, USA. Association for Computational Linguistics.

Marine Carpuat and Dekai Wu. 2007. Improving statistical machine translation using word sense disambiguation. In *The 2007 Joint Conference on Empirical Methods in Natural Language Processing and Computational Natural Language Learning (EMNLP-CoNLL 2007)*, pages 61–72.

Marine Carpuat, Yuval Marton, and Nizar Habash. 2010. Improving arabic-to-english statistical machine translation by reordering post-verbal subjects for alignment. In *Proceedings of the ACL 2010 Conference Short Papers*, ACLShort '10, pages 178–183.

Jinho D. Choi, Martha Palmer, and Nianwen Xue. 2009. Using parallel propbanks to enhance word-alignments. In *Proceedings of ACL-IJCNLP workshop on Linguistic Annotation (LAW'09)*, pages 121–124.

Steve DeNeefe and Kevin Knight. 2009. Synchronous tree adjoining machine translation. In *Proceedings of the 2009 Conference on Empirical Methods in Natural Language Processing (EMNLP'09)*, volume 2, pages 727–736.

R.-E. Fan, K.-W. Chang, C.-J. Hsieh, X.-R. Wang, and C.-J. Lin. 2008. Liblinear: A library for large linear classification. *Journal of Machine Learning Research*, 9:1871–1874.

Christiane Fellbaum. 1998. *WordNet: An Electronic Lexical Database*. MIT Press.

Pascale Fung, Zhaojun Wu, Yongsheng Yang, and Dekai Wu. 2007. Learning bilingual semantic frames: Shallow semantic parsing vs. semantic role projection. In *11th Conference on Theoretical and Methodological Issues in Machine Translation*, pages 75–84.

Eduard Hovy, Mitchell Marcus, Martha Palmer, Lance Ramshaw, and Ralph Weischedel. 2006. Ontonotes: The 90 In *Proceedings of HLT-NAACL 2006*, pages 57–60.

Sean Paul Igo. 2007. Identifying reduced passive voice constructions in shallow parsing environments. Master's thesis, University of Utah.

Philipp Koehn, Hieu Hoang, Alexandra Birch, Chris Callison-Burch, Marcello Federico, Nicola Bertoldi, Brooke Cowan, Wade Shen, Christine Moran, Richard Zens, Chris Dyer, Ondrej Bojar, Alexandra Constantin, and Evan Herbst. 2007. Moses: Open source toolkit for statistical machine translation. In *Proceedings of the Annual Meeting of the Association for Computational Linguistics (ACL'07), demonstration session*, pages 177–180.

Harold W. Kuhn. 1955. The hungarian method for the assignment problem. *Naval Research Logistics Quarterly*, 2:83–97.

Simon Lacoste-Julien, Ben Taskar, Dan Klein, and Michael I. Jordan. 2006. Word alignment via quadratic assignment. In *Proceedings of the main conference on Human Language Technology Conference of the North American Chapter of the Association of Computational Linguistics*, HLT-NAACL '06, pages 112–119, Stroudsburg, PA, USA. Association for Computational Linguistics.

Nitin Madnani, Philip Resnik, Bonnie Dorr, and Richard Schwartz. 2008a. Applying automatically generated semantic knowledge: A case study in machine translation. In *NSF Symposium on Semantic Knowledge Discovery, Organization and Use*.

Nitin Madnani, Philip Resnik, Bonnie Dorr, and Richard Schwartz. 2008b. Are multiple reference translations necessary? investigating the value of paraphrased reference translations in parameter optimization. In *Proceedings of the 8th Conference of the Association for Machine Translation in the Americas (AMTA'08)*.

David Mareček. 2009a. Improving word alignment using alignment of deep structures. In *Proceedings of the 12th International Conference on Text, Speech and Dialogue*, pages 56–63.

David Mareček. 2009b. Using tectogrammatical alignment in phrase-based machine translation. In *Proceedings of WDS 2009 Contributed Papers*, pages 22—27.

Franz Josef Och and Hermann Ney. 2003. A systematic comparison of various statistical alignment models. *Computational Linguistics*, 29(1):19–51.

Sebastian Padó and Mirella Lapata. 2005. Cross-linguistic projection of role-semantic information. In *Proceedings of the conference on Human Language Technology and Empirical Methods in Natural Language Processing*, HLT '05, pages 859–866, Stroudsburg, PA, USA. Association for Computational Linguistics.

Sebastian Padó and Mirella Lapata. 2006. Optimal constituent alignment with edge covers for semantic projection. In *Proceedings of the 21st International Conference on Computational Linguistics and the 44th annual meeting of the Association for Computational Linguistics*, ACL-44, pages 1161–1168, Stroudsburg, PA, USA. Association for Computational Linguistics.

Slav Petrov and Dan Klein. 2007. Improved inference for unlexicalized parsing. In *In HLT-NAACL '07*.

Philip Resnik. 2004. Exploiting hidden meanings: Using bilingual text for monolingual annotation. In Alexander Gelbukh, editor, *Lecture Notes in Computer Science 2945: Computational Linguistics and Intelligent Text Processing*, pages 283–299. Springer.

Mihai Surdeanu and Jordi Turmo. 2005. Semantic role labeling using complete syntactic analysis. In *Proceedings of CoNLL-2005 shared task*, pages 221–224.

Dekai Wu and Pascale Fung. 2009a. Can semantic role labeling improve smt? In *Proceedings of the 13th Annual Conference of the EAMT*, pages 218–225, Barcelona, Spain.

Dekai Wu and Pascale Fung. 2009b. Semantic roles for smt: A hybrid two-pass model. In *Proceedings of the North American Chapter of the Association for Computational Linguistics - Human Language Technologies (NAACL-HLT'09)*, pages 13–16.

Zhaojun Wu, Yongsheng Yang, and Pascale Fung. 2006. C-assert: Chinese shallow semantic parser. `http://hlt030.cse.ust.hk/research/c-assert/`.

Shumin Wu, Jinho D. Choi, and Martha Palmer. 2010. Detecting cross-lingual semantic similarity using parallel propbanks. In *Proceedings of the 9th Conference of the Association for Machine Translation in the Americas*.

Nianwen Xue and Martha Palmer. 2009. Adding semantic roles to the chinese treebank. *Nat. Lang. Eng.*, 15(1):143–172.

Nianwen Xue. 2004. Calibrating features for semantic role labeling. In *Proceedings of EMNLP 2004*, pages 88–94.

Nianwen Xue. 2008. Labeling chinese predicates with semantic roles. *Computational Linguistics*, 34(2):225–255.

Yaqin Yang and Nianwen Xue. 2010. Chasing the ghost: recovering empty categories in the chinese treebank. In *Proceedings of the 23rd International Conference on Computational Linguistics: Posters*, COLING '10, pages 1382–1390, Stroudsburg, PA, USA. Association for Computational Linguistics.

Min Zhang, Hongfei Jiang, Ai Ti Aw, Jun Sun, Sheng Li, and Chew Lim Tan. 2007. A tree-to-tree alignment-based model for statistical machine translation. In *Machine Translation Summit XI*.

Incorporating Source-Language Paraphrases into Phrase-Based SMT with Confusion Networks

Jie Jiang,[†] **Jinhua Du,**[‡] and **Andy Way**[†]

[†]CNGL, School of Computing, Dublin City University, Glasnevin, Dublin 9, Ireland
{jjiang, away}@computing.dcu.ie

[‡]School of Automation and Information Engineering,
Xi'an University of Technology, Xi'an, Shaanxi, China
jhdu@xaut.edu.cn

Abstract

To increase the model coverage, source-language paraphrases have been utilized to boost SMT system performance. Previous work showed that word lattices constructed from paraphrases are able to reduce out-of-vocabulary words and to express inputs in different ways for better translation quality. However, such a word-lattice-based method suffers from two problems: 1) path duplications in word lattices decrease the capacities for potential paraphrases; 2) lattice decoding in SMT dramatically increases the search space and results in poor time efficiency. Therefore, in this paper, we adopt word confusion networks as the input structure to carry source-language paraphrase information. Similar to previous work, we use word lattices to build word confusion networks for merging of duplicated paths and faster decoding. Experiments are carried out on small-, medium- and large-scale English–Chinese translation tasks, and we show that compared with the word-lattice-based method, the decoding time on three tasks is reduced significantly (up to 79%) while comparable translation quality is obtained on the large-scale task.

1 Introduction

With the rapid development of large-scale parallel corpus, research on data-driven SMT has made good progress to the real world applications. Currently, for a typical automatic translation task, the SMT system searches and exactly matches the input sentences with the phrases or rules in the models. Obviously, if the following two conditions could be satisfied, namely:

- the words in the parallel corpus are highly aligned so that the phrase alignment can be performed well;
- the coverage of the input sentence by the parallel corpus is high;

then the "exact phrase match" translation method could bring a good translation.

However, for some language pairs, it is not easy to obtain a huge amount of parallel data, so it is not that easy to satisfy these two conditions. To alleviate this problem, paraphrase-enriched SMT systems have been proposed to show the effectiveness of incorporating paraphrase information. In terms of the position at which paraphrases are incorporated in the MT-pipeline, previous work can be organized into three different categories:

- Translation model augmentation with paraphrases (Callison-Burch et al., 2006; Marton et al., 2009). Here the focus is on the translation of unknown source words or phrases in the input sentences by enriching the translation table with paraphrases.
- Training corpus augmentation with paraphrases (Bond et al., 2008; Nakov, 2008a; Nakov, 2008b). Paraphrases are incorporated into the MT systems by expanding the training data.
- Word-lattice-based method with paraphrases (Du et al., 2010; Onishi et al.,

Proceedings of SSST-5, Fifth Workshop on Syntax, Semantics and Structure in Statistical Translation, pages 31–40,
ACL HLT 2011, Portland, Oregon, USA, June 2011.

2010). Instead of augmenting the translation table, source-language paraphrases are constructed to enrich the inputs to the SMT system. Another directly related work is to use word lattices to deal with multi-source translation (Schroeder et al., 2009), in which paraphrases are actually generated from the alignments of difference source sentences.

Comparing these three methods, the word-lattice-based method has the least overheads because:

- The translation model augmentation method has to re-run the whole MT pipeline once the inputs are changed, while the word-lattice-based method only need to transform the new input sentences into word lattices.

- The training corpus augmentation method requires corpus-scale expansion, which drastically increases the computational complexity on large corpora, while the word-lattice-based method only deals with the development set and test set.

In (Du et al., 2010; Onishi et al., 2010), it is also observed that the word-lattice-based method performed better than the translation model augmentation method on different scales and two different language pairs in several translation tasks. Thus they concluded that the word-lattice-based method is preferable for this task.

However, there are still some drawbacks for the word-lattice-based method:

- In the lattice construction processing, duplicated paths are created and fed into SMT decoders. This decreases the paraphrase capacity in the word lattices. Note that we use the phrase "paraphrase capacity" to represent the amount of paraphrases that are actually built into the word lattices. As presented in (Du et al., 2010), only a limited number of paraphrases are allowed to be used while others are pruned during the construction process, so duplicate paths actually decrease the number of paraphrases that contribute to the translation quality.

- The lattice decoding in SMT decoder have a very high computational complexity which makes the system less feasible in real time application.

Therefore, in this paper, we use confusion networks (CNs) instead of word lattices to carry paraphrase information in the inputs for SMT decoders. CNs are constructed from the aforementioned word lattices, while duplicate paths are merged to increase paraphrase capacity (e.g. by admitting more non-duplicate paraphrases without increasing the input size). Furthermore, much less computational complexity is required to perform CN decoding instead of lattice decoding in the SMT decoder. We carried out experiments on small-, medium- and large-scale English–Chinese translation tasks to compare against a baseline PBSMT system, the translation model augmentation of (Callison-Burch et al., 2006) method and the word-lattice-based method of (Du et al., 2010) to show the effectiveness of our novel approach.

The motivation of this work is to use CN as the compromise between speed and quality, which comes from previous studies in speech recognition and speech translation: in (Hakkani-Tür et al., 2005), word lattices are transformed into CNs to obtain compact representations of multiple aligned ASR hypotheses in speech understanding; in (Bertoldi et al., 2008), CNs are also adopted instead of word lattices as the source-side inputs for speech translation systems. The main contribution of this paper is to show that this compromise also works for SMT systems incorporating source-language paraphrases in the inputs.

Regarding the use of paraphrases SMT system, there are still other two categories of work that are related to this paper:

- Using paraphrases to improve system optimization (Madnani et al., 2007). With an English–English MT system, this work utilises paraphrases to reduce the number of manually translated references that are needed in the parameter tuning process of SMT, while preserved a similar translation quality.

- Using paraphrases to smooth translation models (Kuhn et al., 2010; Max, 2010). Either cluster-based or example-based methods are proposed to obtain better estimation on phrase translation probabilities with paraphrases.

The rest of this paper is organized as follows: In section 2, we present an overview of the word-lattice-based method and its drawbacks. Section 3 proposes the CN-based method, including the building process and its application on paraphrases in SMT. Section 4 presents the experiments and results of the proposed method as well as discussions. Conclusions and future work are then given in Section 5.

2 Word-lattice-based method

Compared with translation model augmentation with paraphrases (Callison-Burch et al., 2006), word-lattice-based paraphrasing for PBSMT is introduced in (Du et al., 2010). A brief overview of this method is given in this section.

2.1 Lattice construction from paraphrases

The first step of the word-lattice-based method is to generate paraphrases from parallel corpus. The algorithm in (Bannard and Callison-Burch, 2005) is used for this purpose by pivoting through phrases in the source- and the target- languages: for each source phrase, all occurrences of its target phrases are found, and all the corresponding source phrases of these target phrases are considered as the potential paraphrases of the original source phrase (Callison-Burch et al., 2006). A paraphrase probability $p(e_2|e_1)$ is defined to reflect the similarities between two phrases, as in (1):

$$p(e_2|e_1) = \sum_f p(f|e_1)p(e_2|f) \qquad (1)$$

where the probability $p(f|e_1)$ is the probability that the original source phrase e_1 translates as a particular phrase f on the target side, and $p(e_2|f)$ is the probability that the candidate paraphrase e_2 translates as the source phrase. Here $p(e_2|f)$ and $p(f|e_1)$ are defined as the translation probabilities estimated using maximum likelihood by counting the observations of alignments between phrases e and f in the parallel corpus, as in (2) and (3):

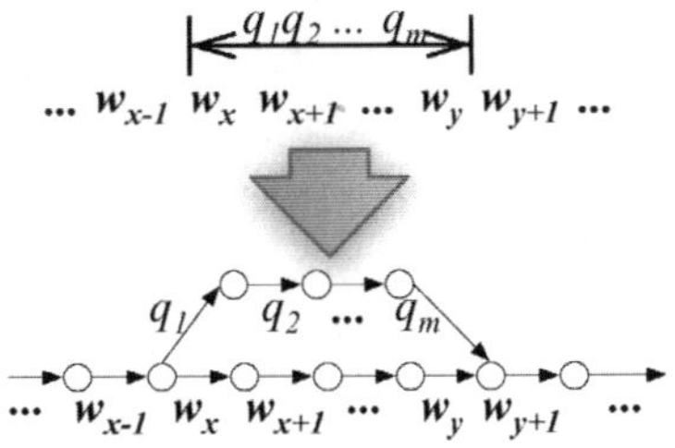

Figure 1: Construct word lattices from paraphrases.

$$p(e_2|f) \approx \frac{count(e_2, f)}{\sum_{e_2} count(e_2, f)} \qquad (2)$$

$$p(f|e_1) \approx \frac{count(f, e_1)}{\sum_f count(f, e_1)} \qquad (3)$$

The second step is to transform input sentences in the development and test sets into word lattices with paraphrases extracted in the first step. As illustrated in Figure 1, given a sequence of words $\{w_1, \ldots, w_N\}$ as the input, for each of the paraphrase pairs found in the source sentence (e.g. $p_i = \{q_1, \ldots, q_m\}$ for $\{w_x, \ldots, w_y\}$), add in extra nodes and edges to make sure those phrases coming from paraphrases share the same start nodes and end nodes with that of the original ones. Subsequently the following empirical methods are used to assign weights on paraphrases edges:

- Edges originating from the input sentences are assigned weight 1.
- The first edges for each of the paraphrases are calculated as in (4):

$$w(e^1_{p_i}) = \frac{1}{k+i} \quad (1 <= i <= k) \qquad (4)$$

  where 1 stands for the first edge of paraphrase p_i, and i is the probability rank of p_i among those paraphrases sharing with a same start node, while k is a predefined constant as a trade-off parameter for efficiency and performance, which is related to the paraphrase capacity.

- The rest of the edges corresponding to the paraphrases are assigned weight 1.

The last step is to modify the MT pipeline to tune and evaluate the SMT system with word lattice inputs, as is described in (Du et al., 2010; Onishi et al., 2010).

For further discussion, a real example of the generated word lattice is illustrated in Figure 2. In the word lattice, double-line circled nodes and solid lined edges come from originated from the original sentence, while others are generated from paraphrases. Word, weight and ranking of each edge are displayed in the figure. By adopting such an input structure, the diversity of the input sentences is increased to provide more flexible translation options during the decoding process, which has been shown to improve translation performance (Du et al., 2010).

2.2 Path duplication and decoding efficiency

As can be seen in Figure 2, the construction process in the previous steps tends to generate duplicate paths in the word lattices. For example, there are two paths from node 6 to node 11 with the same words "secretary of state" but different edge probabilities (the path via node 27 and 28 has the probability $1/12$, while the path via node 26 and 9 has the probability $1/99$). This is because the aforementioned straightforward construction process does not track path duplications from different spans on the source side. Since the number of admitted paraphrases is restricted by parameter k in formula (4), the path duplication will decrease the paraphrase capacity to a certain extend.

Moreover, state of the art PBSMT decoders (e.g. Moses (Koehn et al., 2007)) have a much higher computational complexity for lattice structures than for sentences. Thus even though only the test sentences need to be transformed into word lattices, decoding time is still too slow for real-time applications.

Motivated by transforming ASR word-graphs into CNs (Bertoldi et al., 2008), we adopt CN as the trade-off between efficiency and quality. We aim to merge duplicate paths in the word lattices to increase paraphrase capacity, and to speed up the decoding process via CN decoding. Details of the proposed method are presented in the following section.

3 Confusion-network-based method

CNs are weighted direct graphs where each path from the start node to the end node goes through all the other nodes. Each edge is labelled with a word and a probability (or weight). Although it is commonly required to normalize the probability of edges between two consecutive nodes to sum up to one, from the point of view of the decoder, this is not a strict constraint as long as any score is provided (similar to the weights on the word lattices in the last section, and we prefer to call it "weight" in this case).

The benefits of using CNs are:

1. the ability to represent the original word lattice with a highly compact structure;

2. all hypotheses in the word lattice are totally ordered, so that the decoding algorithm is mostly retained except for the collection of translation options and the handeling of ϵ edges (Bertoldi et al., 2008), which requires much less computational resources than the lattice decoding.

The rest of this section details the construction process of the CNs and the application in paraphrase-enriched SMT.

3.1 Confusion Network building

We build our CN from the aforementioned word lattices. Previous studies provide several methods to do this. (Mangu et al., 2000) propose a method to cluster lattice words on the similarity of pronunciations and frequency of occurrence, and then to create CNs using cluster orders. Although this method has a computational complexity of $O(n^3)$, the SRILM toolkit (Stolcke, 2002) provides a modified algorithm which runs much faster than the original version. In (Hakkani-Tür et al., 2005), a pivot algorithm is proposed to form CNs by normalizing the topology of the input lattices.

In this paper, we use the modified method of (Mangu et al., 2000) provided by the SRILM toolkit to convert word lattices into CNs. Moreover, we aim to obtain CNs with the following guidelines:

- Cluster the lattice words only by topological orders and edge weights without considering word similarity. The objective is to reduce the

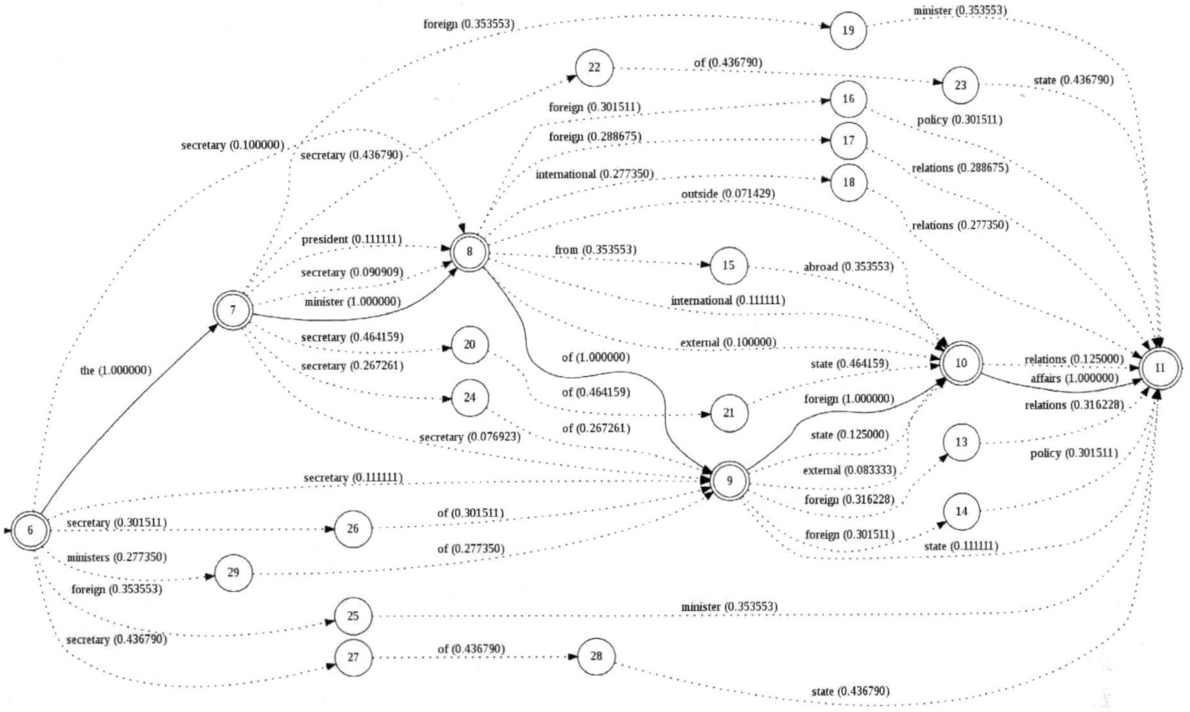

Figure 2: An example of a real paraphrase lattice. Note that it is a subsection of the whole word lattice that is too big to fit into this page, and edge weights have been evenly distributed for CN conversion as specified by formula (5).

impact of path duplications in the building process, since duplicate words will bias the importance of paths.

- Assign edge weights by the ranking of paraphrase probabilities, rather than by posterior probabilities from the modified method of (Mangu et al., 2000). This is similar to that given in formula (4). The reason for this is to reduce the impact of path duplications on the calculation of weights.

Thus, we modified the construction process as follows:

1. For each of the input word lattices, replace word texts with unique identifiers (to make the lattice alignment uncorrelated to the word similarity, since in this case, all words in the lattice are different from each other).

2. Evenly distribute edge weights for each of the lattices by modifying formula (4) as in (5):

$$w(e^j_{p_i}) = \frac{1}{\sqrt[M_i]{(k+i)}} \quad (1 <= i <= k) \qquad (5)$$

where $1 <= j <= M_i$, given $e^j_{p_i}$ is the jth edge of paraphrase p_i, and M_i is the number of words in p_i. This is to avoid large weights on the paraphrase edges for lattice alignments.

3. Transform the weighted word lattices into CNs with the SRILM toolkit, and the paraphrase ranking information is carried on the edges.

4. Replace the word texts in step 1, and then for each column of the CN, merge edges with same words by keeping those with the highest ranking (a smaller number indicates a higher ranking, and edges from the original sentences will always have the highest ranking). Note that to assign ranking for each ϵ edge which does not appear in the word lattice, we use the ranking of non-original edges (in the same column) which have the closest posterior probability to it. (Assign ranking 1 if failed to find a such edge).

5. Reassign the edge weights: 1) edges from original sentences are assigned with weight 1; 2) edges from paraphrases are assigned with an

empirical method as in (6):

$$w(e^{cn}_{p_i}) = \frac{1}{k+i} \quad (1 <= i <= k) \qquad (6)$$

where $e^{cn}_{p_i}$ are edges corresponding with paraphrase p_i, and i is the probability rank of p_i in formula (4), while k is also defined in formula (4).

A real example of a constructed CN is depicted in Figure 3, which is correspondent with the word lattice in Figure 2. Unlike the word lattices, all the nodes in the CN are generated from the original sentence, while solid lined edges come from the original sentence, and dotted lined edges correspond to paraphrases.

As in shown in the Figures, duplicate paths in the word lattices have been merged into CN edges by step 4. For example, the two occurrences of "secretary of state" in the word lattices (one path from node 6 to 11 via 27 and 28, and one path from node 6 to 11 via 26 and 9 in the word lattice) are merged to keep the highest-ranked path in the CN (note there is one ϵ edge between node 9 and 10 to accomplish the merging operation). Furthermore, each edge in the CN is assigned a weight by formula (6). This weight assignment procedure penalizes paths from paraphrases according to the paraphrase probabilities, in a similar manner to the aforementioned word-lattice-based method.

3.2 Modified MT pipeline

By transforming word lattices into CNs, duplicate paths are merged. Furthermore the new features on the edges are introduced by formula (6), which is then tuned on the development set using MERT (Och, 2003) in the log-linear model (Och and Ney, 2002). Since the SMT decoders are able to perform CN decoding (Bertoldi et al., 2008) in an efficient multi-stack decoding way, decoding time is drastically reduced compared to lattice decoding.

The training steps are then modified as follows: 1) Extract phrase table, reordering table, and build target-side language models from parallel and monolingual corpora respectively for the PBSMT model; 2) Transform source sentences in the development set into word lattices, and then transform them into CNs using the method proposed in Section 3.1; 3) Tune the PBSMT model on the CNs via the development set. Note that the overhead of the evaluation steps are: transform each test set sentence into a word lattice, and also transform them into a CN, then feed them into the SMT decoder to obtain decoding results.

4 Experiments

4.1 Experimental setup

Experiments were carried out on three English–Chinese translation tasks. The training corpora comprise 20K, 200K and 2.1 million sentence pairs, where the former two corpora are derived from FBIS corpus[1] which is sentence-aligned by Champollion aligner (Ma, 2006), the latter corpus comes from HK parallel corpus,[2] ISI parallel corpus,[3] other news data and parallel dictionaries from LDC.

The development set and the test set for the 20K and 200K corpora are randomly selected from the FBIS corpus, each of which contains 1,200 sentences, with one reference. For the 2.1 million corpus, the NIST 2005 Chinese–English current set (1,082 sentences) with one reference is used as the development set, and NIST 2003 English–Chinese current set (1,859 sentences) with four references is used as the test set.

Three baseline systems are built for comparison: Moses PBSMT baseline system (Koehn et al., 2007), a realization of the translation model augmentation system described in (Callison-Burch et al., 2006) (named "Para-Sub" hereafter), and the word-lattice based system proposed in (Du et al., 2010).

Word alignments on the parallel corpus are performed using GIZA++ (Och and Ney, 2003) with the "grow-diag-final" refinement. Maximum phrase length is set to 10 words and the parameters in the log-linear model are tuned by MERT (Och, 2003). All the language models are 5-gram built with the SRILM toolkit (Stolcke, 2002) on the monolingual part of the parallel corpora.

4.2 Paraphrase acquisition

The paraphrases data for all paraphrase-enriched system is derived from the "Paraphrase Phrase Ta-

[1]Paragraph-aligned corpus with LDC number LDC2003E14.

[2]LDC number: LDC2004T08.

[3]LDC number: LDC2007T09.

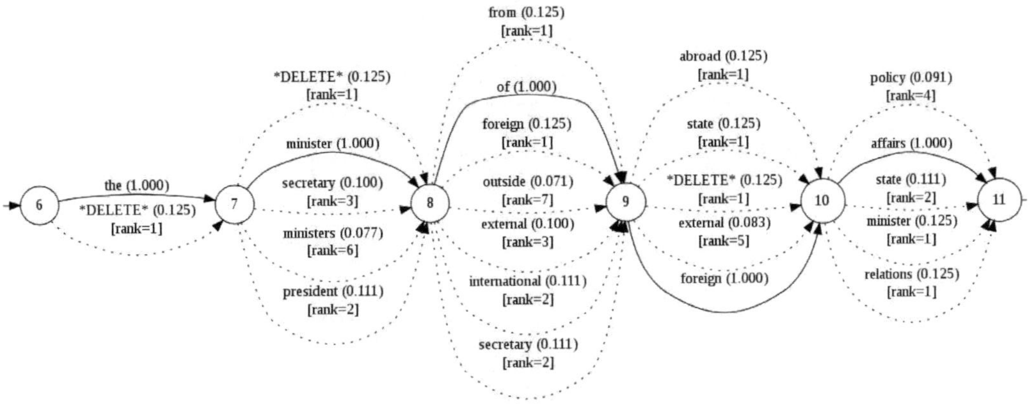

Figure 3: An example of a real CN converted from a paraphrase lattice. Note that it is a subsection of the whole CN that is converted from the word lattice in Figure 2.

ble"[4] of TER-Plus (Snover et al., 2009). Furthermore, the following two steps are taken to filter out noise paraphrases as described in (Du et al., 2010):

1. Filter out paraphrases with probabilities lower than 0.01.

2. Filter out paraphrases which are not observed in the phrase table. This objective is to guarantee that no extra out-of-vocabulary words are introduced into the paraphrase systems.

The filtered paraphrase table is then used to generate word lattices and CNs.

4.3 Experimental results

The results are reported in BLEU (Papineni et al., 2002) and TER (Snover et al., 2006) scores.

Table 1 compares the performance of four systems on three translation tasks. As can be observed from the Table, for 20K and 200K corpora, the word-lattice-based system accomplished the best results. For the 20K corpus, the CN outperformed the baseline PBSMT by 0.31 absolute (2.15% relative) BLEU points and 1.5 absolute (1.99% relative) TER points. For the 200K corpus, it still outperformed the "Para-Sub" by 0.06 absolute (0.26% relative) BLEU points and 0.15 absolute (0.23% relative) TER points. Note that for the 2.1M corpus, although CN underperformed the best word lattice by an insignificant amount (0.06 absolute, 0.41% relative) in terms of BLEU points, it has the best performance in terms of TER points (0.22 absolute, 0.3% relative than word lattice). Furthermore, the CN outperformed "Para-Sub" by 0.36 absolute (2.55% relative) BLEU points and 1.37 absolute (1.84% relative) TER points, and also beat the baseline PBSMT system by 0.45 absolute (3.21% relative) BLEU points and 1.82 absolute (2.43% relative) TER points. The paired 95% confidence interval of significant test (Zhang and Vogel, 2004) between the "Lattice" and "CN" system is [-0.19, +0.38], which also suggests that the two system has a comparable performance in terms of BLEU.

In Table 2, decoding time on test sets is reported to compare the computational efficiency of the baseline PBSMT, word-lattice-based and CN-based methods. Note that word lattice construction time and CN building time (including word lattice construction and conversion from word lattices into CNs with the SRILM toolkit (Stolcke, 2002)) are counted in the decoding time and illustrated in the table within parentheses respectively. Although both word-lattice-based and CN-based methods require longer decoding times than the baseline PBSMT system, it is observed that compared with the word lattices, CNs reduced the decoding time significantly on three tasks, namely 52.06% for the 20K model, 75.75% for the 200K model and 78.88% for the 2.1M model. It is also worth noting that the "Para-Sub" system has a similar decoding time with baseline PBSMT since only the translation table is modified.

[4] `http://www.umiacs.umd.edu/~snover/terp/downloads/terp-pt.v1.tgz`

System	20K		200K		2.1M	
	BLEU	TER	BLEU	TER	BLEU	TER
Baseline PBSMT	14.42	75.30	23.60	63.65	14.04	74.88
Para-Sub	14.78	73.75	23.41	63.84	14.13	74.43
Word-lattice-based	**15.44**	**73.06**	**25.20**	**62.37**	**14.55**	73.28
CN-based	14.73	73.8	23.47	63.69	14.49	**73.06**

Table 1: Comparison on PBSMT, "Para-Sub", word-lattice and CN-based methods.

System	FBIS testset (1,200 inputs)		NIST testset (1,859 inputs)
	20K model	200K model	2.1M model
Baseline	21 min	41 min	37 min
Lattice	102 min (+ 15 sec)	398 min (+ 20 sec)	559 min (+ 21 sec)
CN	48 min (+ 61 sec)	95 min (+ 96 sec)	116 min (+ 129 sec)

Table 2: Decoding time comparison of PBSMT, word-lattice ("Lattice") and CN-based ("CN") methods.

4.4 Discussion

From the performance and decoding time reported in the last section, it is obvious that on large scale corpora, the CN-based method significantly reduced the computational complexity while preserved the system performance of the best lattice-based method. Thus it makes the paraphrase-enriched SMT system more applicable to real-world applications. On the other hand, for small- and medium-scale data, CNs can be used as a compromise between speed and quality, since decoding time is much less than word lattices, and compared with the "Para-Sub" system, the only overhead is the transforming of the input sentences.

It is also interesting that the relative performance of the CNs increases gradually with the size of the training corpus, which indicates that it is more suitable for models built from large scale data. Considering the decoding time, it is preferable to use CNs instead of word lattices for such translation tasks. However, for the small- and medium-scale data, the CN system is not competitive even compared with the baseline. In this case it suggests that, on these two tasks, the *coverage* issue is not solved by incorporating paraphrases with the CN structure. It might because of the ambiguity that introduced by CNs harms the decoder to choose the appropriate source words from paraphrases. On the other hand, this ambiguity could be decreased with translation models trained on a large corpus, which provides enough observations for the decoders to favour paraphrases.

5 Conclusion and future work

In this paper, CNs are used instead of word lattices to incorporate paraphrases into SMT. Transformation from word lattices into CNs is used to merge path duplications, and decoding time is drastically reduced with CN decoding. Experiments are carried out on small-, medium- and large-scale English–Chinese translation tasks and confirm that compared with word lattices, it is much more computationally efficient to use CNs, while no loss of performance is observed on the large-scale task.

In the future, we plan to apply more features such as source-side language models and phrase length (Onishi et al., 2010) on the CNs to obtain better system performance. Furthermore, we will carry out this work on other language pairs to show the effectiveness of paraphrases in SMT systems. We will also investigate the reason for its lower performance on the small- and medium-scale corpora, as well as the impact of the paraphrase filtering procedure on translation quality.

Acknowledgments

This research is supported by the Science Foundation Ireland (Grant 07/CE/I1142) as part of the Centre for Next Generation Localisation (www.cngl.ie) at Dublin City University. Thanks to the reviewers for their invaluable comments and suggestions.

References

Colin Bannard and Chris Callison-Burch. 2005. Paraphrasing with bilingual parallel corpora. In *43rd Annual meeting of the Association for Computational Linguistics*, Ann Arbor, MI, pages 597–604.

Nicola Bertoldi, Richard Zens, Marcello Federico, and Wade Shen 2008. Efficient Speech Translation Through Confusion Network Decoding. In *IEEE Transactions on Audio, Speech, and Language Processing, 16(8)*, pages 1696–1705.

Francis Bond, Eric Nichols, Darren Scott Appling and Michael Paul. 2008. Improving Statistical Machine Translation by Paraphrasing the Training Data. In *Proceedings of the International Workshop on Spoken Language Translation (IWSLT)*, Hawaii, pages 150–157.

Chris Callison-Burch, Philipp Koehn and Miles Osborne. 2006. Improved Statistical Machine Translation Using Paraphrases. In *Proceedings of the Human Language Technology conference - North American chapter of the Association for Computational Linguistics (HLT-NAACL)*, NY, pages 17–24.

Jinhua Du, Jie Jiang and Andy Way. 2010. Facilitating Translation Using Source Language Paraphrase Lattices. In *Proceedings of the Conference on Empirical Methods in Natural Language Processing (EMNLP)*, Cambridge, MA, pages 420–429.

Dilek Hakkani-Tür, Frédéric Béchet, Giuseppe Riccardi and Gokhan Tur. 2005. Beyond ASR 1-best: Using word confusion networks in spoken language understanding. In *Computer Speech and Language (2005): 20(4)*, pages 495–514.

Philipp Koehn, Hieu Hoang, A. Birch, C. Callison-Burch, M. Federico, N. Bertoldi, B. Cowan, Wade Shen, C. Moran, R. Zens, C. Dyer, O. Bojar, A. Constantin and Evan Herbst. 2007. Moses: Open Source Toolkit for Statistical Machine Translation. In *ACL 2007: demo and poster sessions*, Prague, Czech Republic, pages 177–180.

Roland Kuhn, Boxing Chen, George Foster and Evan Stratford. 2010. Phrase Clustering for Smoothing TM Probabilities - or, How to Extract Paraphrases from Phrase Tables. In *Proceedings of the 23rd International Conference on Computational Linguistics (Coling 2010)*, Beijing, China, pages 608–616.

Xiaoyi Ma. 2006. Champollion: A Robust Parallel Text Sentence Aligner. *LREC 2006: Fifth International Conference on Language Resources and Evaluation*, Genova, Italy, pages 489–492.

Nitin Madnani, Necip Fazil Ayan, Philip Resnik and Bonnie J. Dorr. 2007. Using Paraphrases for Parameter Tuning in Statistical Machine Translation. In *Proceedings of the Second Workshop on Statistical Machine Translation*, Prague, Czech Republic, pages 120–127.

Lidia Mangu, Eric Brill and Andreas Stolcke. 2000. Finding Consensus in Speech Recognition: Word Error Minimization and Other Applications of Confusion Networks. In *Computer Speech and Language 14 (4)*, pages 373–400.

Yuval Marton, Chris Callison-Burch and Philip Resnik. 2009. Improved Statistical Machine Translation Using Monolingually-Derived Paraphrases. In *Proceedings of the Conference on Empirical Methods in Natural Language Processing (EMNLP)*, Singapore, pages 381–390.

Aurélien Max. 2010. Example-Based Paraphrasing for Improved Phrase-Based Statistical Machine Translation. In *Proceedings of the 2010 Conference on Empirical Methods in Natural Language Processing*, Cambridge, MA, pages 656–666.

Preslav Nakov. 2008a. Improved Statistical Machine Translation Using Monolingual Paraphrases In *Proceedings of the European Conference on Artificial Intelligence (ECAI)*, Patras, Greece, pages 338–342.

Preslav Nakov. 2008b. Improving English-Spanish statistical machine translation: experiments in domain adaptation, sentence paraphrasing, tokenization, and recasing. In *Proceedings of ACL-08:HLT. Third Workshop on Statistical Machine Translation*, Columbus, Ohio, USA, pages 147–150.

Franz Josef Och. 2003. Minimum Error Rate Training in Statistical Machine Translation. In *Proceedings of the 41st Annual Meeting of the Association for Computational Linguistics (ACL)*, pages 160–167.

Franz Josef Och and Hermann Ney. 2002. Discriminative training and maximum entropy models for statistical machine translation. In *Proceedings of the 40th Annual Meeting of the Association for Computational Linguistics (ACL)*, Philadelphia, PA, pages 295–302.

Franz Och and Hermann Ney. 2003. A systematic comparison of various statistical alignment models. *Computational Linguistics, 29(1)*, pages 19–51.

Takashi Onishi, Masao Utiyama and Eiichiro, Sumita. 2010. Paraphrase Lattice for Statistical Machine Translation. In *Proceedings of the ACL 2010 Conference Short Papers*, Uppsala, Sweden, pages 1–5.

Kishore Papineni, Salim Roukos, Todd Ward, and Wei-Jing Zhu. 2002. BLEU: A Method For Automatic Evaluation of Machine Translation. *ACL-2002: 40th Annual meeting of the Association for Computational Linguistics*, pp.311-318, Philadelphia, PA.

Josh Schroeder, Trevor Cohn and Philipp Koehn. 2009. Word Lattices for Multi-Source Translation. In *Proceedings of the 12th Conference of the European Chapter of the ACL (EACL 2009)*, Athens, Greece, pages 719–727.

Matthew Snover, Bonnie Dorr, Richard Schwartz, Linnea Micciulla and John Makhoul. 2006. A study of translation edit rate with targeted human annotation. In *Proceedings of the 7th Conference of the Association for Machine Translation in the Americas*, Cambridge, pages 223–231.

Matthew Snover, Nitin Madnani, Bonnie J.Dorr and Richard Schwartz. 2009. Fluency, adequacy, or HTER? Exploring different human judgments with a tunable MT metric. In *Proceedings of the Fourth Workshop on Statistical Machine Translation*, Athens, Greece, pages 259–268.

Andreas Stolcke. 2002. SRILM - an extensible language modeling toolkit. In *Proceedings of the International Conference on Spoken Language Processing (ICSLP)*, Denver, Colorado, pages 901–904.

Ying Zhang and Stephan Vogel. 2004. Measuring confidence intervals for the machine translation evaluation metrics. In *Proceedings of the 10th International Conference on Theoretical and Methodological Issues in Machine Translation (TMI)*. pages 85–94.

Multi-Word Unit Dependency Forest-based Translation Rule Extraction

Hwidong Na **Jong-Hyeok Lee**
Department of Computer Science and Engineering
Pohang University of Science and Technology (POSTECH)
San 31 Hyoja Dong, Pohang, 790-784, Republic of Korea
{leona, jhlee}@postech.ac.kr

Abstract

Translation requires non-isomorphic transformation from the source to the target. However, non-isomorphism can be reduced by learning multi-word units (MWUs). We present a novel way of representating sentence structure based on MWUs, which are not necessarily continuous word sequences. Our proposed method builds a simpler structure of MWUs than words using words as vertices of a dependency structure. Unlike previous studies, we collect many alternative structures in a packed forest. As an application of our proposed method, we extract translation rules in form of a source MWU-forest to the target string, and verify the rule coverage empirically. As a consequence, we improve the rule coverage compare to a previous work, while retaining the linear asymptotic complexity.

1 Introduction

Syntax is the hierarchical structure of a natural language sentence. It is generally represented with tree structures using phrase structure grammar (PSG) or dependency grammar (DG). Although the state-of-the-art statistical machine translation (SMT) paradigm is phrase-based SMT (PBSMT), many researchers have attempted to utilize syntax in SMT to overcome the weaknesses of PBSMT. An emerging paradigm alternative to PBSMT is syntax-based SMT, which embeds the source and/or target syntax in its translation model (TM). Utilizing syntax in TM has two advantages over PBSMT.

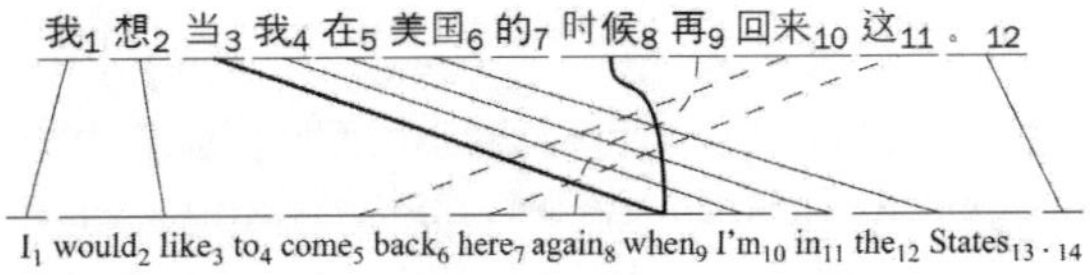

Figure 1: A pair of sentences that require long distance reordering (dashed line) and discontinuous translation (thick line)

The first advantage is that syntax eases global reordering between the source and the target language. Figure 1 shows that we need global reordering in a complex real situation, where a verbal phrase requires a long distance movement. PBSMT often fails to handle global reordering, for example, from subject-verb-object (SVO) to SOV transformation where V should be moved far away from the original position in

Proceedings of SSST-5, Fifth Workshop on Syntax, Semantics and Structure in Statistical Translation, pages 41–51,
ACL HLT 2011, Portland, Oregon, USA, June 2011.

Table 1: Statistics of the corresponding target words for the continuous word sequences in the source language, or vice versa. C denotes consistent, O overlapped, D discontinuous, and N null.

Word Alignment	C	O	D	N
Manual	25	60	10	5
Automatic	20	55	15	5

the source language. This is because of the two distance-based constraints in PBSMT: the distortion model cost and the distortion size limit. For the distortion model cost, PBSMT sets zero cost to the monotone translation and penalizes the distorted translations as the distortion grows larger. For the distortion size limit, a phrase can only be moved from its original position within a limit. Therefore, PBSMT fails to handle long distance reordering. Syntax-based SMT manages global reordering as structural transformation. Because reordering occurs at the sub-structure level such as constituents or treelets in syntax-based SMT, the transformation of the sub-structure eventually yields the reordering of the whole sentence.

The second advantage of using syntax in TM is that syntax guides us to discontinuous translation patterns. Because PBSMT regards only a continuous sequence of words as a translation pattern, it often fails to utilize many useful discontinuous translation patterns. For example, two discontinuous source words correspond to a target word in Figure 1. In our inspection of the training corpus, a continuous word sequence often corresponds to a set of discontinuous words in the target language, or vice versa (Table 1). Discontinuous translation patterns frequently appear in many languages (Søgaard and Kuhn, 2009). Syntax-based SMT overcomes the limitations of PBSMT because it finds discontinuous patterns along with the hierarchical structure. For example, the two discontinuous source words have a head-dependent relation (Figure 3). Especially with the dependency tree, we can easily identify patterns that have non-projectivity (Na et al., 2010). However, syntax-based patterns such as constituents or treelets do not sufficiently cover various useful patterns, even if we have the correct syntactic analysis (Chiang, 2010). For this reason, many researchers have proposed supplementary patterns such as an intra/inter constituent or sequence of treelets (Galley et al., 2006; Shen et al., 2008).

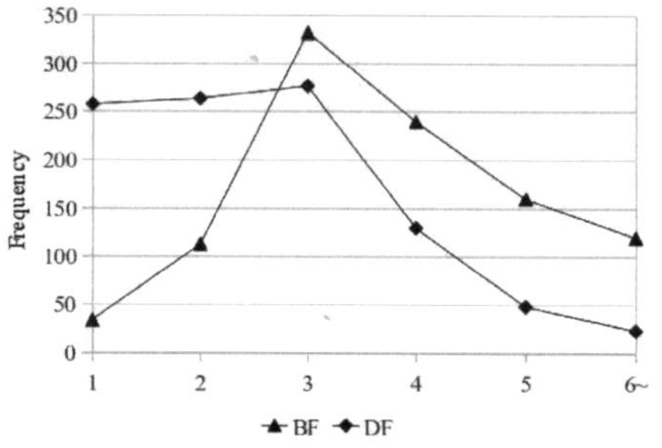

Figure 2: The maximum branching factor (BF) and depth factor (DF) in a dependency tree in our corpus

Unlike PSG, DG does not include non-terminal symbols, which represent constituent information. This makes DG simpler than PSG. For instance, it directly associates syntatic role with the structure, but introduces a difficulty in syntax-based SMT. The branching factor of a dependency tree becomes larger when a head word dominates many dependents. We observe that the maximum branching factor of an automatically parsed dependency tree ranges widely, while most trees have depth under a certain degree (Figure 2). This indicates that we have a horizontally flat dependency tree structure. The translation patterns extracted from the flat dependency tree are also likely to be flat. Unfortunately, the flat patterns are less applicable at the decoding stage. When one of the modifiers does not match, for instance, we fail to apply the translation pattern. Therefore, we need a more generally applicable representation for syntax-based SMT using DG.

We propose a novel representation of DG that regards a set of words as a unit of the dependency relations, similar to (Ding, 2006; Wu et al., 2009; Na et al., 2010). Unlike their work, we consider many alternatives without predefined units, and construct a packed forest of the multi-word units (MWUs) from a dependency tree. For brevity, we denote the forest based on MWUs as an MWU-forest. Because all possible alternatives are exponentially many, we give an efficient algorithm that enumerates the k-best alternatives in section 3. As an application, we extract translation patterns in form of a source MWU-forest to the target string in order to broaden the coverage of the extracted patterns for syntax-based SMT in section 4. We also report empirical results related to the usefulness of the extracted pattern in section 5. The experimental results show that the MWU-forest representation gives more applicable translation patterns than the original word-based tree.

2 Related Work

Previous studies have proposed merging alternative analyses to deal with analysis errors for two reasons: 1) the strongest alternative is not necessarily the correct analysis, and 2) most alternatives contain similar elements such as common sub-trees. For segmentation alternatives, Dyer et al. (2008) proposed a word lattice that represents exponentially large numbers of segmentations of a source sentence, and integrates reordering information into the lattice as well. For parsing alternatives, Mi et al. (2008) suggested a packed forest that encodes alternative PSG derivations. Futher, Mi et al. (2010) combined the two approaches in order to benefit from both.

The translation literature also shows that translation requires non-isomorphic transformation from the source to the target. This yields translation divergences such as head-switching (Dorr, 1994). Ding and Palmer (2005) reported that the percentage of the head-swapping cases is 4.7%, and that of broken dependencies is 59.3% between Chinese and English. The large amount of non-isomorphism, however, will be reduced by learning MWUs such as elementary trees (Eisner, 2003).

There are few studies that consider a dependency structure based on MWUs. Ding (2006) suggested a packed forest which consists of the elementary trees, and described how to find the best decomposition of the dependency tree. However, Ding (2006) did not show how to determine the MWUs and restrict them to form a subgraph from a head. For opinion mining, Wu et al. (2009) also utilized a dependency structure based on MWUs, although they restricted MWUs with predefined relations. Na et al. (2010) proposed an MWU-based dependency tree-to-string translation rule extraction, but considered only one decomposition for efficiency. Our proposed method includes additional units over Ding's method, such as a sequence of subgraphs within a packed forest. It is also more general than Wu et al.'s method because it does not require any predefined relations. We gain much better rule coverage against Na et al.'s method, while retaining linear asymptotical computational time.

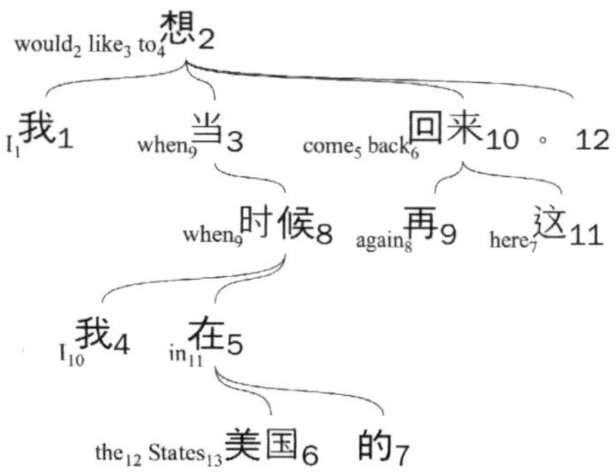

Figure 3: A dependency tree of the source sentence in Figure 1

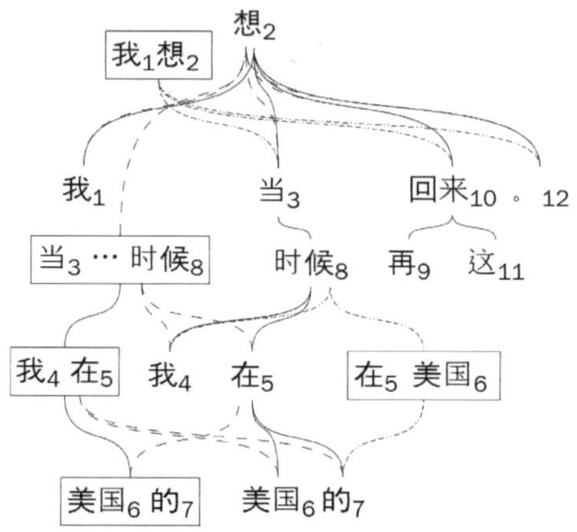

Figure 4: An MWU-forest of Figure 3. The dashed line indicates the alternative hyperedges.

3 MWU-based Dependency Forest

There are two advantages when we use the MWU-forest representaion with DG. First, we express the discontinuous patterns in a vertex, so that we can extract more useful translation patterns beyond continuous ones for syntax-based SMT. Second, an MWU-forest contains many alternative structures which may be simpler structures than the original tree in terms of the branching factor and the maximum depth. Wu et al. (2009) utilized an MWU-tree to identify the product features in a sentence easily.

As in previous literature in syntax-based SMT using DG, we only consider the **well-formed** MWUs where an MWU is either a treelet (a connected sub-graph), or a sequence of treelets under a common head. In other words, each vertex in an MWU-forest is either "fixed on head" or "floating with children". The formal definitions can be found in (Shen et al., 2008).

We propose encoding multiple dependency structures based on MWUs into a hypergraph. A hypergraph is a compact representation of exponetially many variations in a polynomial space. Unlike PSG, DG does not have non-terminals that represent the linguistically motivated, intermediate structure such as noun phrases and verb phrases. For this simplicity, Tu et al. (2010) proposed a dependency forest as a hypergraph, regarding a word as a vertex with a span that ranges for all its descendants. The dependency forest offers tolerence of parsing errors.

Our representation is different from the dependency forest of Tu et al. (2010) since a vertex corresponds to multiple words as well as words. Note that our representation is also capable of incorporating multiple parse trees. Therefore, MWU-forests will also be tolerant of the parsing error if we provide multiple parse trees. In this work, we concentrate on the effectiveness of MWUs, and hence utilize the best dependency parse tree. Figure 4 shows an MWU-forest of the dependency tree in Figure 3.

More formally, a hypergraph $H = \langle V, E \rangle$ consists of the vertices V and hyperedges E. We assume that a length-J sentence has a dependency graph which is single-headed, acyclic, and rooted, i.e. h_j is the index of the head word of the j-th word, or 0 if the word is the root. Each vertex $v = \{j | j \in [1, J]\}$ denotes a set of the indices of the words that satisfies the well-formed constraint. Each hyperedge $e = \langle tails(e), head(e) \rangle$ denotes a set of the dependency relations between $head(e)$ and $\forall v \in tails(e)$. We include a special node $v_0 \in V$ that denotes the dummy root of an MWU-forest. Note that v_0 does not appear in $tails(e)$ for all hyperedges. We denote $|e|$ is the arity of hyperedge e, i.e. the number of tail nodes, and the arity of a hypergraph is the maximum arity over all hyperedges. Also, let $\sigma(v)$ be the indices of the words that the head lays out of the vertex, i.e. $\sigma(v) = \{j | h_j \notin v \wedge j \in v\}$, and $\tau(v)$ be the indices of the direct dependent words of the vertex, i.e. $\tau(v) = \{j | h_j \in v \wedge j \notin v\}$. Let $OUT(v)$ and $IN(v)$ be the outgoing and incoming hyperedges of a vertex v, respectively.

It is challenging to weight the hyperedges based on dependency grammar because a dependency relation is a binary relation from a head to a dependent. Tu et al. (2010) assigned a probability for each hyperedge based on the score of the binary relation. We simply prefer the hyperedges that have lower arity by scoring as follows:

$$c(e) = \frac{\sum_{v \in tails(e)} |v|}{|e|}$$

$$p(e) = \frac{c(e)}{\sum_{e' \in IN(head(e))} c(e')}$$

We convert a dependency tree into a hypergraph in two steps using the Inside-Outside algorithm. Algorithm 1 shows the pseudo code of our proposed method. At the first step, we find the k-best incoming hyperedges for each vertex (line 3-8), and compute the inside probability (line 9), in bottom-up order. At the second step, we compute the outside probability (line 12) for each vertex in a top-down manner. Finally we prune out less probable hyperedges (line 14) similar to (Mi et al., 2008). The inside and outside probabilities are defined as follows:

Algorithm 1 Build Forest

1: Initialize V
2: **for** $v \in V$ in bottom-up order **do**
3:     Create a chart $C = |\tau(v)|^2$
4:     **for** chart span $[p, q]$ **do**
5:         Initialize $C[p, q]$ if $\exists v$ s.t. $[p, q] = v$ or $\sigma(v)$
6:         Combine $C[p, i]$ and $C[i + 1, q]$
7:     **end for**
8:     Set $IN(v)$ to the k-best in $C[TOP]$
9:     Set $\beta(v)$ as in Eq. 1
10: **end for**
11: **for** $v \in V$ in top-down order **do**
12:     Set $\alpha(v)$ as in Eq. 2
13: **end for**
14: Prune out e if $p(e) \leq \delta$
15: **return** v_0

$$\beta(v) = \sum_{e \in IN(v)} p(e) \prod_{d \in tails(e)} \beta(d) \quad (1)$$

where $\beta(v) = 1.0$ if $IN(v) = \emptyset$, and

$$\alpha(v) = \sum_{\substack{h \in OUT(v) \\ e \in IN(head(h))}} \frac{\alpha(head(e)) p(e)}{|OUT(v)|} \cdot \prod_{d \in tails(e) \setminus \{v\}} \beta(d) \quad (2)$$

where $\alpha(v) = 1.0$ if $OUT(v) = \emptyset$.

In practice, we restrict the number of words in a vertex in the initialization (line 1). We approximate all possible alternative MWUs that include each word as follows:

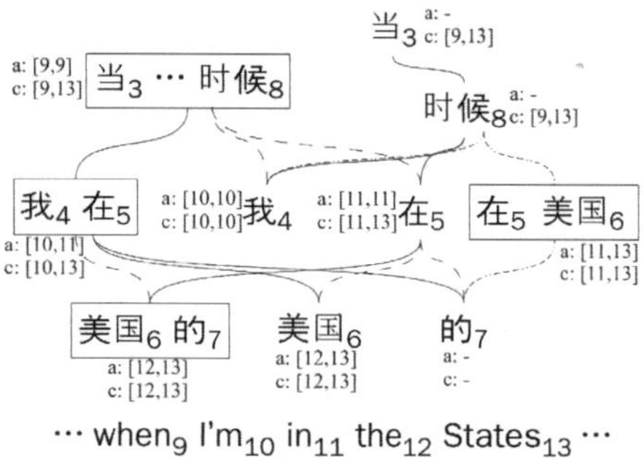

Figure 5: A sub-forest of Figure 4 with annotation of $aspan$ and $cspan$ for each vertex. We omit the span if it is not consistent.

- A horizontal vertex is a sequence of modifiers for a common head word, and
- A vertical vertex is a path from a word to one of the ancestors, and
- A combination of the horizontal vertices and the vertical vertices, and
- A combination of the vertical vertices and the vertical vertices.

The computational complexity of the initializaion directly affects the complexity of the entire procedure. For each word, generating the horizontal vertices takes $O(b^2)$, and the vertical vertices take $O(b^{d-1})$, where b is the maximum branching factor and d is the maximum depth of a dependency tree. The two combinations take $O(b^{d+1})$ and $O(b^{2(d-1)})$ time to initialize the vertices. However, it takes $O(m^{m+1})$ and $O(m^{2(m-1)})$ if we restrict the maximum number of the words in a vertex to a constant m.

Ding and Palmer (2005) insisted that the Viterbi decoding of an MWU-forest takes linear time. In our case, we enumerate the k-best incoming hyperedeges instead of the best one. Because each enumeration takes $O(k^2|\tau(v)|^3)$, the total time complexity also becomes linear to the length of the sentence n similar to Ding and Palmer (2005), i.e. $O(|V|k^2|\tau(v)|^3)$, where $|V| = O(na^{2(a-1)})$ and $a = \min(m, b, d)$.

Table 2: The extracted rules in Figure 5. N denotes the non-lexicalized rules with variables x_i for each $v \in tails(e)$, and L denotes the lexicalized rule.

	$head(e)$	$tails(e)$	$rhs(\gamma)$
N	$\{3\}$	$\{8\} : x_1$	x_1
	$\{8\}$	$\{4\} : x_1, \{5\} : x_2$	when x_1 x_2
	$\{3, 8\}$	$\{4, 5\} : x_1$	when x_1
	$\{3, 8\}$	$\{4\} : x_1, \{5\} : x_2$	when x_1 x_2
	$\{4, 5\}$	$\{6, 7\} : x_1$	I'm in x_1
	$\{5\}$	$\{6, 7\} : x_1$	in x_1
L	$\{6, 7\}$	N/A	the States
	$\{4\}$		I'm
	$\{5\}$		in
	$\{4, 5\}$		I'm in
	$\{5, 6\}$		in the State
	$\{3, 8\}$		When

4 MWU-Forest-to-String Translation Rule Extraction

As an application of our proposed MWU-forest, we extract translation rules for syntax-based SMT. Forest-based translation rule extraction has been suggested by Mi and Huang (2008) although their forest compacts the k-best PSG trees. The extraction procedure is essentially the same as Galley et al. (2004), which identifies the cutting points (frontiers) and extracts the sub-structures from a root to frontiers.

The situation changes in DG because DG does not have intermediate representation. At the dependency structure, a node corresponds to two kinds of target spans. We borrow the definitions of the aligned span ($aspan$), and the covered span ($cspan$) from Na et al. (2010), i.e.

- $aspan(v) = [\min(a_v), \max(a_v)]$, and
- $cspan(v) =$ $aspan(v) \bigcup_{\substack{d \in tails(e) \\ e \in IN(v)}} cspan(d)$

, where $a_v = \{i | j \in v \wedge (i, j) \in A\}$. Figure 5 shows $aspans$ and $cspans$ of a sub-forest of of the MWU-forest in the previous example.

Each span type yields a different rule type: $aspan$ yields a lexicalized rule without any variables, and $cspan$ yields a non-lexicalized rule with variables for the dependents of the head word. For example, Table 2 shows the extracted rule in Figure 5.

In our MWU-forest, the rule extraction procedure is almost identical to a dependency tree-to-string rule extraction except we regard MWUs as vertices. Let f_j and e_i be the j-th source and i-th target word, respectively. As an MWU itself has a internal structure, a lexical rule is a tree-to-string translation rule. Therefore, a lexicalized rule is a pair of the source words s and the target words t as follows:

$$\begin{aligned} s(v) &= \{f_j | j \in v\} \\ t(v) &= \{e_i | i \in aspan(v)\} \end{aligned} \quad (3)$$

In addition, we extract the non-lexicalized rules from a hyperedge e to $cspan$ of the $head(e)$. A non-lexicalized rule is a pair of the source words in the vertices of a hyperedge and the $cspan$ of the target words with substitutions of $cspan(d)$ for each $d \in tails(e)$. We abstract d on the source with $\sigma(d)$ for non-lexicalized rules (row 2 in Table 2). We define the source words s and the target words t as follows:

$$\begin{aligned} s(e) &= \{f_j | j \in head(e) \vee j \in \sigma(d)\} \\ t(e) &= \{e_i | i \in cspan(v) \wedge i \notin cspan(d)\} \\ &\quad \cup \{x_i | d \leftrightarrow x_i\} \end{aligned} \quad (4)$$

Algorithm 2 Extract Rules($H = \langle V, E \rangle$)

```
Γ = ∅
for v ∈ V do
    if aspan(v) is consistent then
        Γ ← Γ ∪ ⟨ s(v) , t(v) ⟩ as in Eq. 3
    end if
    if cspan(v) is consistent then
        for e ∈ IN(v) do
            if cspan(d)∀d ∈ tails(e) then
                Γ ← Γ ∪ ⟨ s(e), t(e) ⟩ as in Eq. 4
            end if
        end for
    end if
end for
return Γ
```

where $d \in tails(e)$.

More formally, we extract a synchronous tree substitution grammar (STSG) which regards the MWUs as non-terminals.

Definition 1 *A STSG using MWU (**STSG-MWU**) is a 6-tuple* $G = \langle \Sigma_S, \Sigma_T, \Delta, \Gamma, S, \phi \rangle$, *where:*

- Σ_S and Σ_T are finite sets of terminals (words, POSs, etc.) of the source and target languages, respectively.
- Δ is a finite set of MWUs in the source language, i.e. $\Delta = \{\Sigma_S\}+$
- Γ is a finite set of production rules where a production rule $\gamma : X \rightarrow \langle\, lhs(\gamma) \,,\, rhs(\gamma),\, \phi \,\rangle$, which is a relationship from Δ to $\{x \cup \Sigma_T\}*$, where ϕ is the bijective function from the source vertices to the variables x in $rhs(\gamma)$. The asterisk represents the Kleenstar operation, and
- S is the start symbol used to represent the whole sentence, i.e. $\gamma_0 : S \rightarrow \langle\, X \,,\, X \,\rangle$.

For each type of span, we only extract the rules if the target span has consistent word alignments, i.e. $span \neq \emptyset \wedge \forall i \in span$, $\{j|(i,j) \in A \cap (i',j) \in A \text{ s.t. } i' \notin span\} = \emptyset$. Algorithm 2 shows the pseudo code of the extraction. Because a vertex has $aspan$ and $csapn$, we extract a lexicalized rule (line 3-5) and/or non-lexicalized rules (line 6-12) for each vertex.

5 Experiment

We used the training corpus provided for the DIALOG Task in IWSLT10 between Chinese and English . The corpus is a collection of 30,033 sentence pairs and consists of dialogs in travel situations (10,061) and parts of the BTEC corpus (19,972). Details about the provided corpus are described in (Paul, 2009). We used the Stanford Parser [1] to obtain word-level dependency structures of Chinese sentences, and GIZA++ [2] to obtain word alignments of the biligual corpus.

We extracted the SCFG-MWU from the biligual corpus with word alignment. In order to investigate the coverage of the extracted rule, we counted the number of the recovered sentences, i.e. counted if the extracted rule for each sentence pair generates the target sentence by combining the extracted rules. As we collected many alternatives in an MWU-forest, we wanted to determine the importance of each source fragment. Mi and Huang (2008) penalized a rule γ by the posterior probability of its tree fragment $lhs(\gamma)$. This posterior probability is also computed in the Inside-Outside fashion that we used in Algorithm 1. Therefore, we regarded the fractional count of a rule γ as

[1]http://nlp.stanford.edu/software/lex-parser.shtml, Version 1.6.4

[2]http://code.google.com/p/giza-pp/

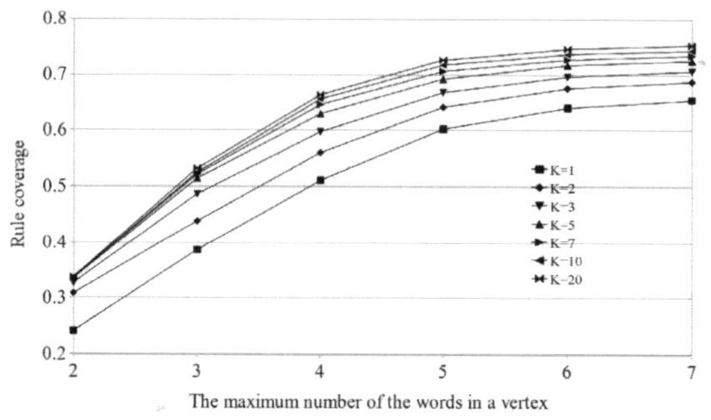

Figure 6: The rule coverage according to the number of the words in a vertex.

$$c(\gamma) = \frac{\alpha\beta(lhs(\gamma))}{\alpha\beta(v_0)}$$

We prioritized the rule according to the fractional count. The priority is used when we combine the rules to restore the target sentence using the extracted rule for each sentence. We varied the maximum size of a vertex m, and the number of incoming hyperedges k. Figure 6 shows the emprical result.

6 Discussion

Figure 6 shows that we need MWU to broaden the coverage of the extracted translation rules. The rule coverage increases as the number of words in an MWU increases, and almost converges at $m = 6$. Our proposed method recover around 75% of the sentences in the corpus when we properly restrict m and k. This is a great improvement over Na et al. (2010), who reported around 60% of the rule coverage without the limitaion of the size of MWUs. They only considered the best decomposition of the dependency tree, while our proposed method collects many alternative MWUs into an MWU-forest. When we considered the best decomposition ($k = 1$), the rule coverage dropped to

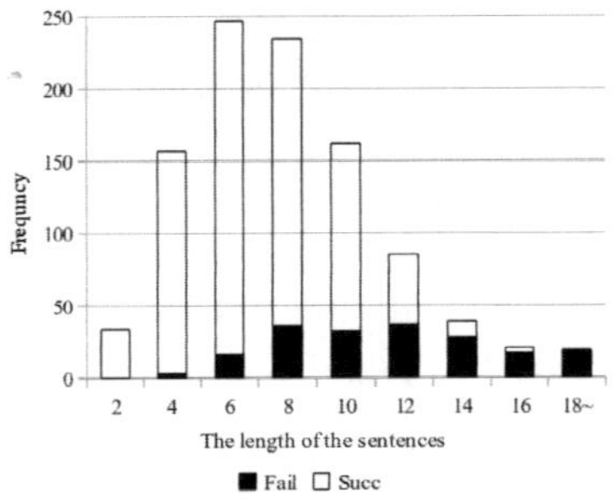

Figure 7: The frequency of the recovery according to the length of the sentences in 1,000 sentences

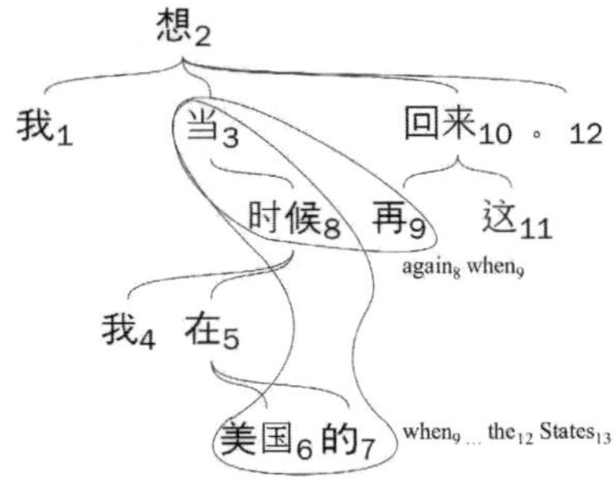

Figure 8: An illustration of ill-formed MWUs

around 65%. This can be viewed as an indirect comparison between Na et al. (2010) and our proposed method in this corpus.

Figure 7 shows that the frequency of success and failure in the recovery depends on the length of the sentences. As the length of sentences increase, the successful recovery occurs less frequently. We investigated the reason of failure in the longer sentences. As a result, the two main sources of the failure are the word alignment error and the dependency parsing error.

Our proposed method does not include all translation rules in PBSMT because of the syntactic constraint. Generally speaking, our proposed method cannot deal with MWUs that do not satisfy the well-formed constraint. However, ill-formed MWUs seems to be useful as well. For example, our proposed method dose not allow ill-formed vertices in an MWU-forest as shown in Figure 8. This would be problematic when we use an erroneuos parsing result. Because dealing with parsing error has been studied in literature, our proposed method has the potential to improve thought future work.

7 Conclusion

We have presented a way of representing sentence structure using MWUs on DG. Because of the absence of the intermdiate representation in DG, we built a simpler structure of MWUs than words using words as vertices of a dependency structure. Unlike previous studies, we collected many alternative structures using MWUs in a packed forest, which is novel. We also extracted MWU-forest-to-string translation rules, and verified the rule coverage empirically. As a consequence, we improvemed the rule coverage compared with a previous work, while retaining the linear asymptotic complexity. We will expand our propose method to develop a syntax-based SMT system in the future, and incoporate the parsing error by considering multiple syntactic analyses.

Acknowledgments

We appreciate the three anonymous reviewers. This work was supported in part by the Korea Science and Engineering Foundation (KOSEF) grant funded by the Korean government (MEST No. 2011-0003029), and in part by the BK 21 Project in 2011.

References

David Chiang. 2010. Learning to translate with source and target syntax. In *Proceedings of the 48th Annual Meeting of the Association for Computational Linguistics*, pages 1443–1452, Uppsala, Sweden, July. Association for Computational Linguistics.

Yuan Ding and Martha Palmer. 2005. Machine translation using probabilistic synchronous dependency insertion grammars. In *ACL '05: Proceedings of the 43rd Annual Meeting on Association for Computational Linguistics*, pages 541–548, Morristown, NJ, USA. Association for Computational Linguistics.

Yuan Ding. 2006. *Machine Translation Using Probabilistic Synchronous Dependency Insertion Grammars*. Ph.D. thesis, August.

Bonnie J. Dorr. 1994. Machine translation divergences: a formal description and proposed solution. *Comput. Linguist.*, 20:597–633, December.

Christopher Dyer, Smaranda Muresan, and Philip Resnik. 2008. Generalizing word lattice translation. In *Proceedings of ACL-08: HLT*, pages 1012–1020, Columbus, Ohio, June. Association for Computational Linguistics.

Jason Eisner. 2003. Learning non-isomorphic tree mappings for machine translation. In *ACL '03: Proceedings of the 41st Annual Meeting on Association for Computational Linguistics*, pages 205–208, Morristown, NJ, USA. Association for Computational Linguistics.

Michel Galley, Mark Hopkins, Kevin Knight, and Daniel Marcu. 2004. What's in a translation rule? In Daniel Marcu Susan Dumais and Salim Roukos, editors, *HLT-NAACL 2004: Main Proceedings*, pages 273–280, Boston, Massachusetts, USA, May 2 - May 7. Association for Computational Linguistics.

Michel Galley, Jonathan Graehl, Kevin Knight, Daniel Marcu, Steve DeNeefe, Wei Wang, and Ignacio Thayer. 2006. Scalable inference and training of context-rich syntactic translation models. In *Proceedings of the 21st International Conference on Computational Linguistics and 44th Annual Meeting of the Association for Computational Linguistics*, pages 961–968, Sydney, Australia, July. Association for Computational Linguistics.

Haitao Mi and Liang Huang. 2008. Forest-based translation rule extraction. In *Proceedings of the 2008 Conference on Empirical Methods in Natural Language Processing*, pages 206–214, Honolulu, Hawaii, October. Association for Computational Linguistics.

Haitao Mi, Liang Huang, and Qun Liu. 2008. Forest-based translation. In *Proceedings of ACL-08: HLT*, pages 192–199, Columbus, Ohio, June. Association for Computational Linguistics.

Haitao Mi, Liang Huang, and Qun Liu. 2010. Machine translation with lattices and forests. In *Coling 2010: Posters*, pages 837–845, Beijing, China, August. Coling 2010 Organizing Committee.

Hwidong Na, Jin-Ji Li, Yeha Lee, and Jong-Hyeok Lee. 2010. A synchronous context free grammar using dependency sequence for syntax-base statistical machine translation. In *The Ninth Conference of the Association for Machine Translation in the Americas (AMTA 2010)*, Denver, Colorado, October.

Michael Paul. 2009. Overview of the iwslt 2009 evaluation campaign.

Libin Shen, Jinxi Xu, and Ralph Weischedel. 2008. A new string-to-dependency machine translation algorithm with a target dependency language model. In *Proceedings of ACL-08: HLT*, pages 577–585, Columbus, Ohio, June. Association for Computational Linguistics.

Anders Søgaard and Jonas Kuhn. 2009. Empirical lower bounds on aligment error rates in syntax-based machine translation. In *Proceedings of the Third Workshop on Syntax and Structure in Statistical Translation (SSST-3) at NAACL HLT 2009*, pages 19–27, Boulder, Colorado, June. Association for Computational Linguistics.

Zhaopeng Tu, Yang Liu, Young-Sook Hwang, Qun Liu, and Shouxun Lin. 2010. Dependency forest for statistical machine translation. In *Proceedings of the 23rd International Conference on Computational Linguistics (Coling 2010)*, pages

1092–1100, Beijing, China, August. Coling 2010 Organizing Committee.

Yuanbin Wu, Qi Zhang, Xuangjing Huang, and Lide Wu. 2009. Phrase dependency parsing for opinion mining. In *Proceedings of the 2009 Conference on Empirical Methods in Natural Language Processing*, pages 1533–1541, Singapore, August. Association for Computational Linguistics.

An Evaluation and Possible Improvement Path for Current SMT Behavior on Ambiguous Nouns

Els Lefever[1,2] and Véronique Hoste[1,2,3]

[1]LT3, Language and Translation Technology Team, University College Ghent
Groot-Brittanniëlaan 45, 9000 Gent, Belgium
[2]Dept. of Applied Mathematics and Computer Science, Ghent University
Krijgslaan 281 (S9), 9000 Gent, Belgium
[3]Dept. of Linguistics, Ghent University
Blandijnberg 2, 9000 Gent, Belgium

Abstract

Mistranslation of an ambiguous word can have a large impact on the understandability of a given sentence. In this article, we describe a thorough evaluation of the translation quality of ambiguous nouns in three different setups. We compared two statistical Machine Translation systems and one dedicated Word Sense Disambiguation (WSD) system. Our WSD system incorporates multilingual information and is independent from external lexical resources. Word senses are derived automatically from word alignments on a parallel corpus. We show that the two WSD classifiers that were built for these experiments (English–French and English–Dutch) outperform the SMT system that was trained on the same corpus. This opens perspectives for the integration of our multilingual WSD module in a statistical Machine Translation framework, in order to improve the automated translation of ambiguous words, and by consequence make the translation output more understandable.

1 Introduction

Word Sense Disambiguation (WSD) is the NLP task that consists in assigning a correct sense to an ambiguous word in a given context. Traditionally, WSD relies on a predefined monolingual sense-inventory such as WordNet (Fellbaum, 1998) and WSD modules are trained on corpora, which are manually tagged with senses from these inventories. A number of issues arise with these monolingual supervised approaches to WSD. First of all, there is a lack of large sense-inventories and sense-tagged corpora for languages other than English. Furthermore, sense inventories such as WordNet contain very fine-grained sense distinctions that make the sense disambiguation task very challenging (even for human annotators), whereas very detailed sense distinctions are often irrelevant for practical applications. In addition to this, there is a growing feeling in the community that WSD should be used and evaluated in real application such as Machine Translation (MT) or Information Retrieval (IR) (Agirre and Edmonds, 2006).

An important line of research consists in the development of dedicated WSD modules for MT. Instead of assigning a sense label from a monolingual sense-inventory to the ambiguous words, the WSD system has to predict a correct translation for the ambiguous word in a given context. In (Vickrey et al., 2005), the problem was defined as a word translation task. The translation choices of ambiguous words are gathered from a parallel corpus by means of word alignment. The authors reported improvements on two simplified translation tasks: word translation and blank filling. The evaluation was done on an English-French parallel corpus but is confronted with the important limitation of having only one valid translation (the aligned translation in the parallel corpus) as a gold standard translation. Cabezas and Resnik (2005) tried to improve an SMT system by adding additional translations to the phrase table, but were confronted with tuning problems of this dedicated WSD feature. Specia (2006) used an inductive logic programming-based WSD system which was tested on seven ambiguous verbs in English-Portuguese translation. The latter systems already present promising results for the use of WSD in MT, but really significant improvements in terms of general machine translation qual-

Proceedings of SSST-5, Fifth Workshop on Syntax, Semantics and Structure in Statistical Translation, pages 52–60,
ACL HLT 2011, Portland, Oregon, USA, June 2011.

ity were for the first time obtained by Carpuat and Wu (2007) and Chan et al. (2007). Both papers describe the integration of a dedicated WSD module in a Chinese-English statistical machine translation framework and report statistically significant improvements in terms of standard MT evaluation metrics.

Stroppa et al. (2007) take a completely different approach to perform some sort of implicit Word Sense Disambiguation in MT. They introduce context-information features that exploit source similarity, in addition to target similarity that is modeled by the language model, in an SMT framework. For the estimation of these features that are very similar to the typical WSD local context features (left and right context words, Part-of-Speech of the focus phrase and context words), they use a memory-based classification framework.

The work we present in this paper is different from previous research in two aspects. Firstly, we evaluate the performance of two state-of-the-art SMT systems and a dedicated WSD system on the translation of ambiguous words. The comparison is done against a manually constructed gold-standard for two language pairs, viz. English–French and English–Dutch. Although it is crucial to measure the general translation quality after integrating a dedicated WSD module in the SMT system, we think it is equally interesting to conduct a dedicated evaluation of the translation quality on ambiguous nouns. Standard SMT evaluation metrics such as BLEU (Papineni et al., 2002) or edit-distance metrics (e.g. Word Error Rate) measure the global overlap of the translation with a reference, and are thus not very sensitive to WSD errors. The mistranslation of an ambiguous word might be a subtle change compared to the reference sentence, but it often drastically affects the global understanding of the sentence.

Secondly, we explore the potential benefits of a real multilingual approach to WSD. The idea to use translations from parallel corpora to distinguish between word senses is based on the hypothesis that different meanings of a polysemous word are often lexicalized across languages (Resnik and Yarowsky, 2000). Many WSD studies have incorporated this cross-lingual evidence idea and have successfully applied bilingual WSD classifiers (Gale and Church, 1993; Ng et al., 2003; Diab and Resnik, 2002) or systems that use a combination of existing WordNets with multilingual evidence (Tufiş et al., 2004). Our WSD system is different in the sense that it is independent from a predefined sense-inventory (it only uses the parallel corpus at hand) and that it is truly multilingual as it incorporates information from four other languages (French, Dutch, Spanish, Italian and German depending on the target language of the classifier). Although our classifiers are still very preliminary in terms of the feature set and parameters that are used, we obtain interesting results on our test sample of ambiguous nouns. We therefore believe our system can have a real added value for SMT, as it can easily be trained for different language pairs on exactly the same corpus which is used to train the SMT system, which should make the integration a lot easier.

The remainder of this paper is organized as follows. Section 2 introduces the two machine translation systems we evaluated, while section 3 describes the feature construction and learning algorithm of our multilingual WSD system. Section 4 gives an overview of the experimental setup and results. We finally draw conclusions and present some future research in Section 5.

2 Statistical Machine Translation Systems

For our experiments, we analyzed the behavior of two phrase-based statistical machine translation (SMT) systems on the translation of ambiguous nouns. SMT generates translations on the basis of statistical models whose parameters are derived from the analysis of sentence-aligned parallel text corpora. Phrase-based SMT is considered as the dominant paradigm in MT research today. It combines a phrase translation model (which is based on the noisy channel model) and a phrase-based decoder in order to find the most probable translation e of a foreign sentence f (Koehn et al., 2003). Usually the Bayes rule is used to reformulate this translation probability:

$$argmax_e p(e|f) = argmax_e p(f|e)p(e)$$

This allows for a language model $p(e)$ that guarantees the fluency and grammatical correctness of the translation, and a separate translation model $p(f|e)$ that focusses on the quality of the translation. Training of both the language model (on monolingual data) as well as the translation model (on bilingual text corpora) requires large amounts of text data.

Research has pointed out that adding more training data, both for the translation as for the language models, results in better translation quality, (Callison-Burch et al., 2009). Therefore it is important to notice that our comparison of the two SMT systems is somewhat unfair, as we compared the Moses research system (that was trained on the Europarl corpus) with the Google commercial system that is trained on a much larger data set. It remains an interesting exercise though, as we consider the commercial system as the upper bound of how far current SMT can get in case it has unlimited access to text corpora and computational resources.

2.1 Moses

The first statistical machine translation system we used is the off-the-shelf Moses toolkit (Koehn et al., 2007). As the Moses system is open-source, well documented, supported by a very lively users forum and reaches state-of-the-art performance, it has quickly been adopted by the community and highly stimulated development in the SMT field. It also features factored translation models, which enable the integration of linguistic and other information at the word level. This makes Moses a good candidate to experiment with for example a dedicated WSD module, that requires more enhanced linguistic information (such as lemmas and Part-of-Speech tags).
We trained Moses for English–French and English–Dutch on a large subsection of the Europarl corpus (See Section 3 for more information on the corpus), and performed some standard cleaning. Table 1 lists the number of aligned sentences after cleaning the bilingual corpus, and the number of uni-, bi- and trigrams that are comprised by the language model.

2.2 Google

In order to gain insights in the upper bounds for current SMT, we also analyzed the output of the Google Translate API[1] for our set of ambiguous nouns. Google Translate currently supports 57 languages. As both the amount of parallel and monolingual training data as well as the computer power are crucial for statistical MT, Google (that disposes of large computing clusters and a network of data centers for Web search) has very valuable assets at its disposal for this task. We can only speculate about the amount of resources that Google uses to train its translation engine. Part of the training data comes from transcripts of United Nations meetings (in six official languages) and those of the European Parliament (Europarl corpus). Google research papers report on a distributed infrastructure that is used to train on up to two trillion tokens, which result in language models containing up to 300 billion ngrams (Brants et al., 2007).

	French	Dutch
Number of bilingual sentence pairs		
	872.689	873.390
Number of ngrams		
unigrams	103.027	173.700
bigrams	1.940.925	2.544.554
trigrams	2.054.906	1.951.992

Table 1: Statistics resulting from the Moses training phase

3 ParaSense

This section describes the ParaSense WSD system: a multilingual classification-based approach to Word Sense Disambiguation. Instead of using a predefined monolingual sense-inventory such as WordNet, we use a language-independent framework where the word senses are derived automatically from word alignments on a parallel corpus. We used the sentence-aligned Europarl corpus (Koehn, 2005) for the construction of our WSD module. The following six languages were selected: English (our focus language), Dutch, French, German, Italian and Spanish. We only considered the 1-1 sentence alignments between English and the five other languages. This way we obtained a six-lingual sentence-aligned subcorpus of Europarl, that contains 884.603 sentences per language. For our experiments we used the lexical sample of twenty ambiguous nouns that was also used in the SemEval-2010 "Cross-Lingual Word Sense Disambiguation" (CLWSD) task (Lefever and Hoste, 2010b), which consists in assigning a

[1] `http://code.google.com/apis/language/translate/overview.html`

correct translation in five supported target languages (viz. French, Italian, Spanish, German and Dutch) for an ambiguous focus word in a given context.

In order to detect all relevant translations for the twenty ambiguous focus words, we ran GIZA++ (Och and Ney, 2003) with its default settings on our parallel corpus. The obtained word alignment output was then considered to be the classification label for the training instances for a given classifier (e.g. the French translation resulting from the word alignment is the label that is used to train the French classifier). This way we obtained all class labels (or oracle translations) for all training instances for our five classifiers (English as an input language and French, German, Dutch, Italian and Spanish as target languages). For the experiments described in this paper, we focused on the English–French and English–Dutch classifiers.

We created two experimental setups. The first training set contains the automatically generated word alignment translations as labels. A postprocessing step was applied on these translations in order to automatically filter leading and trailing determiners and prepositions from the GIZA++ output. For the creation of the second training set, we manually verified all word alignment correspondences of the ambiguous words. This second setup gives an idea of the upperbound performance in case the word alignment output could be further improved for our ambiguous nouns.

3.1 Classifier

To train our WSD classifiers, we used the memory-based learning (MBL) algorithms implemented in TIMBL (Daelemans and van den Bosch, 2005), which has successfully been deployed in previous WSD classification tasks (Hoste et al., 2002). We performed very basic heuristic experiments to define the parameter settings for the classifier, leading to the selection of the Jeffrey Divergence distance metric, Gain Ratio feature weighting and $k = 7$ as number of nearest neighbours. In future work, we plan to use an optimized word-expert approach in which a genetic algorithm performs joint feature selection and parameter optimization per ambiguous word (Daelemans et al., 2003).

3.2 Feature Construction

For the feature vector construction, we combine local context features that were extracted from the English sentence and a set of binary bag-of-words features that were extracted from the aligned translations in the four other languages (that are not the target language of the classifier).

3.2.1 Local Context Features

We extract the same set of local context features from both the English training and test instances. All English sentences were preprocessed by means of a memory-based shallow parser (MBSP) (Daelemans and van den Bosch, 2005) that performs tokenization, Part-of-Speech tagging and text chunking. The preprocessed English instances were used as input to build a set of commonly used WSD features:

- features related to the **focus word itself** being the word form of the focus word, the lemma, Part-of-Speech and chunk information,
- **local context features** related to a window of three words preceding and following the focus word containing for each of these words their full form, lemma, Part-of-Speech and chunk information

These local context features are to be considered as a basic feature set. The Senseval evaluation exercises have shown that feeding additional information sources to the classifier results in better system performance (Agirre and Martinez, 2004). In future experiments we plan to integrate a.o. lemma information on the surrounding content words and semantic analysis (e.g. Singular Value Decomposition (Gliozzo et al., 2005)) in order to detect latent correlations between terms.

3.2.2 Translation Features

In addition to the commonly deployed local context features, we also extracted a set of binary bag-of-words features from the aligned translations that are not the target language of the classifier (e.g. for the French classifier, we extract bag-of-words features from the Italian, Spanish, Dutch and German aligned translations). We preprocessed all aligned translations by means of the Treetagger tool (Schmid, 1994) that outputs Part-of-Speech and lemma information. Per ambiguous focus word, a list of all content words (nouns, adjectives, adverbs and verbs) that occurred in the aligned translations of the English sentences containing this word, was extracted. This resulted in one binary feature per selected content word per language. For the construction of the translation features for the training set, we used the Europarl aligned translations.

As we do not dispose of similar aligned translations for our test instances (where we only have the English test sentences at our disposal), we had to adopt a different strategy. We decided to use the Google Translate API to automatically generate translations for all English test instances in the five target languages. This automatic translation process can be done using whatever machine translation tool, but we chose the Google API because of its easy integration. Online machine translation tools have already been used before to create artificial parallel corpora that were used for NLP tasks such as for instance Named Entity Recognition (Shah et al., 2010). Similarly, Navigli and Ponzetto (2010) used the Google Translate API to enrich BabelNet, a wide-coverage multilingual semantic network, with lexical information for all languages.

Once the automatic aligned translations were generated, we preprocessed them in the same way as we did for the aligned training translations. In a next step, we again selected all content words from these translations and constructed the binary bag-of-words features.

4 Evaluation

To evaluate the two machine translation systems as well as the ParaSense system on their performance on the lexical sample of twenty ambiguous words, we used the sense inventory and test set of the SemEval Cross-Lingual Word Sense Disambiguation task. The sense inventory was built up on the basis of the Europarl corpus: all retrieved translations of a polysemous word were manually grouped into clusters, which constitute different senses of that given word. The test instances were selected from the JRC-ACQUIS Multilingual Parallel Corpus[2] and BNC[3]. There were in total 50 test instances for each of the twenty ambiguous words in the sample. To label the test data, native speakers assigned three valid translations from the predefined clusters of Europarl translations to each test instance. A more detailed description of the construction of the data set can be found in (Lefever and Hoste, 2010a). As evaluation metric, we used a straightforward accuracy measure that divides the number of correct answers by the total amount of test instances. As a baseline, we selected the most frequent lemmatized translation that resulted from the automated word alignment (GIZA++).

The output of the ParaSense WSD module consists of a lemmatized translation of the ambiguous focus word in the target language. The output of the two statistical machine translation systems, however, is a translation of the full English input sentence. Therefore we manually selected the translation of the ambiguous focus word from the full translation, and made sure the translation was put in its base form (masculine singular form for nouns and adjectives, infinitive form for verbs).

Table 2 lists the accuracy figures for the baseline, two flavors of the ParaSense system (with and without correction of the word alignment output), Moses and Google for English–French and English–Dutch.

A first conclusion is that all systems beat the most frequent sense baseline. As expected, the Google system (where there was no limitation on the training data) achieves the best results, but for French the considerable difference in training size only leads to modest performance gains compared to the ParaSense System. Another interesting observation is that the ParaSense system that uses manually verified translation labels hardly beats the system that uses automatically generated class labels. This is promising as it makes the manual interventions on the data superfluous and leads to a fully automatic system development process.

Figure 1 illustrates the accuracy figures for French for all three systems (for the ParaSense system we used the flavor that incorporates the non-validated translation labels) on all individual test words.

The three curves follow a similar pattern, except for some words where Moses (*mood, scene, side*) or both Moses and ParaSense (*figure*) perform worse. As the curves show, some words (e.g. *coach, figure,*

[2]http://wt.jrc.it/lt/Acquis/

[3]http://www.natcorp.ox.ac.uk/

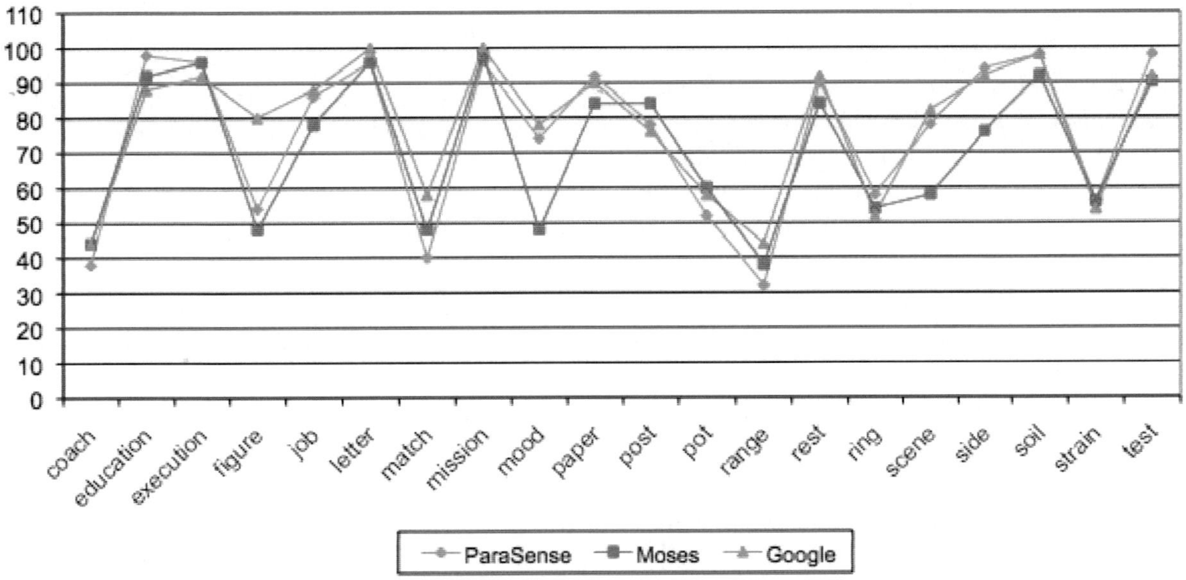

Figure 1: Accuracy figures per system for all 20 test words

	French	Dutch
Baseline	63%	59%
ParaSense system		
Non Corrected word alignment labels	75%	68%
Corrected word alignment labels	76%	68%
SMT Systems		
Moses	71%	63%
Google	78%	74%

Table 2: Accuracy figures averaged over all twenty test words

match, range) are particularly hard to disambiguate, while others obtain very high scores (e.g. *letter, mission, soil*). The almost perfect scores for the latter can be explained by the fact that these words all have a very generic translation in French (respectively *lettre, mission, sol*) that can be used for all senses of the word, although there might be more suited translations for each of the senses depending on the context. As the manual annotators could pick three good translations for each test instance, the most generic translation often figures between the gold standard translations.

The low scores for some other words can often be explained through the relationship with the number of training instances (corresponding to the frequency of the word in the training corpus) and the ambiguity (number of translations) per word. As is shown in Table 3, both for *coach* and *match* there are very few examples in the corpus, while *figure* and *range*

	Number of Instances	Number of Translations
coach	66	11
education	4380	55
execution	489	26
figure	2298	167
job	7531	184
letter	1822	75
match	109	21
mission	1390	46
mood	100	26
paper	3650	94
post	998	68
pot	63	27
range	1428	145
rest	1739	80
ring	143	46
scene	284	50
side	3533	261
soil	287	16
strain	134	40
test	1368	92

Table 3: Number of instances and classes for all twenty test words in French

are very ambiguous (respectively 167 and 145 translations to choose from).

The main novelty of our ParaSense system lies in the application of a multilingual approach to perform WSD, as opposed to the more classical approach that only uses monolingual local context features. Consequently we also ran a set of additional experiments to examine the contribution of the different translation features to the WSD performance. Table 4 shows the accuracy figures for French and Dutch for a varying number of translation features including the other four languages: Italian, Spanish, French and Dutch for the French classifier or French for the Dutch classifier. The scores clearly confirm the validity of our hypothesis: the classifiers using translation features are constantly better than the one that merely uses English local context features. For French, the other two romance languages seem to contribute most: the classifier that uses Italian and Spanish bag-of-words features achieves the best performance (75.50%), whereas the classifier that incorporates German and Dutch translations obtains the worst scores (71.90%). For Dutch, the interpretation of the scores is less straightforward: the Italian-German combination achieves the best result (69%), but the difference with the other classifiers that use two romance languages (Italian-Spanish: 67.70% and Italian-French: 67.20%) is less salient than for French. In order to draw final conclusions on the contribution of the different languages, we probably first need to optimize our feature base and classification parameters. For the current experiments, we use very sparse bag-of-words features that can be optimized in different ways (e.g. feature selection, reduction of the bag-of-words features by applying semantic analysis such as Singular Value Decomposition, etc.).

	French	**Dutch**
Baseline	63.10	59.40
All four translation features		
It, Es, De, Nl/Fr	75.20	68.10
Three translation features		
It, Es, De	75.00	67.80
Es, De, Nl/Fr	74.70	66.30
It, De, Nl/Fr	75.20	68.20
It, Es, Nl/Fr	75.30	67.90
Average	75.05	67.55
Two translation features		
Es, De	74.70	67.80
It, De	75.10	69.00
De, Nl/Fr	71.90	68.00
It, Es	75.50	67.70
Es, Nl/Fr	74.20	68.10
It, Nl/Fr	75.30	67.20
Average	74.45	67.96
One translation feature		
De	74.50	66.50
Es	75.20	68.40
It	74.90	66.70
Nl/Fr	73.80	66.20
Average	74.60	66.95
No translation features		
None	73.50	63.90

Table 4: Accuracy figures for French and Dutch for a varying number of translation features including the other four languages viz. Italian (It), Spanish (Es), German (De) and French (Fr) or Dutch (Nl)

5 Conclusion

We presented a thorough evaluation of two statistical Machine Translation systems and one dedicated WSD system on a lexical sample of English ambiguous nouns. Our WSD system incorporates both monolingual local context features and bag-of-words features that are built from aligned translations in four additional languages. The best results are obtained by Google, the SMT system that is built with no constraints on data size or computational resources. Although there is still a lot of room for improvement on the feature base and optimization of the WSD classifiers, our results show that the ParaSense system outperforms Moses that is built with the same training corpus.

We also noticed large differences among the test words, often related to the number of training instances and the number of translations the classifier (or decoder) has to choose from.

Additional experiments with the ParaSense system incorporating a number of varying translations features allow us to confirm the validity of our hypothesis. The classifiers that use the multilingual bag-of-words features clearly outperform the classifier that only uses local context features.

In future work, we want to expand our feature set and apply a genetic algorithm to perform joint feature selection, parameter optimization and instance selection. In addition, we will apply semantic analysis tools (such as SVD or LSA) on our multilingual bag-of-words sets in order to detect latent semantic topics in the multilingual feature base. Finally, we want to evaluate to which extent the integration of our WSD output helps the decoder to pick the correct translation in a real SMT framework.

References

E. Agirre and P. Edmonds, editors. 2006. *Word Sense Disambiguation. Algorithms and Applications*. Text, Speech and Language Technology. Springer, Dordrecht.

E. Agirre and D. Martinez. 2004. Smoothing and Word Sense Disambiguation. In *Proceedings of EsTAL - España for Natural Language Processing*, Alicante, Spain.

Th. Brants, A.C. Popat, P. Xu, F.J. Och, and J. Dean. 2007. Large Language Models in Machine Translation. In *Proceedings of the 2007 Joint Conference on Empirical methods in Natural Language Processing and Computational Natural Language Learning*, pages 858–867.

C. Cabezas and P. Resnik. 2005. Using wsd techniques for lexical selection in statistical machine translation. Technical report, Institute for Advanced Computer Studies, University of Maryland.

C. Callison-Burch, Ph. Koehn, Ch. Monz, and J. Schroeder. 2009. Findings of the 2009 Workshop on Statistical Machine Translation. In *Proceedings of the 4th EACL Workshop on Statistical Machine Translation*, pages 1–28, Athens, Greece.

M. Carpuat and D. Wu. 2007. Improving statistical machine translation using word sense disambiguation. In *Proceedings of the 2007 Joint Conference on Empirical Methods in Natural Language Processing and Computational Natural Language Learning (EMNLP-CoNLL)*, pages 61–72, Prague, Czech Republic.

Y.S. Chan, H.T. Ng, and D. Chiang. 2007. Word sense disambiguation improves statistical machine translation. In *Proceedings of the 45th Annual Meeting of the Association of Computational Linguistics*, pages 33–40, Prague, Czech Republic.

W. Daelemans and A. van den Bosch. 2005. *Memory-based Language Processing*. Cambridge University Press.

W. Daelemans, V. Hoste, F. De Meulder, and B. Naudts. 2003. Combined optimization of feature selection and algorithm parameters in machine learning of language. *Machine Learning*, pages 84–95.

M. Diab and P. Resnik. 2002. An Unsupervised Method for Word Sense Tagging Using Parallel Corpora. In *Proceedings of ACL*, pages 255–262.

C. Fellbaum. 1998. *WordNet: An Electronic Lexical Database*. MIT Press.

W.A. Gale and K.W. Church. 1993. A program for aligning sentences in bilingual corpora. *Computational Linguistics*, 19(1):75–102.

A.M. Gliozzo, C. Giuliano, and C. Strapparava. 2005. Domain Kernels for Word Sense Disambiguation. In

43nd Annual Meeting of the Association for Computational Linguistics. (ACL-05).

V. Hoste, I. Hendrickx, W. Daelemans, and A. van den Bosch. 2002. Parameter Optimization for Machine-Learning of Word Sense Disambiguation. *Natural Language Engineering, Special Issue on Word Sense Disambiguation Systems*, 8:311–325.

P. Koehn, F.J. Och, and D. Marcu. 2003. Statistical Phrase-based translation. In *HLT-NAACL 2003: conference combining Human Language Technology conference series and the North American Chapter of the Association for Computational Linguistics conference series*, pages 48–54, Edmonton, Canada.

P. Koehn, H. Hoang, A. Birch, C. Callison-Burch, M. Federico, N. Bertoldi, B. Cowan, W. Shen, C. Moran, R. Zens, C. Dyer, O. Bojar, A. Constantin, and E. Herbst. 2007. Moses: Open Source Toolkit for Statistical Machine Translation. In *Proceedings of the ACL 2007 Demo and Poster Sessions*, pages 177–180, Prague, Czech Republic.

P. Koehn. 2005. Europarl: a parallel corpus for statistical machine translation. In *Tenth Machine Translation Summit*, pages 79–86, Phuket, Thailand.

E. Lefever and V. Hoste. 2010a. Construction of a Benchmark Data Set for Cross-Lingual Word Sense Disambiguation. In Nicoletta Calzolari, Khalid Choukri, Bente Maegaard, Joseph Mariani, Jan Odijk, Stelios Piperidis, and Daniel Tapias, editors, *Proceedings of the seventh International Conference on Language Resources and Evaluation (LREC'10)*, Valletta, Malta, May. European Language Resources Association (ELRA).

E. Lefever and V. Hoste. 2010b. SemEval-2010 Task 3: Cross-Lingual Word Sense Disambiguation. In *Proceedings of the 5th International Workshop on Semantic Evaluation, ACL 2010*, pages 15–20, Uppsala, Sweden.

R. Navigli and S.P. Ponzetto. 2010. BabelNet: Building a very large multilingual semantic network. In *Proceedings of the 48th Annual Meeting of the Association for Computational Linguistics*, pages 216–225, Uppsala, Sweden.

H.T. Ng, B. Wang, and Y.S. Chan. 2003. Exploiting parallel texts for word sense disambiguation: An empirical study. In *41st Annual Meeting of the Association for Computational Linguistics (ACL)*, pages 455–462, Sapporo, Japan.

F. J. Och and H. Ney. 2003. A systematic comparison of various statistical alignment models. *Computational Linguistics*, 29(1):19–51.

K. Papineni, S. Roukos, T. Ward, and Zhu W.-J. 2002. BLEU: a method for automatic evaluation of machine translation. In *Proceedings of the 40th Annual Meeting of the Association for Computational Linguistics*.

Ph. Resnik and D. Yarowsky. 2000. Distinguishing systems and distinguishing senses: New evaluation methods for word sense disambiguation. *Natural Language Engineering*, 5(3):113–133.

H. Schmid. 1994. Probabilistic part-of-speech tagging using decision trees. In *Proceedings of the International Conference on new methods in Language Processing*, Manchester, UK.

R. Shah, B. Lin, A. Gershman, and R. Frederking. 2010. SYNERGY: A Named Entity Recognition System for Resource-scarce Languages such as Swahili using Online Machine Translation. In *Proceedings of the Second Workshop on African Language Technology (AFLAT 2010)*, Valletta, Malt.

L. Specia. 2006. A Hybrid Relational Approach for WSD - First Results. In *Proceedings of the COLING/ACL 2006 Student Research Workshop*, pages 55–60, Sydney, Australia.

N. Stroppa, A. van den Bosch, and A. Way. 2007. Exploiting source similarity for smt using context-informed features. In *Proceedings of the 11th Conference on Theoretical and Methodological Issues in Machine Translation (TMI 2007)*.

D. Tufiş, R. Ion, and N. Ide. 2004. Fine-Grained Word Sense Disambiguation Based on Parallel Corpora, Word Alignment, Word Clustering and Aligned Wordnets. In *Proceedings of the 20th International Conference on Computational Linguistics (COLING 2004)*, pages 1312–1318, Geneva, Switzerland, August. Association for Computational Linguistics.

D. Vickrey, L. Biewald, M. Teyssier, and D. Koller. 2005. Word-sense disambiguation for machine translation. In *Proceedings of EMNLP05*, pages 771–778.

Improving Reordering for Statistical Machine Translation with Smoothed Priors and Syntactic Features

Bing Xiang, Niyu Ge, and Abraham Ittycheriah
IBM T. J. Watson Research Center
Yorktown Heights, NY 10598
{bxiang,niyuge,abei}@us.ibm.com

Abstract

In this paper we propose several novel approaches to improve phrase reordering for statistical machine translation in the framework of maximum-entropy-based modeling. A smoothed prior probability is introduced to take into account the distortion effect in the priors. In addition to that we propose multiple novel distortion features based on syntactic parsing. A new metric is also introduced to measure the effect of distortion in the translation hypotheses. We show that both smoothed priors and syntax-based features help to significantly improve the reordering and hence the translation performance on a large-scale Chinese-to-English machine translation task.

1 Introduction

Over the past decade, statistical machine translation (SMT) has evolved into an attractive area in natural language processing. SMT takes a source sequence, $S = [s_1\ s_2\ \ldots\ s_K]$ from the source language, and generates a target sequence, $T^* = [t_1\ t_2\ \ldots\ t_L]$, by finding the most likely translation given by:

$$T^* = \arg\max_T p(T|S) \tag{1}$$

In most of the existing approaches, following (Brown et al., 1993), Eq. (1) is factored using the source-channel model into

$$T^* = \arg\max_T p(S|T)p^\lambda(T), \tag{2}$$

where the two models, the translation model, $p(S|T)$, and the language model (LM), $p(T)$, are estimated separately: the former using a parallel corpus and a hidden alignment model and the latter using a typically much larger monolingual corpus. The weighting factor λ is typically tuned on a development test set by optimizing a translation accuracy criterion such as BLEU (Papineni et al., 2002).

In recent years, among all the proposed approaches, the phrase-based method has become the widely adopted one in SMT due to its capability of capturing local context information from adjacent words. Word order in the translation output relies on how the phrases are reordered based on both language model scores and distortion cost/penalty (Koehn et al., 2003), among all the features utilized in a maximum-entropy (log-linear) model (Och and Ney, 2002). The distortion cost utilized during the decoding is usually a penalty linearly proportional to the number of words in the source sentence that are skipped in a translation path.

In this paper, we propose several novel approaches to improve reordering in the phrase-based translation with a maximum-entropy model. In Section 2, we review the previous work that focused on the distortion and phrase reordering in SMT. In Section 3, we briefly review the baseline of this work. In Section 4, we introduce a smoothed prior probability by taking into account the distortions in the priors. In Section 5, we present multiple novel distortion features based on syntactic parsing. A new distortion evaluation metric is proposed in Section 6 and experimental results on a large-scale Chinese-English machine translation task are reported in Section 7. Section 8 concludes the paper.

Proceedings of SSST-5, Fifth Workshop on Syntax, Semantics and Structure in Statistical Translation, pages 61–69,
ACL HLT 2011, Portland, Oregon, USA, June 2011.

2 Previous Work

Significant amount of research has been conducted in the past on the word reordering problem in SMT. In (Brown et al., 1993) IBM Models 3 through 5 model reordering based on the surface word information. For example, Model 4 attempts to assign target-language positions to source-language words by modeling $d(j|i, K, L)$ where j is the target-language position, i is the source-language position, K and L are respectively source and target sentence lengths. These models are not effective in modeling reordering because they do not have enough context and lack structural information.

Phrase-based SMT systems such as (Koehn et al., 2003) move from using words as translation units to using phrases. One of the advantages of phrase-based SMT systems is that the local reordering is inherent in the phrase translations. However, phrase-based SMT systems capture reordering instances and not reordering phenomena. It has trouble to produce the right translation order if the training data does not contain the specific phrase pairs. For example, phrases do not capture the phenomenon that Arabic adjectives and nouns need to be reordered.

Instead of directly modeling the distance of word movement, some phrase-level reordering models indicate how to move phrases, also called orientations. Orientations typically apply to the adjacent phrases. Two adjacent phrases can be either placed monotonically (sometimes called straight) or swapped (non-monotonically or inverted). In (Och and Ney, 2004; Tillmann, 2004; Kumar and Byrne, 2005; Al-Onaizan and Papineni, 2006; Xiong et al., 2006; Zens and Ney, 2006; Ni et al., 2009), people presented models that use lexical features from the phrases to predict their orientations. These models are very powerful in predicting local phrase placements. In (Galley and Manning, 2008) a hierarchical orientation model is introduced that captures some non-local phrase reordering by a shift reduce algorithm. Because of the heavy use of lexical features, these models tend to suffer from data sparseness problems.

Syntax information has been used for reordering, such as in (Xia and McCord, 2004; Collins et al., 2005; Wang et al., 2007; Li et al., 2007; Chang et al., 2009). More recently, in (Ge, 2010) a probabilistic reordering model is presented to model directly the source translation sequence and explicitly assign probabilities to the reordering of the source input with no restrictions on gap, length or adjacency. The reordering model is used to generate a reordering lattice which encodes many reordering and their costs (negative log probability). Another recent work is (Green et al., 2010), which estimates future linear distortion cost and presents a discriminative distortion model that predicts word movement during translation based on multiple features.

This work differentiates itself from all the previous work on the phrase reordering as the following. Firstly, we propose a smoothed distortion prior probability in the maximum-entropy-based MT framework. It not only takes into account the distortion in the prior, but also alleviates the data sparseness problem. Secondly, we propose multiple syntactic features based on the source-side parse tree to capture the reordering phenomena between two different languages. The correct reordering patterns will be automatically favored during the decoding, due to the higher weights obtained through the maximum entropy training on the parallel data. Finally, we also introduce a new metric to quantify the effect on the distortions in different systems. The experiments on a Chinese-English MT task show that these proposed approaches additively improve both the distortion and translation performance significantly.

3 Maximum-Entropy Model for MT

In this section we give a brief review of a special maximum-entropy (ME) model as introduced in (Ittycheriah and Roukos, 2007). The model has the following form,

$$p(\mathbf{t}, j|\mathbf{s}) = \frac{p_0(\mathbf{t}, j|\mathbf{s})}{Z} exp \sum_i \lambda_i \phi_i(\mathbf{t}, j, \mathbf{s}), \quad (3)$$

where $\mathbf{s}$ is a source phrase, and $\mathbf{t}$ is a target phrase. j is the jump distance from the previously translated source word to the current source word. During training j can vary widely due to automatic word alignment in the parallel corpus. To limit the sparseness created by long jumps, j is capped to a window of source words (-5 to 5 words) around the last translated source word. Jumps outside the window are treated as being to the edge of the window. In

Eq. (3), p_0 is a prior distribution, Z is a normalizing term, and $\phi_i(\mathbf{t}, j, \mathbf{s})$ are the features of the model, each being a binary question asked about the source and target streams. The feature weights λ_i can be estimated with the Improved Iterative Scaling (IIS) algorithm.

Several categories of features have been proposed:

- Lexical features that examine source word, target word and jump;
- Lexical context features that examine the previous and next source words, and also the previous two target words;
- Segmentation features based on morphological analysis;
- Part-of-speech (POS) features that collect the syntactic information from the source and target words;
- Coverage features that examine the coverage status of the source words to the left and to the right. They fire only if the left source is open (untranslated) or the right source is closed.

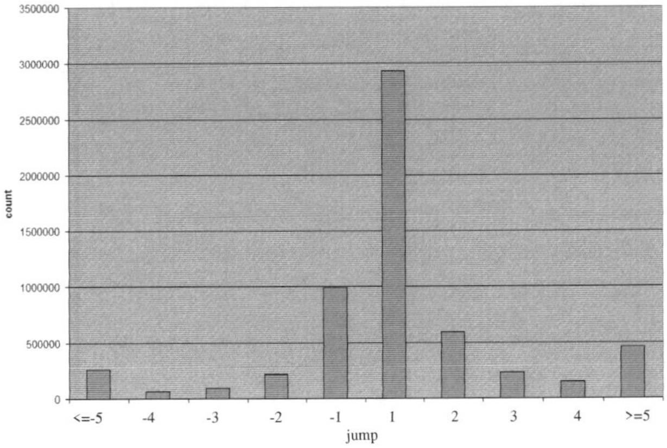

Figure 1: Counts of jumps for words with POS *NN*.

4 Distortion Priors

Generally the prior distribution in Eq. (3) can contain any information we know about the future.

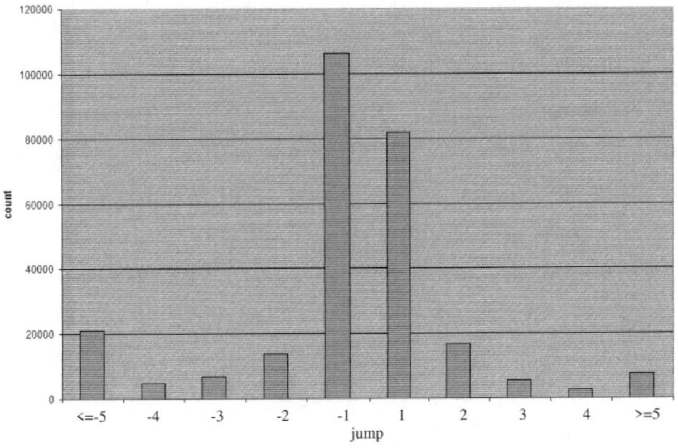

Figure 2: Counts of jumps for words with POS *NT*.

In (Ittycheriah and Roukos, 2007), the normalized phrase count is utilized as the prior, i.e.

$$p_0(\mathbf{t}, j|\mathbf{s}) \approx \frac{1}{l} p_0(\mathbf{t}|\mathbf{s}) = \frac{C(\mathbf{s}, \mathbf{t})}{l * C(\mathbf{s})} \qquad (4)$$

where l is the jump window size (a constant), $C(\mathbf{s}, \mathbf{t})$ is the co-ocurrence count of phrase pair ($\mathbf{s}$, $\mathbf{t}$), and $C(\mathbf{s})$ is the source phrase count of $\mathbf{s}$. It can be seen that distortion j is not taken into account in Eq. (4). The contribution of distortion solely comes from the features. In this work, we estimate the prior probability with distortion included,

$$p_0(\mathbf{t}, j|\mathbf{s}) = p_0(\mathbf{t}|\mathbf{s}) p(j|\mathbf{s}, \mathbf{t}) \qquad (5)$$

where $p(j|\mathbf{s}, \mathbf{t})$ is the distortion probability for a given phrase pair ($\mathbf{s}$, $\mathbf{t}$).

Due to the sparseness issue in the estimation of $p(j|\mathbf{s}, \mathbf{t})$, we choose to smooth it with the global distortion probability through

$$p(j|\mathbf{s}, \mathbf{t}) = \alpha p_l(j|\mathbf{s}, \mathbf{t}) + (1 - \alpha) p_g(j), \qquad (6)$$

where p_l is the local distortion probability estimated based on the counts of jumps for each phrase pair in the training, p_g is the global distortion probability estimated on all the training data, and α is the interpolation weight. In this work, p_g is estimated based on either source POS (if it's a single-word source phrase) or source phrase size (if it's more than one word long), as shown below.

$$p_g(j) = \begin{cases} P_g(j|POS), & \text{if } |\mathbf{s}| = 1 \\ P_g(j||\mathbf{s}|), & \text{if } |\mathbf{s}| > 1 \end{cases} \qquad (7)$$

In this way, the system can differentiate the distortion distributions for single source words with different POS tags, such as adjectives versus nouns. And in the meantime, we also differentiate the distortion distribution with different source phrase lengths. We show several examples of the jump distributions in Fig. 1 and 2 collected from 1M sentence pairs in a Chinese-to-English parallel corpus with automatic parsing and word alignment. Fig. 1 shows the count histogram for single-word phrases with POS tag as *NN*. The distortion with $j = 1$, i.e. monotone, dominates the distribution with the highest count. The reordering with $j = -1$ has the second highest count. Such pattern is shared by most of the other POS tags. However, Fig. 2 shows that the distribution of jumps for *NT* is quite different from *NN*. The jump with $j = -1$ is actually the most dominant, with higher counts than monotone translation. This is due to the different order in English when translating Chinese temporal nouns.

5 Distortion Features

Although the maximum entropy translation model has an explicit indicator of distortion, j, built into the features, we discuss in this section some novel features that try to capture the distortion phenomena of translation. These features are questions about the parse tree of the source language and in particular about the local parse node neighborhood of the current source word being translated. Figure 3 shows an example sentence from the Chinese-English Parallel Treebank (LDC2009E83) and the source language parse is displayed on the left. The features below can be viewed as either being within a parse node or asking about the coverage status of neighborhood nodes.

Since these features are asking about the current coverage, they are specific to a path in the search lattice during the decoding phase of translation. Training these features is done by evaluating on the path defined by the automatic word alignment of the parallel corpus sentence.

5.1 Parse Tree Modifications

The 'de' construction in Chinese is by now famous. In order to ask more coherent questions about the parse neighborhood, we modify the parse structures to "raise" the 'de' structure. The parse trees annotated by the LDC have a structure as shown in Fig. 4. After raising the 'de' structure we obtain the tree in Fig. 5.

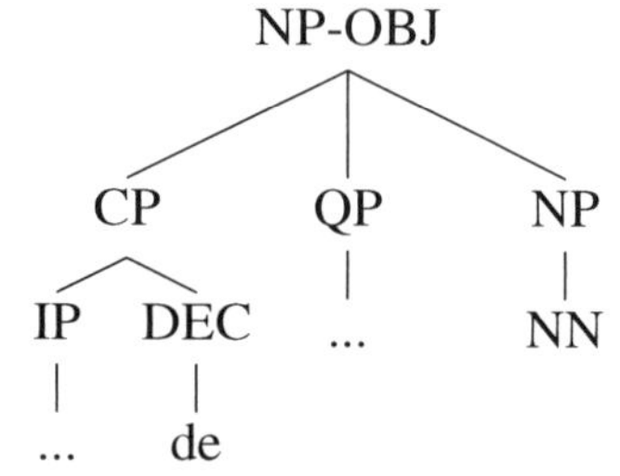

Figure 4: Original parse tree from LDC.

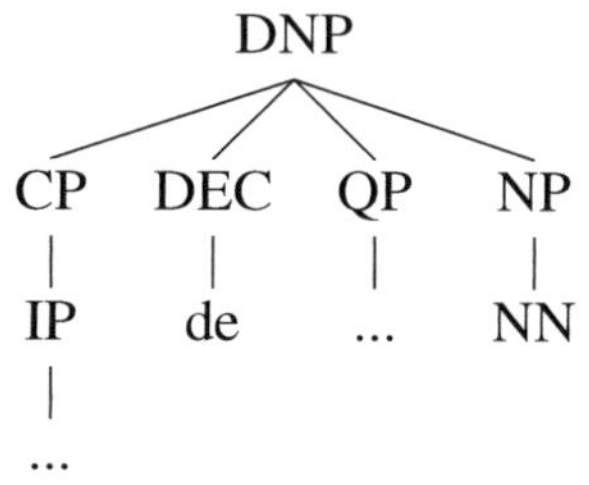

Figure 5: The parse tree after transformation.

The transformation has been applied to the example shown in Figure 3. The resulting flat structure facilitates the parse sibling feature discussed below.

5.2 Parse Coverage Feature

The first set of new features we will introduce is the source parse coverage feature. This feature is interior to a source parse node and asks if the leaves under this parse node are covered (translated) or not so far. The feature has the following components:

ϕ_i(*SourceWord, TargetWord, SourceParseParent, jump, Coverage*).

Unary parents in the source parse tree are excluded since the feature has no ambiguity in coverage. In Figure 3, the 'PP' node above position 5 has two children, P, NP. When translating source position 6, this feature indicates that the PP node has a leaf that is already covered.

5.3 Parse Sibling Feature

The second set of new features is the source parse sibling feature. This feature asks whether the neigh-

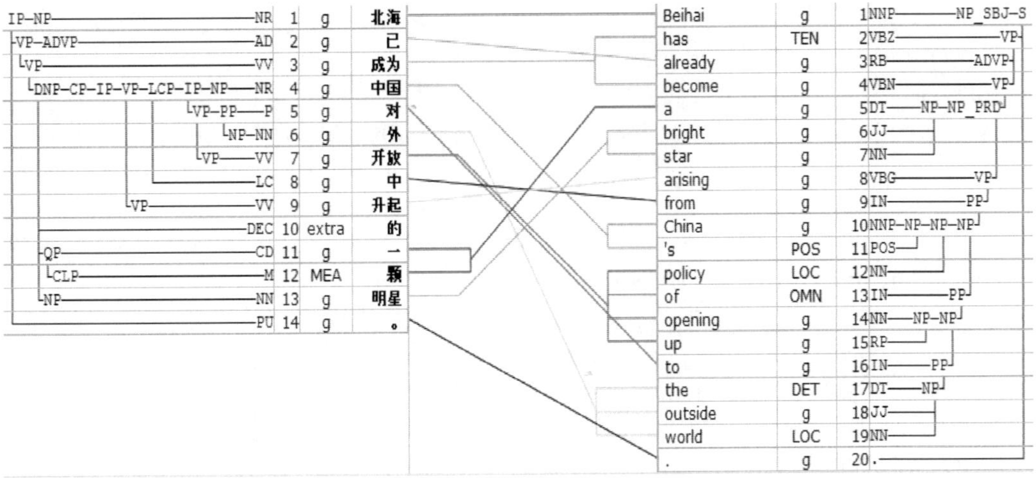

Figure 3: Chinese-English example.

boring parse node has been covered or not. The feature includes two types:

ϕ_i(*SourceWord, TargetWord, SourceParseSibling, jump, SiblingCoverage, SiblingOrientation*)

and

ϕ_i(*SourcePOS, TargetPOS, SourceParseSibling, jump, SiblingCoverage, SiblingOrientation*).

Some example features for the first type are shown in Table 1, where $\alpha_i = e^{\lambda_i}$. The coverage status (Cov) of the parse sibling node indicates if the node is covered completely (1), partially (2) or not covered (0). In order to capture the relationship of the neighborhood node, we indicate the orientation which can be either of {left (-1), right (1)}. Given the example shown in Figure 3, at source position 10, the system can now ask about the 'CP' structure to the left and the 'QP' and 'NP' structures to the right. An α_i of greater than 1.0 (meaning $\lambda_i > 0$) indicates that the feature increases the probability of the related target block. From these examples, it's clear that the system prefers to produce an empty translation for the Chinese word "de" when the 'QP' and 'NP' nodes to the right of it are already covered (the first two features in Table 1) and when the 'CP' node to left is still uncovered (the third feature). The last feature in the table shows α_i for the case when 'CP' has already been covered.

These features are able to capture neighborhoods that are much larger than the original baseline model which only asked questions about the immediate lexical neighborhood of the current source word.

Cnt	α_i	Tgt	Src	Parse Node	Cov	Orientation
18065	2.06	e_0	de	QP	1	1
366153	1.99	e_0	de	NP	1	1
143433	3.41	e_0	de	CP	0	-1
99297	1.05	e_0	de	CP	1	-1

Table 1: Parse Sibling Word Features (e_0 represents empty target).

6 A New Distortion Evaluation Metric

MT performance is usually measured by such metric as BLEU which measures the MT output as a whole including word choice and reordering. It is useful to measure these components separately. Unigram BLEU (BLEUn1) measures the precision of word choice. We need a metric for measuring reordering accuracy. The naive way of counting accuracy at every source position does not account for the case of the phrasal movement. If a phrase is moved to the wrong place, every source word in the phrase would be penalized whereas a more reasonable metric would penalize the phrase movement only once if the phrase boundary is correct.

We propose the following pair-wise distortion metric. From an MT output, we first extract the source visit sequence:

Hyp: $\{h_1, h_2, \ldots h_n\}$

where h_i are the visit order of the source sentence. From the reference, we extract the true visit sequence:

Ref: $\{r_1, r_2, \ldots r_n\}$

The Pair-wise Distortion metric PDscore can be computed as follows:

$$PDscore(\vec{H}) = \sum_{i=1}^{n} \frac{I(h_i = r_j \wedge h_{i-1} = r_{j-1})}{n} \tag{8}$$

It measures how often the translation output gets the pair-wise source visit order correct. We notice that an MT metric named LRscore was proposed in (Birch and Osborne, 2010). It computes the distance between two word order sequences, which is different from the metric we proposed here.

7 Experiments

7.1 Data and Baseline

We conduct a set of experiments on a Chinese-to-English MT task. The training data includes the UN parallel corpus and LDC-released parallel corpora, with about 11M sentence pairs, 320M words in total (counted at the English side). To evaluate the smoothed distortion priors and different features, we use an internal data set as the development set and the NIST MT08 evaluation set as the test set, which includes 76 documents (691 sentences) in newswire and 33 documents (666 sentences) in weblog, both with 4 sets of references for each sentence. Instead of using all the training data, we sample the training corpus based on the dev/test set to train the system more efficiently. The most recent and good-quality corpora are sampled first. For the given test set, we obtain the first 20 instances of n-grams (length from 1 to 15) from the test that occur in the training universe and the resulting sentences then form the training sample. In the end, 1M sentence pairs are selected for the sampled training for each genre of the MT08 test set.

A 5-gram language model is trained from the English Gigaword corpus and the English portion of the parallel corpus used in the translation model training. The Chinese parse trees are produced by a maximum entropy based parser (Ratnaparkhi, 1997). The baseline decoder is a phrase-based decoder that employs both normal phrases and also non-contiguous phrases. The value of maximum skip is set to 9 in all the experiments. The smoothing parameter α for distortion prior is set to 0.9 empirically based on the results on the development set.

7.2 Distortion Evaluation

We evaluate the MT distortion using the metric in Eq. (8) on two hand-aligned test sets. Test-278 includes 278 held-out sentences. Test-52 contains the first 52 sentences from the MT08 Newswire set, with the Chinese input sentences manually aligned to the first set of reference translations. From the hand alignment, we extract the true source visit sequence and this is the reference.

The evaluation results are in Table 2. It is shown that the smoothed distortion prior, parse coverage feature and parse sibling feature each provides improvement on the PDscore on Test-278 and Test-52. The final system scores are 2 to 3 points absolute higher than the baseline scores. The state visit sequence in the final system is closer to the true visit sequence than that of the baseline. This indicates the advantage of using both parse-based syntactic features and also the smoothed prior that takes into account of the distortion effect. We also provide an upper-bound in the last row by computing the PDscore between the first and second set of references for Test-52. The number shows the agreement between two human translators in terms of PDscore is around 71%.

System	Test-278	Test-52
ME Baseline	44.58	48.96
+Prior	45.12	49.22
+COV	45.00	49.03
+SIB	45.43	49.20
+COV+SIB	46.16	49.45
+Prior+COV+SIB	47.68	51.04
Ref1 vs. Ref2	-	70.99

Table 2: Distortion accuracy PDscore (Prior:smoothed distortion prior; COV:parse coverage feature; SIB:parse sibling feature).

7.3 Translation Results

Translation results on the MT08 Newswire set and MT08 Weblog set are listed in Table 3 and Table 4 respectively. The MT performance is measured with the widely adopted BLEU and TER (Snover et al., 2006) metrics. We also compare the results from different configurations with a normal phrase-based

System	Number of Features	BLEU	TER
PBT	n/a	29.71	59.40
ME	9,008,382	32.12	56.78
+Prior	9,008,382	32.46	56.41
+COV	9,202,431	32.48	56.50
+SIB	10,088,487	32.73	56.26
+COV+SIB	10,282,536	32.94	55.97
+Prior+COV+SIB	10,282,536	33.15	55.62

Table 3: MT results on MT08 Newswire set (PBT:normal phrase-based MT; ME:Maximum-entropy baseline; Prior:smoothed distortion prior; COV:parse coverage feature; SIB:parse sibling feature).

System	Number of Features	BLEU	TER
PBT	n/a	20.07	62.90
ME	9,192,617	22.42	60.36
+Prior	9,192,617	22.70	60.11
+COV	9,306,967	22.69	60.14
+SIB	9,847,445	22.91	59.92
+COV+SIB	9,961,795	23.04	59.78
+Prior+COV+SIB	9,961,795	23.25	59.56

Table 4: MT results on MT08 Weblog set (PBT:normal phrase-based MT; ME:Maximum-entropy baseline; Prior:smoothed distortion prior; COV:parse coverage feature; SIB:parse sibling feature).

SMT system (Koehn et al., 2003) that is trained on the same training data. The number of features used in the systems are listed in the tables.

We start from the maximum-entropy baseline, a system implemented similarly as in (Ittycheriah and Roukos, 2007). It utilizes multiple features as listed in Section 3, including lexical reordering features, and produces an already significantly better performance than the normal phrase-based MT system (PBT). It is around 2.5 points better in both BLEU and TER than the PBT baseline. By adding smoothed priors, parse coverage features or parse sibling features each separately, the MT performance is improved by 0.3 to 0.6. The parse sibling feature alone provides the largest individual contribution. When adding both types of new features, the improvement is around 0.6 to 0.8 on two genres. Finally, applying all three results in the best performance (the last row). On the Newswire set, the final system is more than 3 points better than the PBT baseline and 1 point better than the ME baseline. On the Weblog set, it is more than 3 points better than PBT and 0.8 better than the ME baseline. All the MT results above are statistically significant with p-value < 0.0001 by using the tool described in (Zhang and Vogel, 2004).

7.4 Analysis

To better understand the distortion and translation results, we take a closer look at the parse-based features. In Table 5, we list the most frequent parse sibling features that are related to the Chinese phrases with "PP VV" structures. It is known that in Chinese usually the preposition phrases ("PP") are written/spoken before the verbs ("VV"), with a different order from English. Table 5 shows how such reordering phenomenon is captured by the parse sibling features. Recall that when α_i is greater than 1, the system prefers the reordering with that feature fired. When α_i is smaller than 1, the system will penalize the corresponding translation order during the decoding search. When the coverage is equal to 1, it means "PP" has been translated before translating current "VV". As shown in the table, those features with coverage equal to 1 have α_i lower than 1, which will result in penalties on incorrect translation orders.

In Fig. 6, we show the comparison between the

Count	α_i	j	TgtPOS	SrcPOS	ParseSib Node	Cov	Orien-tation
3052	1.10	5	VBD	VV	PP	0	-1
2662	1.10	-1	VBD	VV	PP	0	-1
2134	1.25	4	VBD	VV	PP	0	-1
50	0.73	5	VBD	VV	PP	1	-1
39	0.84	-5	VBD	VV	PP	1	-1
18	0.95	-2	VBD	VV	PP	1	-1

Table 5: Parse Sibling Word Features related to Chinese "PP VV".

Src1	瑞士 科学院 冰川 专家 长期 跟踪 研究 发现 , 1850 年 至 2005 年间 , 瑞士 的 1800 余 条 冰川 **正(were) 以(at) 年均(annual) 3% 的 速度(rate) 缩减 (shrinking)**。
Ref	a long-term follow-up research by glacier experts at the swiss academy of sciences found that from 1850 to 2005 the 1,800 plus glaciers in switzerland **were shrinking at an annual rate of 3 %** .
Baseline	the swiss academy of sciences glacier experts long-term follow-up study found that from 2005 to 1850 , with **an average** of more than 1800 glaciers in switzerland is the **reduced rate of 3 %** .
New	the swiss academy of sciences glacier experts long-term follow-up study found that from 1850 to 2005 , more than 1800 of swiss glaciers **shrinking at an annual rate of 3 %**.
Src2	但 在 此 同时 塔利班 组织 说 , 另 一 名 **遭到(had been) 绑架(kidnapped) 的(who) 德国(german) 人质(hostage)** 身体 非常 虚弱 , 开始 陷入 昏迷 并 失去 意识 。
Ref	but at the same time the taliban said that another **german hostage who had been kidnapped** was in extremely poor health , and had started to become comatose and to lose consciousness .
Baseline	but at the same time , another one **was kidnapped** by the taliban of the **german hostage** body very weak , began to fall into a coma and lost consciousness .
New	but at the same time , the taliban said that the body of another **german hostage who was kidnapped** very weak , began to fall into a coma and lost consciousness .

Figure 6: Chinese-English MT examples(Baseline:Maximum-entropy baseline; New:System with smoothed priors and syntactic features).

ME baseline output and those from the improved system with the parse-based features and smoothed distortion priors. The differences are highlighted in bold for easy understanding. The first example shows that the new system fixes the order for "PP VV", while the second one shows the fix for the translation of "CP de NP". This is consistent with the features we showed in Table 1 and 5. The new features help to translate the Chinese text in the right order.

8 Conclusion

In this paper we have presented several novel approaches that improved phrase reordering in the framework of maximum entropy based translation. A smoothed prior probability was proposed to take into account the distortions in the priors. Several novel distortion features were presented based on the syntactic parsing. A new metric PDscore was also introduced to measure the effect of distortion in the translation hypotheses. We showed that both smoothed prior and syntax-based features additively improved the distortion and also the translation performance significantly on a large-scale Chinese-English machine translation task. How to further take advantage of the syntactic information to improve the reordering in SMT will continue to be an interesting topic in the future.

Acknowledgments

We would like to acknowledge the support of DARPA under Grant HR0011-08-C-0110 for funding part of this work. The views, opinions, and/or findings contained in this article/presentation are those of the author/presenter and should not be interpreted as representing the official views or policies, either expressed or implied, of the Defense Advanced Research Projects Agency or the Department of Defense.

References

Yaser Al-Onaizan and Kishore Papineni. 2006. Distortion models for statistical machine translation. In *Proceedings of the 21st International Conference on Computational Linguistics and 44th Annual Meeting of the ACL*, pages 529–536, Sydney, Australia.

Alexandra Birch and Miles Osborne. 2010. Lrscore for evaluating lexical and reordering quality in mt. In *Proceedings of the Joint 5th Workshop on Statistical Machine Translation and MetricsMATR*.

Peter F. Brown, Vincent J. Della Pietra, Stephen A. Della Pietra, and Robert L. Mercer. 1993. The mathematics of statistical machine translation: parameter estimation. *Computational Linguistics*, 19(2):263–311.

Pi-Chuan Chang, Huihsin Tseng, Dan Jurafsky, and Christopher D. Manning. 2009. Discriminative reordering with chinese grammatical relations features. In *Proceedings of the Third Workshop on Syntax and Structure in Statistical Translation*.

Michael Collins, Philipp Koehn, and Ivona Kučerová. 2005. Clause restructuring for statistical machine translation. In *Proceedings of ACL*, pages 531–540.

Michel Galley and Christoph D. Manning. 2008. A simple and effective hierarchical phrase reordering model. In *Proceedings of the EMNLP*.

Niyu Ge. 2010. A direct syntax-driven reordering model for phrase-based machine translation. In *Proceedings of HLT-NAACL*, pages 849–857.

Spence Green, Michel Galley, and Christopher D. Manning. 2010. Improved models of distortion cost for statistical machine translation. In *Proceedings of HLT-NAACL*.

Abraham Ittycheriah and Salim Roukos. 2007. Direct translation model 2. In *Proceedings HLT/NAACL*, pages 57–64, April.

Philipp Koehn, Franz Och, and Daniel Marcu. 2003. Statistical phrase-based translation. In *Proceedings of NAACL/HLT*.

Shankar Kumar and William Byrne. 2005. Local phrase reordering models for statistical machine translation. In *Proceedings of HLT/EMNLP*, pages 161–168.

Chi-Ho Li, Dongdong Zhang, Mu Li, Ming Zhou, Minghui Li, and Yi Guan. 2007. A probabilistic approach to syntax-based reordering for statistical machine translation. In *Proceedings of ACL*.

Yizhao Ni, Craig J.Saunders, Sandor Szedmak, and Mahesan Niranjan. 2009. Handling phrase reorderings for machine translation. In *Proceedings of ACL*.

Franz-Josef Och and Hermann Ney. 2002. Discriminative training and maximum entropy models for statistical machine translations. In *40th Annual Meeting of the ACL*, pages 295–302, Philadelphia, PA, July.

Franz Josef Och and Hermann Ney. 2004. The alignment template approach to statistical machine translation. *Computational Linguistics*, 30(4):417–449.

Kishore Papineni, Salim Roukos, Todd Ward, and Weijing Zhu. 2002. Bleu: a method for automatic evaluation of machine translation. In *Proceedings of ACL*, pages 311–318.

Adwait Ratnaparkhi. 1997. A linear observed time statistical parser based on maximum entropy models. In *Proceedings of EMNLP*, pages 1–10.

Matthew Snover, Bonnie Dorr, Richard Schwartz, Linea Micciulla, and John Makhoul. 2006. A study of translation edit rate with targeted human annotation. In *Proceedings of Association for Machine Translation in the Americas*.

Christoph Tillmann. 2004. A unigram orientation model for statistical machine translation. In *Proceedings of HLT-NAACL*.

Chao Wang, Michael Collins, and Philipp Koehn. 2007. Chinese syntactic reordering for statistical machine translation. In *Proceedings of EMNLP*, pages 737–745.

Fei Xia and Michael McCord. 2004. Improving a statistical mt system with automatically learned rewrite patterns. In *Proceedings of COLING*.

Deyi Xiong, Qun Liu, and Shouxun Lin. 2006. Maximum entropy based phrase reordering model for statistical machine translation. In *Proceedings of ACL*.

Richard Zens and Hermann Ney. 2006. Discriminative reordering models for statistical machine translation. In *Proceedings of the Workshop on Statistical Machine Translation*.

Ying Zhang and Stephan Vogel. 2004. Measuring confidence intervals for the machine translation evaluation metrics. In *Proceedings of The 10th International Conference on Theoretical and Methodological Issues in Machine Translation*.

Reestimation of Reified Rules in Semiring Parsing and Biparsing

Markus Saers and **Dekai Wu**
Human Language Technology Center
Dept. of Computer Science and Engineering
Hong Kong University of Science and Technology
{masaers|dekai}@cs.ust.hk

Abstract

We show that reifying the rules from hyperedge weights to first-class graph nodes automatically gives us rule expectations in any kind of grammar expressible as a deductive system, without any explicit algorithm for calculating rule expectations (such as the inside-outside algorithm). This gives us expectation maximization training for any grammar class with a parsing algorithm that can be stated as a deductive system, for free. Having such a framework in place accelerates turnover time for experimenting with new grammar classes and parsing algorithms—to implement a grammar learner, only the parse forest construction has to be implemented.

1 Introduction

We propose *contextual probability* as a quantity that measures how often something has been used in a corpus, and when calculated for rules, it gives us everything needed to calculate rule expectations for expectation maximization. For labeled spans in context-free parses, this quantity is called *outside probability*, and in semiring (bi-) parsing, it is called *reverse value*. The inside-outside algorithm for reestimating context-free grammar rules uses this quantity for the symbols occurring in the parse forest. Generally, the contextual probability is:

> The *contextual probability* of ***something***
> is the sum of the probabilities
> of all contexts where it was used.

For symbols participating in a parse, we could state it like this:

> The *contextual probability* of ***an item***
> is the sum of the probabilities
> of all contexts where it was used.

...which is exactly what we mean with outside probability. In semiring (bi-) parsing, this quantity is called reverse value, but in this framework it is also defined for rules, which means that we could restate our boxed statement as:

> The *contextual probability* of ***a rule***
> is the sum of the probabilities
> of all contexts where it was used.

This opens up an interesting line of inquiry into what this quantity might represent. In this paper we show that the contextual probabilities of the rules contain precisely the new information needed in order to calculate the expectations needed to reestimate the rule probabilities. This line of inquiry was discovered while working on a preterminalized version of linear inversion transduction grammars (LITGs), so we will use these preterminalized LITGs (Saers and Wu, 2011) as an example throughout this paper.

We will start by examining semiring parsing (parsing as deductive systems over semirings, Section 3), followed by a section on how this relates to weighted hypergraphs, a common representation of parse forests (Section 4). This reveals a disparity between weighted hypergraphs and semiring parsing. It seems like we are forced to choose between the inside-outside algorithm for context-free grammars

Proceedings of SSST-5, Fifth Workshop on Syntax, Semantics and Structure in Statistical Translation, pages 70–78,
ACL HLT 2011, Portland, Oregon, USA, June 2011.

on the one side, and the flexibility of grammar formalism and parsing algorithm development afforded by semiring (bi-) parsing. It is, however, possible to have both, which we will show in Section 5. An integral part of this unification is the concept of contextual probability. Finally, we will offer some conclusions in Section 6.

2 Background

A common view on probabilistic parsing—be it bilingual or monolingual—is that it involves the construction of a *weighted hypergraph* (Billot and Lang, 1989; Manning and Klein, 2001; Huang, 2008). This is an appealing conceptualization, as it separates the construction of the parse forest (the actual hypergraph) from the probabilistic calculations that need to be carried out. The calculations are, in fact, given by the hypergraph itself. To get the probability of the sentence (pair) being parsed, one simply have to query the hypergraph for the value of the *goal node*. It is furthermore possible to abstract away the calculations themselves, by defining the hypergraph over an arbitrary *semiring*. When the *Boolean semiring* is used, the value of the goal node will be *true* if the sentence (pair) is a member of the language (or transduction) defined by the grammar, and *false* otherwise. When the *probabilistic semiring* is used, the probability of the sentence (pair) is attained, and with the *tropical semiring*, the probability of the most likely tree is attained. To further generalize the building of the hypergraph—the parsing algorithm—a *deductive system* can be used. By defining a hand-full of deductive rules that describe how *items* can be constructed, the full complexities of a parsing algorithm can be very succinctly summarized. Deductive systems to represent parsers and semirings to calculate the desired values for the parses were introduced in Goodman (1999).

In this paper we will reify the grammar rules by moving them from the meta level to the object level—effectively making them first-class citizens of the parse trees, which are no longer weighted hypergraphs, but *mul/add-graphs*. This move allows us to calculate rule expectations for expectation maximization (Dempster et al., 1977) as part of the parsing process, which significantly shortens turn-over time for experimenting with different grammar formalisms.

Another approach which achieve a similar goal is to use a *expectation semiring* (Eisner, 2001; Eisner, 2002; Li and Eisner, 2009). In this semiring, all values are pairs of probabilities and expectations. The inside-outside algorithm with the expectation semiring requires the usual inside and outside calculations over the probability part of the semiring values, followed by a third traversal over the parse forest to populate the expectation part of the semiring values. The approach taken in this paper also requires the usual inside and outside calculations, but o third traversal of the parse forest. Instead, the proposed approach requires two passes over the rules of the grammar per EM iteration. The asymptotic time complexities are thus equivalent for the two approaches.

2.1 Notation

We will use $\mathbf{w}$ to mean a monolingual sentence, and index the individual tokens from 0 to $|\mathbf{w}| - 1$. This means that $\mathbf{w} = w_0, \ldots, w_{|\mathbf{w}|-1}$. We will frequently use spans from this sentence, and denote them $w_{i..j}$, which is to be interpreted as array slices, that is: including the token at position i, but excluding the token at position j (the interval $[i, j)$ over $\mathbf{w}$, or $w_i, \ldots, w_{j-1}$). A sentence $\mathbf{w}$ thus corresponds to the span $w_{0..|\mathbf{w}|}$. We will also assume that there exists a grammar $G = \langle N, \Sigma, S, R \rangle$ or a transduction grammar (over languages L_0 and L_1) $G = \langle N, \Sigma, \Delta, S, R \rangle$ (depending on the context), where N is the set of nonterminal symbols, Σ is a set of (L_0) terminal symbols, Δ is a set of (L_1) terminal symbols, $S \in N$ is the dedicated start symbol and R is a set of rules appropriate to the grammar. A stochastic grammar is further assumed to have a parameterization function θ, that assigns probabilities to all the rules in R. For general L_0 tokens we will use lower case letters from the beginning of the alphabet, and for L_1 from the end of the alphabet. For specific sentences we will use $\mathbf{e} = e_{0..|\mathbf{e}|}$ to represent an L_0 sentence and $\mathbf{f} = f_{0..|\mathbf{f}|}$ to represent an L_1 sentence.

3 Semiring parsing

Semiring parsing was introduced in Goodman (1999), as a unifying approach to parsing. The general idea is that any parsing algorithm can be expressed as a deductive system. The same algorithm can then be used for both traditional grammars and stochastic grammars by changing the semiring used in the deductive system. This approach thus separates the algorithm from the specific calculations it is used for.

Definition 1. *A semiring is a tuple* $\langle \mathbb{A}, \oplus, \otimes, \mathbf{0}, \mathbf{1} \rangle$*, where* $\mathbb{A}$ *is the set the semiring is defined over,* $\oplus$ *is an associative, commutative operator over* $\mathbb{A}$*, with identity element* $\mathbf{0}$ *and* $\otimes$ *is an associative operator over* $\mathbb{A}$ *distributed over* $\oplus$*, with identity element* $\mathbf{1}$.

Semirings can be intuitively understood by considering the *probabilistic semiring*: $\langle \mathbb{R}^+, +, \times, 0, 1 \rangle$, that is: the common meaning of addition and multiplication over the positive real numbers (including zero). Although this paper will have a heavy focus on the probabilistic semiring, several other exists. Among the more popular are the *Boolean semiring* $\langle \{\top, \bot\}, \vee, \wedge, \bot, \top \rangle$ and the *tropical semiring* $\langle \mathbb{R}^+ \cup \{\infty\}, min, +, \infty, 0 \rangle$ (or $\langle \mathbb{R}^- \cup \{-\infty\}, max, +, -\infty, 0 \rangle$ which can be used for probabilities in the logarithmic domain).

The deductive systems used in semiring parsing have three components: an *item* representation, a *goal item* and a set of *deductive rules*. Taking CKY parsing (Cocke, 1969; Kasami and Torii, 1969; Younger, 1967) as an example, the items would have the form $A_{i,j}$, which is to be interpreted as the span $w_{i..j}$ of the sentence being parsed, labeled with the nonterminal symbol A. The goal item would be $S_{0,|\mathbf{w}|}$: the whole sentence labeled with the start symbol of the grammar. Since the CKY algorithm is a very simple parsing algorithm, it only has two deductive rules:

$$\frac{A \rightarrow a,\ \mathbb{I}_a(w_{i..j})}{A_{i,j}} \; {}_{0 \leq i \leq j \leq |\mathbf{w}|} \tag{1}$$

$$\frac{B_{i,k},\ C_{k,j},\ A \rightarrow BC}{A_{i,j}} \tag{2}$$

Where $\mathbb{I}_a(\cdot)$ is the terminal indicator function for the semiring. The general form of a deductive rule is that the *conditions* (entities over the line) yield the *consequence* (the entity under the line) given that the *side conditions* (to the right of the line) are satisfied. We will make a distinction between conditions that are themselves items, and conditions that are not. The non-item conditions will be called *axioms*, and are exemplified above by the indicator function ($\mathbb{I}_a(w_{i..j})$ which has a value that depends only on the sentence) and the rules ($A \rightarrow a$ and $A \rightarrow BC$ which have values that depends only on the grammar).

The indicator function might seem unnecessary, but allows us to reason under uncertainty regarding the input. In this paper, we will assume that we have perfect knowledge of the input (but for generality, we will not place it as a side condition). The function is defined such that:

$$\forall a \in \Sigma^* : \mathbb{I}_a(w) = \begin{cases} \mathbf{1} & \text{if } a = w \\ \mathbf{0} & \text{otherwise} \end{cases}$$

An important concept of semiring parsing is that the deductive rules also specify how to arrive at the value of the consequence. Since it is the first value computed for a node, we will call it α, and the general way to calculate it given a deductive rule and the α-values of the conditions is:

$$\alpha(b) = \bigotimes_{i=1}^{n} \alpha(a_i) \quad \text{iff} \quad \frac{a_1, \ldots, a_n}{b} \; {}_{c_1,\ldots,c_m}$$

If the same consequence can be produced in several ways, the values are summed using the $\oplus$ operator:

$$\alpha(b) = \bigoplus_{\substack{n, a_1, \ldots, a_n \\ \text{such that} \\ \frac{a_1, \ldots, a_n}{b}}} \bigotimes_{i=1}^{n} \alpha(a_i)$$

The α-values of axioms depend on what kind of axiom it is. For the indicator function, the α-value is the value of the function, and for grammar rules, the α-value is the value assigned to the rule by the parameterization function θ of the grammar.

The α-value of a consequence corresponds to the value of everything leading up to that consequence. If we are parsing with a context-free grammar and the probabilistic semiring, this corresponds to the inside probability.

3.1 Reverse values

When we want to reestimate rule probabilities, it is not enough to know the probabilities of arriving at different consequences, we also need to know how likely we are to need the consequences as a condition for other deductions. These values are called

$$\frac{S \to A}{A_{0,|\mathbf{e}|,0,|\mathbf{f}|}}, \qquad \frac{A_{s,s,u,u},\ A \to {}^{\epsilon}/_{\epsilon}}{\mathcal{G}},$$

$$\frac{B_{s',t,u',v},\ B \to [XA],\ X \to {}^{a}/_{x},\ \mathbb{I}_{a/x}\left({}^{e_{s..s'}}/_{f_{u..u'}}\right)}{A_{s,t,u,v}}\ \begin{matrix}0\leq s\leq s',\\ 0\leq u\leq u',\end{matrix}$$

$$\frac{B_{s,t',u,v'},\ B \to [AX],\ X \to {}^{a}/_{x},\ \mathbb{I}_{a/x}\left({}^{e_{t'..t}}/_{f_{v'..v}}\right)}{A_{s,t,u,v}}\ \begin{matrix}t'\leq t\leq |\mathbf{e}|,\\ v'\leq v\leq |\mathbf{f}|,\end{matrix}$$

$$\frac{B_{s',t,u,v'},\ B \to \langle XA\rangle,\ X \to {}^{a}/_{x},\ \mathbb{I}_{a/x}\left({}^{e_{s..s'}}/_{f_{v'..v}}\right)}{A_{s,t,u,v}}\ \begin{matrix}0\leq s\leq s',\\ v'\leq v\leq |\mathbf{f}|,\end{matrix}$$

$$\frac{B_{s,t',u',v},\ B \to \langle AX\rangle,\ X \to {}^{a}/_{x},\ \mathbb{I}_{a/x}\left({}^{e_{t'..t}}/_{f_{u..u'}}\right)}{A_{s,t,u,v}}\ \begin{matrix}t'\leq t\leq |\mathbf{e}|,\\ 0\leq u\leq u'\end{matrix}$$

Figure 2: Deductive system describing a PLITG parser. The symbols A, B and S are nonterminal symbols, while X represents a *preterminal* symbol.

$$\frac{S \to A}{A_{0,|\mathbf{e}|,0,|\mathbf{f}|}}, \qquad \frac{A_{s,s,u,u},\ A \to {}^{\epsilon}/_{\epsilon}}{\mathcal{G}},$$

$$\frac{B_{s',t,u',v},\ B \to [{}^{a}/_{x}\ A],\ \mathbb{I}_{a/x}\left({}^{e_{s..s'}}/_{f_{u..u'}}\right)}{A_{s,t,u,v}}\ \begin{matrix}0\leq s\leq s',\\ 0\leq u\leq u',\end{matrix}$$

$$\frac{B_{s,t',u,v'},\ B \to [A\ {}^{a}/_{x}],\ \mathbb{I}_{a/x}\left({}^{e_{t'..t}}/_{f_{v'..v}}\right)}{A_{s,t,u,v}}\ \begin{matrix}t'\leq t\leq |\mathbf{e}|,\\ v'\leq v\leq |\mathbf{f}|,\end{matrix}$$

$$\frac{B_{s',t,u,v'},\ B \to \langle {}^{a}/_{x}\ A\rangle,\ \mathbb{I}_{a/x}\left({}^{e_{s..s'}}/_{f_{v'..v}}\right)}{A_{s,t,u,v}}\ \begin{matrix}0\leq s\leq s',\\ v'\leq v\leq |\mathbf{f}|,\end{matrix}$$

$$\frac{B_{s,t',u',v},\ B \to \langle A\ {}^{a}/_{x}\rangle,\ \mathbb{I}_{a/x}\left({}^{e_{t'..t}}/_{f_{u..u'}}\right)}{A_{s,t,u,v}}\ \begin{matrix}t'\leq t\leq |\mathbf{e}|,\\ 0\leq u\leq u'\end{matrix}$$

Figure 1: Deductive system describing an LITG parser.

reverse values in Goodman (1999), and outside probabilities in the inside-outside algorithm (Baker, 1979). In this paper we will call them contextual values, or β-values (since they are the second value we calculate).

The way to calculate the reverse values is to start with the goal node and work your way back to the axioms. The reverse value is calculated to be:

$$\beta(x) = \bigoplus_{\substack{n,i,b,a_1,\ldots,a_n\\ \text{such that}\\ \frac{a_1,\ldots,a_n}{b}\wedge x=a_i}} \beta(b) \otimes \bigotimes_{\{j|1\leq j\leq n, j\neq i\}} \alpha(a_j)$$

That is: the reverse value of the consequence combined with the values of all sibling conditions is calculated and summed for all deductive rules where the item is a condition.

3.2 SPLITG

After we introduced stochastic preterminalized LITGs (Saers, 2011, SPLITG), the idea of expressing them in term of semiring parsing occurred. This is relatively straight forward, producing a compact set of deductive rules similar to that of LITGs. For LITGs, the items take the form of bispans labeled with a symbol. We will represent these bispans as $A_{s,t,u,v}$, where A is the label, and the two spans being labeled are $e_{s..t}$ and $f_{u..v}$. Since we usually do top-down parsing, the goal item is a virtual item ($\mathcal{G}$) than can only be reached by rewriting a nonterminal to the empty bistring (${}^{\epsilon}/_{\epsilon}$). Figure 1 shows the deductive rules for LITG parsing.

A preterminalized LITG promote preterminal symbols to a distinct class of symbols in the grammar, which is only allowed to rewrite into biterminals. Factoring out the terminal productions in this fashion allows the grammar to define one probability distribution over all the biterminals, which is useful for bilexica induction. It also means that the LITG rules that produce biterminals have to be replaced by two rules in a PLITG, resulting in the deductive rules in Figure 2.

4 Weighted hypergraphs

A hypergraph is a graph where the nodes are connected with *hyperedges*. A hyperedge is an edge that can connect several nodes with one node—it has

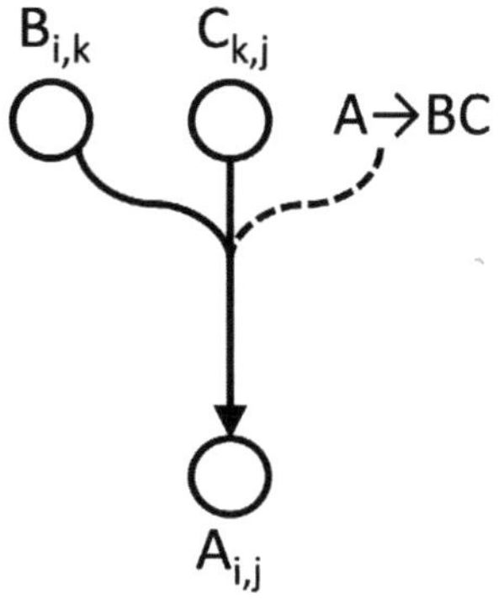

Figure 3: A weighted hyperedge between three nodes, based on the rule $A \rightarrow BC$. The tip of the arrow points to the head of the edge, and the two ends are the tails. The dashed line idicates where the weight of the edge comes from.

one head, but may have any number of tails. Intuitively, this is a good match to context-free grammars, since each rule connects one symbol on the left hand side (the head of the hyperedge) with any number of symbols on the right hand side (the tails of the hyperedge). During parsing, one node is constructed for each labeled (bi-) span, and the nodes are connected with hyperedges based on the valid applications of rules. A hyperedge will be represented as $[h : t_1, \ldots, t_n]$ where h is the head and t_i are the tails.

When this is applied to weighted grammar, each hyperedge can be associated with a weight, making the hypergraph weighted. Every time an edge is traversed, its weight is combined with the value travelling through the edge. Weights are assigned to hyperedges via a weighting function $w(\cdot)$.

Figure 3 contains an illustration of a weighted hyperedge. The arrow indicates the edge itself, whereas the dotted line indicates where the weight comes from. Since each hyperedge corresponds to exactly one rule from a stochastic context-free grammar, we can use the inside-outside algorithm (Baker, 1979) to calculate inside and outside probabilities as well as to reestimate the probabilities of the rules. What we cannot easily do, however, is to change the parsing algorithm or grammar formalism.

If the weighted hyperedge approach was a one-to-one mapping to the semiring parsing approach, we could, but it is not. The main difference is that rules are part of the object level in semiring parsing, but

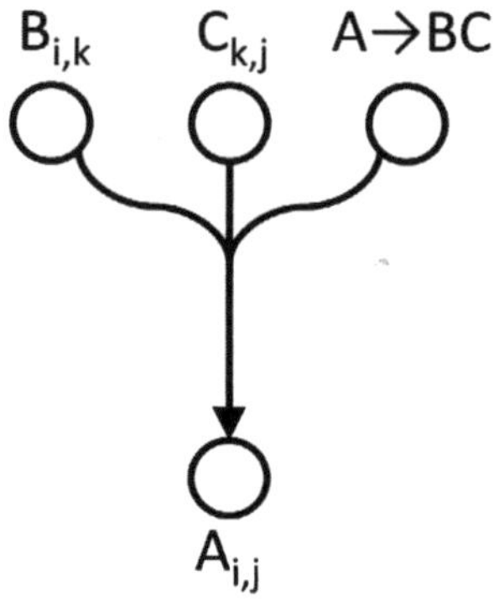

Figure 4: The same hyperedge as in Figure 3, where the rule has been promoted to first-class citizen. The hyperedge is no longer weighted.

part of the meta level in weighted hypergraphs. To address this disparity, we will reify the rules in the weighted hypergraph to make them nodes. Figure 4 shows the same hyperedge as Figure 3, but with the rule as a proper node rather than a weight associated with the hyperedge. These hyperedges are agnostic to what the tail nodes represent, so we can no longer use the inside-outside algorithm to reestimate the rule probabilities. We can, however, still calculate inside probabilities. In the weighted hyperedge approach, the inside probability of a node is:

$$\alpha(p) = \bigoplus_{\substack{n,q_1,\ldots,q_n \\ \text{such that} \\ [p:q_1,\ldots q_n]}} w([p:q_1,\ldots,q_n]) \otimes \bigotimes_{i=1}^{n} \alpha(q_i)$$

Whereas with the rules reified, the weight simply moved into the tail product:

$$\alpha(p) \bigoplus_{\substack{n,q_1,\ldots,q_n \\ \text{such that} \\ [p:q_1,\ldots q_n]}} \bigotimes_{i=1}^{n} \alpha(q_i)$$

By virtue of the deductive system used to build the hypergraph, we also have the reverse values, which correspond to outside probability:

$$\beta(x) = \bigoplus_{\substack{i,p,n,q_1,\ldots,q_n \\ \text{such that} \\ [p:q_1,\ldots q_n]\wedge x=q_i}} \beta(p) \otimes \bigotimes_{\{j|1\leq j\leq n, j\neq i\}} \alpha(q_j)$$

This means that we have the inside and outside probabilities of the nodes, and we could shoe-horn it into the reestimation part of the inside-outside algorithm.

It also means that we have β-values for the rules, which we are calculating as a side-effect of moving them into the object level. In Section 5, we will take a closer look at the semantics of the contextual probabilities that we are in fact calculating for the reified rules, and see how they can be used in reestimation of the rules.

4.1 SPLITG

Using the hypergraph parsing framework for SPLITGs turns out to be non-trivial. Where the standard LITG uses one rule to rewrite a nonterminal into another nonterminal and a biterminal, the SPLITG rewrites a nonterminal to a preterminal and a nonterminal, *and* rewrites the preterminal into a biterminal. This causes problems within the hypergraph framework, where each rule application should correspond to one hyperedge. As it stands we have two options:

1. Let each rule correspond to one hyperedge, which means that we need to introduce preterminal nodes into the hypergraph. This has a clear drawback for bracketing grammars,[1] since it is now necessary to keep different symbols apart. It also produces larger hypergraphs, since the number of nodes is inflated.

2. Let hypergraphs be associated with one or two rules, which means that we need to redefine hyperedges so that there are two different weighting functions: one for the nonterminal weight and one for the preterminal weight. Although all hyperedges are associated with one nonterminal rule, some hyperedges are not associated with any preterminal rule, making the preterminal weighting function partly defined.

Both of these approaches work in practice, but neither is completely satisfactory since they both represent work-arounds to shoe-horn the parsing algorithm (as stated in the deductive system) into a formalism that is not completely compatible. By reifying the rules into the object level, we rid ourselves of this inconvenience, as we no longer differentiate between different types of conditions.

[1] A bracketing grammar is a grammar where $|N| = 1$.

5 Reestimation of reified rules

As has been amply hinted at, the contextual probabilities (outside probabilities, reverse values or β-values) contain all new information we need about the rules to reestimate their probability in an expectation maximization (Dempster et al., 1977) framework. To show that this is indeed the case, we will rewrite the reestimation formulas of the inside-outside algorithm (Baker, 1979) so that they are stated in terms of contextual probability for the rules.

In general, a stochastic context-free grammar can be estimated from examples of trees generated by the grammar by means of relative frequency. This is also true for expectation maximization with the caveat that we have multiple hypotheses over each sentence (pair), and therefore calculate expectations rather than discrete frequency counts. We thus compute the updated parameterization function $\hat{\theta}$ based on expectations from the current parameterization function:

$$\hat{\theta}\left(\varphi|p\right) = \frac{E_\theta\left[p \to \varphi\right]}{E_\theta\left[p\right]}$$

Where $p \in N$ and $\varphi \in \{\Sigma \cup N\}^+$ (or $\varphi \in \{(\Sigma^* \times \Delta^*) \cup N\}^+$ for transduction grammars). The expectations are calculated from the sentences in a corpus $\mathcal{C}$:

$$E_\theta\left[x\right] = \sum_{\mathbf{w} \in \mathcal{C}} E_\theta\left[x|\mathbf{w}\right]$$

The exact way of calculating the expectation on x given a sentence depends on what x is. For nonterminal symbols, the expectations are given by:

$$\begin{aligned}
E_\theta\left[p|\mathbf{w}\right] &= \frac{E_\theta\left[p, \mathbf{w}\right]}{E_\theta\left[\mathbf{w}\right]} \\
&= \frac{\sum_{0 \le i \le j \le |\mathbf{w}|} \Pr\left(p_{i,j}, \mathbf{w}|G\right)}{\Pr\left(\mathbf{w}|G\right)} \\
&= \frac{\sum_{0 \le i \le j \le |\mathbf{w}|} \alpha(p_{i,j})\beta(p_{i,j})}{\alpha(S_{0,|\mathbf{w}|})\beta(S_{0,|\mathbf{w}|})}
\end{aligned}$$

For nonterminal rules, the expectations are shown in Figure 5. The most noteworthy step is the last one, where we use the fact that the summation is over the equivalence of the rule's reverse value. Each

$$E_\theta[p \to qr|\mathbf{w}] = \frac{E_\theta[p \to qr, \mathbf{w}]}{E_\theta[\mathbf{w}]}$$
$$= \frac{\sum_{0\le i\le k\le j\le|\mathbf{w}|} \Pr\left(w_{0..i}, p_{i,j}, w_{j..|\mathbf{w}|}\middle|G\right) \Pr\left(w_{i..k}|q_{i,k}, G\right) \Pr\left(w_{k..j}|r_{k,j}, G\right) \theta\left(qr|p\right)}{\Pr\left(\mathbf{w}|G\right)}$$
$$= \frac{\sum_{0\le i\le k\le j\le|\mathbf{w}|} \beta(p_{i,j})\alpha(q_{i,k})\alpha(r_{k,j})\theta\left(qr|p\right)}{\alpha(S_{0,|\mathbf{w}|})\beta(S_{0,|\mathbf{w}|})}$$
$$= \frac{\theta\left(qr|p\right)\sum_{0\le i\le k\le j\le|\mathbf{w}|} \beta(p_{i,j})\alpha(q_{i,k})\alpha(r_{k,j})}{\alpha(S_{0,|\mathbf{w}|})\beta(S_{0,|\mathbf{w}|})} = \boxed{\frac{\alpha(p\to qr)\beta(p\to qr)}{\alpha(S_{0,|\mathbf{w}|})\beta(S_{0,|\mathbf{w}|})}}$$

Figure 5: Expected values for nonterminal rules in a specific sentence.

$$E_\theta[p \to a|\mathbf{w}] = \frac{E_\theta[p \to a, \mathbf{w}]}{E_\theta[\mathbf{w}]}$$
$$= \frac{\sum_{0\le i\le j\le|\mathbf{w}|} \Pr\left(w_{0..i}, p_{i,j}, w_{j..|\mathbf{w}|}\middle|G\right) \mathbb{I}_a(w_{i..j})\theta\left(a|p\right)}{\Pr\left(\mathbf{w}|G\right)}$$
$$= \frac{\sum_{0\le i\le j\le|\mathbf{w}|} \beta(p_{i,j})\mathbb{I}_a(w_{i..j})\theta\left(a|p\right)}{\alpha(S_{0,|\mathbf{w}|})\beta(S_{0,|\mathbf{w}|})}$$
$$= \frac{\theta\left(a|p\right)\sum_{0\le i\le j\le|\mathbf{w}|} \beta(p_{i,j})\mathbb{I}_a(w_{i..j})}{\alpha(S_{0,|\mathbf{w}|})\beta(S_{0,|\mathbf{w}|})} = \boxed{\frac{\alpha(p\to a)\beta(p\to a)}{\alpha(S_{0,|\mathbf{w}|})\beta(S_{0,|\mathbf{w}|})}}$$

Figure 6: Expected values of terminal rules in a specific sentence.

$\beta(p_{i,j})\alpha(q_{i,k})\alpha(r_{k,j})$ term of the summation corresponds to one instance where the rule was used in the parse. Furthermore, the β value is the outside probability of the consequence of the deductive rule applied, and the two α values are the inside probabilities of the sibling conditions of that deductive rule. The entire summation thus corresponds to our definition of the reverse value of a rule, or its outside probability.

In Figure 6, the same process is carried out for terminal rules. Again, the summation is over all possible ways that we can combine the inside probability of the sibling conditions of the rule with the outside probability of the consequence.

Since the expected values of both terminal and nonterminal rules have the same form, we can generalize the formula for any production φ:

$$E_\theta[p \to \varphi|\mathbf{w}] = \frac{\alpha(p\to\varphi)\beta(p\to\varphi)}{\alpha(S_{0,|\mathbf{w}|})\beta(S_{0,|\mathbf{w}|})}$$

Finally, plugging it all into the original rule estimation formula, we have:

$$\hat{\theta}\left(\varphi|p\right) = \frac{E_\theta[p\to\varphi]}{E_\theta[p]}$$
$$= \frac{\sum\limits_{\mathbf{w}\in C} \frac{\alpha(p\to\varphi)\beta(p\to\varphi)}{\alpha(S_{0,|\mathbf{w}|})\beta(S_{0,|\mathbf{w}|})}}{\sum\limits_{\mathbf{w}\in C} \frac{\sum_{0\le i\le j\le|\mathbf{w}|}\alpha(p_{i,j})\beta(p_{i,j})}{\alpha(S_{0,|\mathbf{w}|})\beta(S_{0,|\mathbf{w}|})}}$$
$$= \alpha(p\to\varphi)\frac{\sum\limits_{\mathbf{w}\in C} \frac{\beta(p\to\varphi)}{\alpha(S_{0,|\mathbf{w}|})\beta(S_{0,|\mathbf{w}|})}}{\sum\limits_{\mathbf{w}\in C} \frac{\sum_{0\le i\le j\le|\mathbf{w}|}\alpha(p_{i,j})\beta(p_{i,j})}{\alpha(S_{0,|\mathbf{w}|})\beta(S_{0,|\mathbf{w}|})}}$$

Rather than keeping track of the expectations of nonterminals, they can be calculated from the rule expectations by marginalizing the productions:

$$E_\theta[p] = \sum_\varphi E_\theta[p\to\varphi]$$

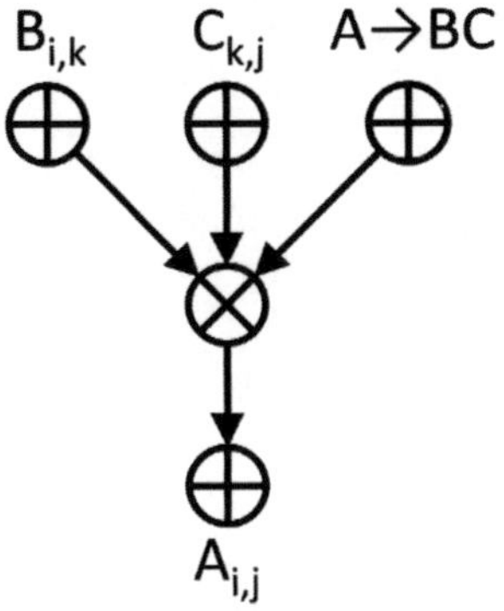

Figure 7: The same hyperedge as in Figures 3 and 4, represented as a mul/add-subgraph.

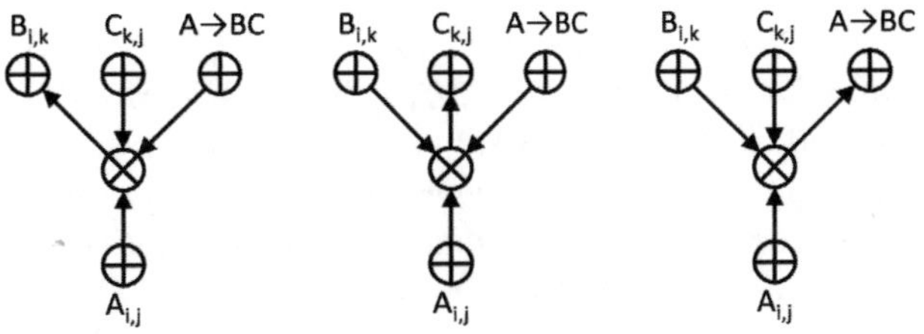

Figure 8: Reverse values (β) are calculated by tracking backwards through all possible paths. This produces three different paths for the mul/add-subgraph from Figure 7. Arrows pointing downward propagate α-values while arrows pointing upward propagate β-values.

5.1 SPLITG

Since this view of EM and parsing generalizes to deductive systems with multiple rules as conditions, we can apply it to the deductive system of SPLITGs. It is, however, also interesting to note how the hypergraph view of parsing is changed by this. We effectively removed the weights from the edges, but kept the feature that values of nodes depend entirely on the values connected by incoming hyperedges. If we assume the values to be from the Boolean semiring, the hypergraphs we ended up with are in fact *and/or-graphs*. That is: each node in the hypergraph corresponds to an *or-node*, and each hyperedge corresponds to an *and-node*. We note that this can be generalized to any semiring, since *or* is equivalent to $\oplus$ and *and* is equivalent to $\otimes$ for the Boolean semiring, we can express a hypergraph over an arbitrary semiring as a *mul/add-graph*.[2] Figure 7 shows how a hyperedge looks in this new graph form. The α-value of a node is calculated by combining the values of all incoming edges using the operator of the node. The β-values are also calculated using the operator of the node, but with the edges reversed. For this to work properly, the *mul-nodes* need to behave somewhat different from *add-nodes*: each incoming edge has to be reversed one at a time, as illustrated in Figure 8.

6 Conclusions

We have shown that the reification of rules into the parse forest graphs allows for a unified framework where all calculations are performed the same way, and where the calculations for the rules encompass all information needed to reestimate them using expectation maximization. The contextual probability of a rule—its outside probability—holds all information needed to calculate expectations, which can be exploited by promoting the rules to first-class citizens of the parse forest. We have also seen how this reification of the rules helped solve a real translation problem—induction of stochastic preterminalized linear inversion transduction grammars using expectation maximization.

[2]Because it is much easier to pronounce than $\otimes$/$\oplus$-graph.

Acknowledgments

This work was funded by the Defense Advanced Research Projects Agency (DARPA) under GALE Contract Nos. HR0011-06-C-0023 and HR0011-06-C-0023, and the Hong Kong Research Grants Council (RGC) under research grants GRF621008, GRF612806, DAG03/04.EG09, RGC6256/00E, and RGC6083/99E. Any opinions, findings and conclusions or recommendations expressed in this material are those of the authors and do not necessarily reflect the views of the Defense Advanced Research Projects Agency. We would also like to thank the three anonymous reviewers, whose feedback made this a better paper.

References

James K. Baker. 1979. Trainable grammars for speech recognition. In *Speech Communication Papers for the 97th Meeting of the Acoustical Society of America*, pages 547–550, Cambridge, Massachusetts.

Sylvie Billot and Bernard Lang. 1989. The structure of shared forests in ambiguous parsing. In *Proceedings of the 27th annual meeting on Association for Computational Linguistics*, ACL'89, pages 143–151, Stroudsburg, Pennsylvania, USA.

John Cocke. 1969. *Programming languages and their compilers: Preliminary notes*. Courant Institute of Mathematical Sciences, New York University.

Arthur Pentland Dempster, Nan M. Laird, and Donald Bruce Rubin. 1977. Maximum likelihood from incomplete data via the em algorithm. *Journal of the Royal Statistical Society. Series B (Methodological)*, 39(1):1–38.

Jason Eisner. 2001. Expectation semirings: Flexible EM for finite-state transducers. In Gertjan van Noord, editor, *Proceedings of the ESSLLI Workshop on Finite-State Methods in Natural Language Processing (FSMNLP)*. Extended abstract (5 pages).

Jason Eisner. 2002. Parameter estimation for probabilistic finite-state transducers. In *Proceedings of the 40th Annual Meeting of the Association for Computational Linguistics (ACL)*, pages 1–8, Philadelphia, July.

Joshua Goodman. 1999. Semiring parsing. *Computational Linguistics*, 25(4):573–605.

Liang Huang. 2008. *Forest-based Algorithms in Natural Language Processing*. Ph.D. thesis, University of Pennsylvania.

Tadao Kasami and Koji Torii. 1969. A syntax-analysis procedure for unambiguous context-free grammars. *Journal of the Association for Computing Machinery*, 16(3):423–431.

Zhifei Li and Jason Eisner. 2009. First- and second-order expectation semirings with applications to minimum-risk training on translation forests. In *Proceedings of the Conference on Empirical Methods in Natural Language Processing (EMNLP)*, pages 40–51, Singapore, August.

Christopher D. Manning and Dan Klein. 2001. Parsing and hypergraphs. In *Proceedings of the 2001 International Workshop on Parsing Technologies*.

Markus Saers and Dekai Wu. 2011. Principled induction of phrasal bilexica. In *Proceedings of the 15th Annual Conference of the European Association for Machine Translation*, Leuven, Belgium, May.

Markus Saers. 2011. *Translation as Linear Transduction: Models and Algorithms for Efficient Learning in Statistical Machine Translation*. Ph.D. thesis, Uppsala University, Department of Linguistics and Philology.

Daniel H. Younger. 1967. Recognition and parsing of context-free languages in time n^3. *Information and Control*, 10(2):189–208.

A Dependency Based Statistical Translation Model

Giuseppe Attardi
Università di Pisa
Dipartimento di Informatica
attardi@di.unipi.it

Atanas Chanev
Università di Pisa
Dipartimento di Informatica
chanev@di.unipi.it

Antonio Valerio Miceli Barone
Università di Pisa
Dipartimento di Informatica
miceli@di.unipi.it

Abstract

We present a translation model based on dependency trees. The model adopts a tree-to-string approach and extends Phrase-Based translation (PBT) by using the dependency tree of the source sentence for selecting translation options and for reordering them. Decoding is done by translating each node in the tree and combining its translations with those of its head in alternative orders with respect to its siblings. Reordering of the siblings exploits a heuristic based on the syntactic information from the parse tree which is learned from the corpus. The decoder uses the same phrase tables produced by a PBT system for looking up translations of single words or of partial sub-trees. A mathematical model is presented and experimental results are discussed.

1 Introduction

Several efforts are being made to incorporate syntactic analysis into phrase-base statistical translation (PBT) (Och 2002; Koehn et. al. 2003), which represents the state of the art in terms of robustness in modeling local word reordering and efficiency in decoding. Syntactic analysis is meant to improve some of the pitfalls of PBT:

- Translation options selection: candidate phrases for translation are selected as consecutive n-grams. This may miss to consider certain syntactic phrases if their component words are far apart.
- Phrase reordering: especially for languages with different word order, e.g. subject-verb-object (SVO) and subject-object-verb (SVO) languages, long distance reordering is a problem. This has been addressed with a distance based distortion model (Och 2002; Koehn et al. 2003), lexicalized phrase reordering (Tillmann, 2004; Koehn, et.al., 2005; Al-Onaizan and Papineni, 2006), by hierarchical phrase reordering model (Galley and Manning, 2008) or by reordering the nodes in a dependency tree (Xu et al., 2009)
- Movement of translations of fertile words: a word with fertility higher than one can be translated into several words that do not occur consecutively. For example, the Italian sentence "*Lui partirà domani*" translates into German as "*Er wird morgen abreisen*". The Italian word "*partirà*" (meaning "*will leave*") translates into "*wird gehen*" in German, but the infinite "*abreisen*" goes to the end of the sentence with a movement that might be quite long.

Reordering of phrases is necessary because of different word order typologies of languages: constituent word order like SOV for Hindi vs. SVO for English; order of modifiers like noun–adjective for French, Italian vs. adjective-noun in English. Xu et al. (2009) tackle this issue by introducing a reordering approach based on manual rules that are applied to the parse tree produced by a dependency parser.

However the splitting phenomenon mentioned above requires more elaborate solutions than simple reordering grammatical rules.

Several schemes have been proposed for improving PBMT systems based on dependency trees. Our approach extends basic PBT as de-

Proceedings of SSST-5, Fifth Workshop on Syntax, Semantics and Structure in Statistical Translation, pages 79–87,
ACL HLT 2011, Portland, Oregon, USA, June 2011. ©2011 Association for Computational Linguistics

scribed in (Koehn et. al., 2003) with the following differences:

- we perform tree-to-string translation. The dependency tree of the source language sentence allows identifying syntactically meaningful phrases as translation options, instead of n-grams. However these phrases are then still looked up in a Phrase Translation Table (PT) quite similarly to PBT. Thus we avoid the sparseness problem that other methods based on treelets suffer (Quirk et al., 2005).
- reordering of phrases is carried out traversing the dependency tree and selecting as options phrases that are children of each head. Hence a far away but logically connected portion of a phrase can be included in the reordering.
- phrase combination is performed by combining the translations of a node with those of its head. Hence only phrases that have a syntactic relation are connected. The Language Model (LM) is still consulted to ensure that the combination is proper, and the overall score of each translation is carried along.
- when all the links in the parse tree have been reduced, the root node contains candidate translations for the whole sentences
- alternative visit orderings of the tree may produce different translations so the final translation is the one with the highest score.

Some of the benefits of our approach include:

1) reordering is based on syntactic phrases rather than arbitrary chunks
2) computing the future cost estimation can be avoided, since the risk of choosing an easier n-gram is mitigated by the fact that phrases are chosen according to the dependency tree
3) since we are translating from tree to string, we can directly exploit the standard phrase tables produced by PBT tools such as giza++ (Och and Ney, 2000) and Moses (Koehn, 2007)
4) integration with the parser: decoding can be performed incrementally while a dependency Shift/Reduce parser builds the parse tree (Attardi, 2006).

2 The Dependency Based Decoder

We describe in more detail the approach by presenting a simple example.

The translation of an input sentence is generated by reducing the dependency tree one link at a time, i.e. merging one node with its parent and combining their translations, until a single node remains. Links must be chosen in an order that preserves the connectivity of the dependency tree. Since there is a one-to-one correspondence between links and nodes (i.e. the link between a node and its head), we can use any ordering that corresponds to a *topological ordering* of the nodes of the tree.

A sentence is a sequence of words $(w_1, \dots, w_n)$, so we can use their index to identify words and hence each ordering is a permutation of those indexes.

Consider for example the dependency tree for the Italian sentence: *Il ragazzo alto* ("*The tall boy*").

There are only two possible topological orderings for this tree: 1-3-2 and 3-1-2.

In principle the decoding process should explore all possible topological orderings for generating translations, but their number is too big, being proportional to the factorial of the number of words, so we will introduce later a criterion for selecting a subset of these, which conform best with the rules of the languages.

Given a permutation we obtain a translation by merging in that order each node with its parent.

The initialization step of the decoder creates nodes corresponding to the parse tree and collects translations for each individual word from the PT.

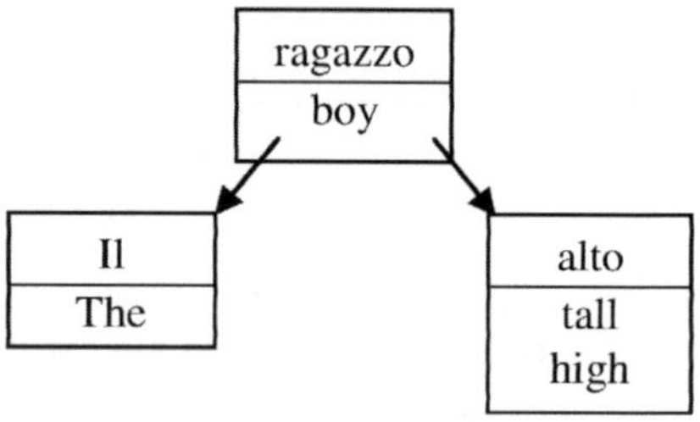

Case 1: Permutation 1-3-2

The first merge step is applied to the nodes for w_1 and its head w_2, performing the concatenation of the translations of nodes *il* (*the*) and *ragazzo* (*boy*), both in normal and reverse order. Hence expansion of this hypothesis reduces the tree to the following, where we show also the partial translations associated to each node. Each translation has associated weights (i.e. the LM weight, the translation model weight, etc.) and a cumulative score. The score is the dot product of the weights for the sentence and the vector of tuning parameters for the model. The score is used to rank the sentences and also to limit how many of them are kept according to the beam size parameter of the algorithm.

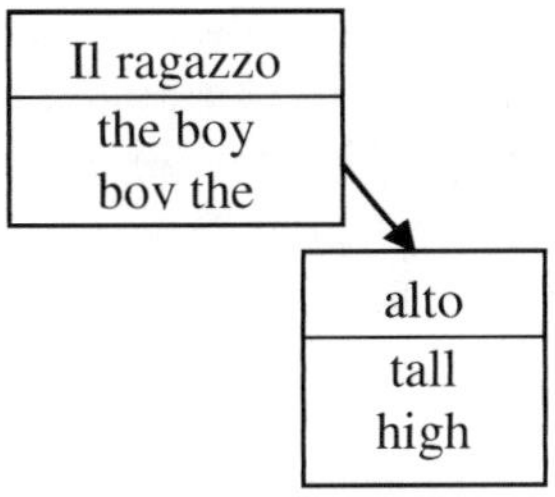

The second step merges the node for word w_3 ("*alto*") with that of its head w_2 ("*ragazzo*") producing a single node with four translations: "*the boy tall*", "*boy the tall*", "*tall the boy*" and "*tall boy the*".

Case 2: Permutation 3-1-2

The first merge between w_3 and w_2 generates two translation fragments: "*boy tall*" and "*tall boy*". The second one creates four translations: "*the boy tall*", "*boy tall the*", "*the tall boy*", "*tall boy the*".

When the tree has been reduced to a single root node and the results of both permutations are collected, the node will contain all eight alternative translations ranked according to the language model, so that the best one, possibly "*the tall boy*", can be selected as overall sentence translation.

3 Node Merge

The operation of node merge consists of taking all possible translations for the two nodes and concatenating them in either sequential or reverse order, adding them to the translation of the parent node and dropping the child.

In certain cases though, for example idiomatic phrases, the best translation is not obtained by combining the individual translations of each word, but instead a proper translation might be found in the Phrase Translation Table (PT). Hence besides performing combination of translations, we also consider the sub-tree rooted at the head node h_{ri} of node r_i. We consider the phrase corresponding to the leaves of the sub-tree rooted at h_{ri} and all children already merged into it, including r_i: if this phrase is present in the PT, then its translations are also added to the node.

This is sometimes useful, since it allows the decoder to exploit phrases that only correspond to partial sub-trees that it will otherwise miss.

4 Reordering Rules

In order to restrict the number of permutations to consider, we introduce a reordering step based on rules that examine the dependency tree of the source sentence.

The rules are dependent on the language pair and they can be learned automatically from the corpus.

We report first a simple set of hand crafted rules devised for the pair Italian-English that we used as a baseline.

The default ordering is to start numbering the left children of a node backwards, i.e. the node closer to the head comes first, then continuing with the right children in sequential order.

Special rules handle these cases:

1) The head is a verb: move an adverb child to first position. This lets a sequence of VA VM V R be turned into VA VM R V, where VA is the POS for auxiliary verbs, VM for modals, V for main verb and R for adverbs.
2) The head is a noun: move adjectives or prepositions immediately following the head to the beginning.

4.1 Learning Reordering Rules

In order to learn the reordering rules we created a word-aligned parallel corpus from 1.3 million source sentences selected from the parallel corpus. The corpus is parsed and each parse tree is analyzed using the giza++ word alignments of its translation to figure out node movements.

For each source-language word, we estimate a unique alignment to a target-language word. If the source word is aligned to more than one target word we select the first one appearing in the alignment file. If a source word is not aligned to any word, we choose the first alignment in its descendants in the dependency tree. If no alignment can be found in the descendants, we assume that the word stays in its original position.

We reorder the source sentence according to this alignment, putting it in target-language order.

We produce a training event consisting of a pair (*context, offset*) for each non-root word. The context of the event consists of a set of features (the POS tag of a word, its dependency tag and the POS of its head) extracted for the word and its children. The outcome of the event is the offset of the word relative to its parent (negative for words that appear on the left of their parent in target-language order, positive otherwise).

We calculate the relative frequency of each event conditioned on the *context*, deriving rules of the form:

(*context, offset, Pr*[*Offset = offset* | *Context = context*]).

During decoding, we compute a reordering position for each source word by adding to the word position to the offset predicted by the most likely reordering rule matching the word context (or 0 if no matching context is found).

The reordering position drives the children combination procedure in the decoder.

Our reordering rules are similar to those proposed by Xu at al. (2009), except that we derive them automatically from the training set, rather than being hand-coded.

4.2 Beam Search

Search through the space of hypotheses generated is performed using beam search that keeps in each node the list of the top best translations for the node. The score for the translation is computed using the weights of the individual phrases that make up the translation and the overall LM probability of the combination.

The scores are computed querying the standard Moses Phrase Table and the LM for the target language; other weights uses by moses such as the reordering weights or the future cost estimates are discarded or not computed.

5 The Model

A mathematical model of the dependency based translation process can be formulated as follows.

Consider the parse of a sentence f of length n. Let R denote all topological ordering of the nodes according to the dependency tree.

Let f_r denote the parse tree along with a consistent node ordering r. Each ordering gives rise to several different translations. Let E_r denote the set of translations corresponding to f_r. We assign to each translation $e_r \in E_r$ a probability according to the formula below. The final translation is the best result obtained through combinations over all orderings.

Error! Objects cannot be created from editing field codes.

Where e_r denotes any of the translations of f obtained when nodes are combined according to node ordering r.

The probability of a translation e_r corresponding to a node ordering r for a phrase f, $p(e_r \mid f)$ is defined as:

Error! Objects cannot be created from editing field codes.

where

Error! Objects cannot be created from editing field codes. and**Error! Objects cannot be created from editing field codes.**denote the leaf words from node r_i and those of its head node h_{ri}, respectively.

Error! Objects cannot be created from editing field codes.is either **Error! Objects cannot**

be created from editing field codes.or **Error! Objects cannot be created from editing field codes.**

$p(f, e) = p_{PT}(str(f), e)$ if $str(f) \in PT$

$str(f)$ is the sentence at the leaves of node r_i

p_{LM} is the Language Model probability

p_{PT} is the Phrase Table probability

6 Related Work

Yamada and Knight (2001) introduced a syntax-based translation model that incorporated source-language syntactic knowledge within statistical translation. Many similar approaches are based on constituent grammars, among which we mention (Chiang, 2005) who introduced hierarchical translation models.

The earliest approach based on dependency grammars is the work by Ashlawi et al. (2000), who developed a tree-to-tree translation model, based on middle-out string transduction capable of phrase reordering. It translated transcribed spoken utterances from English to Spanish and from English to Japanese. Improvements were reported over a word-for-word baseline.

Ambati (2008) presents a survey of other approaches based on dependency trees.

Quirk et. al. (2005) explore a *tree-to-tree* approach, called treelet translation, that extracts treelets, i.e. sub-trees, from both source and target language by means of a dependency parser. A word aligner is used to align the parallel corpus. The source dependency is projected onto the target language sentence in order to extract treelet translation pairs. Given a foreign input sentence, their system first generates its dependency tree made of treelets. These treelets are translated into treelets of the target language, according to the dependency treelet translation model. Translated treelets are then reordered according to a reorder model.

The ordering model is trained on the parallel corpus. Treelet translation pairs are used for decoding. The reordering is done at the treelet level where all the child nodes of a node are allowed all possible orders. The results show marginal improvements in the BLEU score (40.66) in comparison with Pharaoh and MSR-MT. But the treelet translation algorithm is more than an order of magnitude slower.

Shen et. al. (2008) present a hierarchical machine translation method from *string to trees*. The scheme uses the dependency structure of the target language to use transfer rules while generating a translation. The scheme uses well-formed dependency structure which involves fixed and floating type structures. The floating structures allow the translation scheme to perform different concatenation, adjoining and unification operations still being within the definition of well-formed structures. While decoding the scheme uses the probability of a word being the root, and also the left-side, right-side generative probabilities. The number of rules used varies from 27 M (for a string to dependency system) to 140 M (baseline system). The performance reached 37.25% for the system with 3-grams, 39.47% for 5-grams.

Marcu and Wong (2002) propose a joint- probability model. The model establishes a correspondence between a source phrase and a target phrase through some concept. The reordering is integrated into the joint probability model with the help of:

3) Phrase translation probabilities **Error! Objects cannot be created from editing field codes.** denoting the probability that concept c_i generates the translation **Error! Objects cannot be created from editing field codes.** for the English and **Error! Objects cannot be created from editing field codes.** for the foreign language inputs.
4) Distortion probabilities based on absolute positions of the phrases.

Decoding uses a hill-climbing algorithm. Performance wise the approach records an average BLEU score of 23.25%, with about 2% of improvement over the baseline IBM system.

Zhang et. al. (2007) present a reordering model that uses linguistic knowledge to guide both phrase reordering and translation between linguistically correct phrases by means of rules. Rules are encoded in the form of weighted synchronous grammar and express transformations on the parse trees. They experiment also mixing constituency and dependency trees achieving some improvements in BLEU score (27.37%) over a baseline system (26.16%).

Cherry (2008) introduces a cohesion feature into a traditional phrase based decoder. It is implemented as a soft constraint which is based on the dependency syntax of the source language. He reports a BLEU score improvement on French-English translation.

The work by Xu et al. (2009) is the closest to our approach. They perform preprocessing of the foreign sentences by parsing them with a dependency parser and applying a set of hand written rules to reorder the children of certain nodes. The preprocessing is applied to both the training corpus and to the sentences to translate, hence after reordering a regular hierarchical system can be applied. Translation experiments between English and five non SVO Asian languages show significant improvements in accuracy in 4 out of 5 languages. With respect to our approach the solution by Xu et al. does not require any intervention on the translation tools, since the sentences are rewritten before being passed to the processing chain: on the other hand the whole collection has to undergo full parsing with higher performance costs and higher dependency on the accuracy of the parser.

Dyer and Resnik (2010) introduce a translation model based on a Synchronous Context Free Grammar (SCFG). In their model, translation examples are stored as a context-free forest. The process of translation comprise two steps: tree-based reordering and phrase transduction. While reordering is modeled with the context-free forest, the reordered source is transduced into the target language by a Finite State Transducer (FST). The implemented model is trained on those portions of the data which it is able to generate. An increase of BLEU score is achieved for Chinese-English when compared to the phrase based baseline.

Our approach is a true *tree-to-string* model and differs from (Xu et al., 2009), which uses trees only as an intermediate representation to rearrange the original sentences. We perform parsing and reordering only on the phrases to be translated. The training collection is kept in the original form, and this has two benefits: training is not subject to parsing errors and our system can share the same model of a regular hierarchical system.

Another difference is in the selection of translation options: our method exploits the parse tree to select grammatical phrases as translation options.

7 Implementation

The prototype decoder consists of the following components:

1) A specialized table lookup server, providing an XML-RPC interface for querying both the phrase table and the LM
2) A parser engine based on DeSR (DeSR, 2009)
3) A reordering algorithm that adds ordering numbers to the output produced by DeSR in CoNLL-X format. Before reordering, this step also performs a restructuring of the parse tree, converting from the conventions of the Italian Tanl Treebank to a structure that helps the analysis. In particular it converts conjunctions, which are represented as chains, where each conjunct connects to the previous, to a tree where they are all dependent of the same head word. Compound verbs are also revised: in the dependency tree each auxiliary of a verb is a direct child of the main verb. For example in "*avrebbe potuto vedere*", both the auxiliary "*avrebbe*" and the modal "*potuto*" depend on the verb "*vedere*". This steps groups all auxiliaries of a verb under the first one, i.e. "*potuto*". This helps so that the full auxiliary can be looked up separately from the verb in the phrase table.
4) A decoder that uses the output produced by the reordering algorithm, queries the phrase table and performs a beam search on the hypotheses produced according to the suggested reordering.

8 Experimental Setup and Results

Moses (Koehn et al., 2007) is used as a baseline phrase-based SMT system. The following tools and data were used in our experiments:

1) the IRSTLM toolkit (Marcello and Cettolo, 2007) is used to train a 5-gram language mod-

el with *Kneser-Ney* smoothing on a set of 4.5 million sentences from the Italian Wikipedia.

2) the Europarl version 6 corpus, consisting of 1,703,886 sentence pairs, is used for training. A tuning set of 2000 sentences from ACL WMT 2007 is used to tune the parameters.
3) the model is trained with lexical reordering.
4) the model is tuned with mert (Bertoldi, et al.)
5) the official test set from ACL WMT 2008 (Callison-Burch et al., 2008), consisting of 2000 sentences, is used as test set.
6) the open-source parser DeSR (DeSR, 2009) is used to parse Italian sentences, trained on the Evalita 2009 corpus (Bosco et al., 2009). Parser domain adaptation is obtained by adding to this corpus a set of 1200 sentences from the ACL WMT 2005 test set, parsed by DeSR and then corrected by hand.

Both the training corpora and the test set had to be cleaned in order to normalize tokens: for example the English versions contained possessives split like this "*Florence' s*". We applied the same tokenizer used by the parser which conforms to the PTB standard.

DeSR achieved a Labeled Accuracy Score of 88.67% at Evalita 2009, but for the purpose of translation, just the Unlabeled Accuracy is relevant, which was 92.72%.

The table below shows the results of our decoder (Desrt) in the translation from Italian to English, compared to a baseline Moses system trained on the same corpora and to the online version of Google translate.

Desrt was run with a beam size of 10, since experiments showed no improvements with a larger beam size.

We show two versions of Desrt, one with parse trees as obtained by the parser and one (Desrt gold) where the trees were corrected by hand. The difference is minor and this confirms that the decoder is robust and not much affected by parsing errors.

System	*BLEU*	*NIST*
Moses	**29.43**	**7.22**
Moses tree phrases	28.55	7.10
Desrt gold	26.26	6.88
Desrt	26.08	6.86
Google Translate	24.96	6.86
Desrt learned	24.37	6.76

Table 1. Results of the experiments.

Since we used the same phrase table produced by Moses also for Desrt, Moses has an advantage, because it can look up n-grams that do not correspond to grammatical phrases, which Desrt never considers. In order to determine how this affects the results, we tested Moses restricting its choice to phrases corresponding to treelets form the parse tree. The result is shown in the row in the table labeled as "Moses tree phrases". The score is lower, as expected, but this confirms that Desrt makes quite good use of the portion of the phrase table it uses.

Since the version of the reordering algorithm we used produces a single reordering, the Desrt decoder has linear complexity on the length of the sentence. Indeed, despite being written in Python and having to query the PT as a network service, it is quite faster than Moses.

9 Error Analysis

Despite that fact that Desrt is driven by the parse tree, it is capable of selecting fairly good and even long sentences for look up in the phrase table.

How close is the Desrt translation from those of the Moses baseline can be seen from this table:

	1-gram	2-gram	3-gram	4-gram	5-gram
NIST	7.28	3.05	1.0	0.27	0.09
BLEU	84.73	67.69	56.94	48.59	41.78

Sometimes Desrt fails to select a better translation for a verb, since it looks up prepositional phrases separately from the verb, while Moses often connects the preposition to the verb.

This could be improved by performing a check and scoring higher translations which include the translation of the preposition dependent on the verb.

Another improvement could come from creating phrase tables limited to treelet phrases, i.e. phrases corresponding to treelets from the parser.

10 Enhancements

The current algorithm needs to be improved to fully deal with certain aspects of long distance dependencies. Consider for example the sentence "*The grass around the house is wet*". The dependency tree of the sentence contains the non-contiguous phrases "*The grass*" and "*wet*", whose Italian translation must obey a morphological gender agreement between the subject "*grass*" ("*erba*", feminine), and the adjective "*wet*" ("*bagnata*").

However, the current combination algorithm does not exploit this dependence, because the last phases of node merge will occur when the tree has been reduced to this:

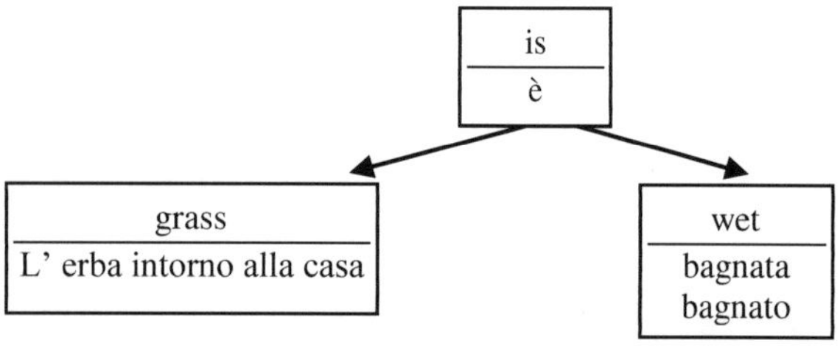

The PT however could tell us that "*erba bagnata*" is more likely than "*erba bagnato*" and allow us to score the former higher.

11 Conclusions

We have described a decoding algorithm guided by the dependency tree of the source sentence. By exploiting the dependency tree and deterministic reordering rules among the children of a node, the decoder is fast and can be kept simple by avoiding to consider multiple reorderings, to use reordering weights and to estimate future costs.

There is still potential for improving the algorithm exploiting information implicit in the PT in terms of morphological constraints, while maintaining a simple decoding algorithm that does not involve complex grammatical transformation rules.

The experiments show encouraging results with respect to state of the art PBT systems. We plan to test the system on other language pairs to see how it generalizes to other situations where phrase reordering is relevant.

Acknowledgments

Zauhrul Islam helped setting up our baseline system and Niladri Chatterjie participated in the early design of the model.

References

G. Attardi. 2006. Experiments with a Multilanguage Non-Projective Dependency Parser. *Proc. of the Tenth Conference on Natural Language Learning*, New York, (NY).

H. Alshawi, S. Douglas and S. Bangalore. 2000. Learning Dependency Translation Models as Collections of Finite State Head Transducers. *Computational Linguistics* 26(1), 45–60.

N. Bertoldi, B. Haddow, J-B. Fouet. 2009. Improved Minimum Error Rate Training in Moses. In *Proc. of 3rd MT Marathon*, Prague, Czech Republic.

V. Ambati. 2008. Dependency Structure Trees in Syntax Based Machine Translation. Adv. MT Seminar Course Report.

C. Bosco, S. Montemagni, A. Mazzei, V. Lombardo, F. Dell'Orletta and A. Lenci. 2009. Evalita'09 Parsing Task: comparing dependency parsers and treebanks. *Proc. of Evalita 2009.*

P. F. Brown, V. J. Della Pietra, S. A. and R. L. Mercer. 1993. The Mathematics of Statistical Machine Translation: Parameter Estimation. *Computational Linguistics*, 19(2), 263–311.

Callison-Burch et al. 2008. Further Meta-Evaluation of Machine Translation. *Proc. of ACL WMT 2008.*

C. Cherry. 2008. Cohesive phrase-based decoding for statistical machine translation. *Proc. of ACL 2008: HLT.*

D. Chiang. 2005. A hierarchical phrase-based model for statistical machine translation. In *Proc. of ACL 2005.*

DeSR. Dependency Shift Reduce parser. http://sourceforge.net/projects/desr/

Y. Ding, and M. Palmer. 2005. Machine Translation using Probabilistic Synchronous Dependency Insertion Grammar. *Proc. of ACL '05*, 541–548.

C. Dyer and P. Resnik. 2010. Context-free reordering, finite-state translation. *Proc. of HLT: The 2010 Annual Conference of the North American Chapter of the ACL,* 858–866.

F. Marcello, M. Cettolo. 2007. Efficient Handling of N-gram Language Models for Statistical Machine Translation. *Workshop on Statistical Machine Translation 2007*.

M. Galley and C. D. Manning. 2008. A Simple and Effective Hierarchical Phrase Reordering Model. In *Proc. of EMNLP 2008*.

R. Hwa, P. Resnik, A. Weinberg, C. Cabezas and O. Kolak, 2005. Bootstrapping Parsers via Syntactic Projection across Parallel texts. *Natural Language Engineering* 11(3), 311-325.

P. Koehn, F. J. Och and D. Marcu. 2003. Statistical Phrase-Based Translation. *Proc. of Human Language Technology and North American Association for Computational Linguistics Conference* (HLT/NAACL), 127–133.

P. Koehn, H. Hoang, A. Birch, C. Callison-Burch, M. Federico, N. Bertoldi, B. Cowan, W. Shen, C. Moran, R. Zens, C. Dyer, O. Bojar, A. Constantin, and E. Herbst. 2007. Moses: Open source toolkit for statistical machine translation. In *Proc. of the 45th Annual Meeting of the ACL*, demonstration session, 177–180, Prague, Czech Republic.

P. Koehn. 2009. *Statistical Machine Translation*. Cambridge University Press.

Y. Liu, Q. Liu and S. Lin. 2006. Tree-to-string Alignment Template for Statistical Machine Translation, In *Proc. of COLING-ACL*.

D. Marcu and W. Wong. 2002. A Phrase-Based Joint Probability Model for Statistical Machine Translation. *Proc. Empirical Methods in Natural Language Processing* (EMNLP), 133–139.

C. Quirk, A. Menzes and C. Cherry. 2005. Dependency Treelet Translation: Syntactically Informed Phrasal SMT. *Proc. 43rd Annual Meeting of the ACL*, 217–279.

S. Libin, J. Xu and R. Weischedel. 2008. A New String-to-Dependency Machine Translation Algorithm with a Target Dependency Language Model. *Proc. ACL-08*, 577–585.

F. J. Och 2002. Statistical Machine Translation: From Single Word Models to Alignment Template. Ph.D. Thesis, RWTH Aachen, Germany.

F.J. Och, H. Ney. 2000. Improved Statistical Alignment Models. *Proc. of the 38th Annual Meeting of the ACL*. Hong Kong, China. 440-447.

K. Yamada and K. Knight. 2001. A Syntax-Based Statistical Translation Model. *Proc. 39th Annual Meeting of ACL* (ACL-01), 6–11.

P. Xu, J. Kang, M. Ringgaard and F. Och. 2009. Using a Dependency Parser to Improve SMT for Subject-Object-Verb Languages. *Proc. of NAACL 2009*, 245–253, Boulder, Colorado.

D. Zhang, Mu Li, Chi-Ho Li and M. Zhou. 2007. Phrase Reordering Model Integrating Syntactic Knowledge for SMT. *Proc. Joint Conference on Empirical Methods in Natural Language Processing and Computational Natural Language Processing*: 533–540.

Improving MT Word Alignment Using Aligned Multi-Stage Parses

Adam Meyers[†], **Michiko Kosaka**[‡], **Shasha Liao**[†] **and Nianwen Xue**[◇]
[†] New York University, [‡]Monmouth University, [◇]Brandeis University

Abstract

We use hand-coded rules and graph-aligned logical dependencies to reorder English text towards Chinese word order. We obtain a 1.5% higher F-score for Giza++ compared to running with unprocessed text. We describe this research and its implications for SMT.

1 Introduction

Some statistical machine translation (SMT) systems use pattern-based rules acquired from linguistically processed bitexts. They acquire these rules through the alignment of a parsed structure in one language with a raw string in the other language (Yamada and Knight, 2001; Shen et al., 2008) or the alignment of source/target language parse trees (Zhang et al., 2008; Cowan, 2008). This paper shows that machine translation (MT) can also benefit by aligning a "deeper" level of analysis than parsed text, which includes semantic role labeling, regularization of passives and wh constructions, etc. We create GLARF representations (Meyers et al., 2009) for English and Chinese sentences, in the form of directed acyclic graphs. We describe two graph-based techniques for reordering English sentences to be closer to that of corresponding Chinese sentences. One technique is based on manually created rules and the other is based on an automatic alignment of GLARF representations of Chinese/English sentences. After reordering, we align words of the reordered English with the words of the Chinese, using the Giza++ word aligner(Och and Ney, 2003). For both techniques, the resulting alignment has a higher F-score than Giza++ on raw text (a 0.7% to 1.5% absolute improvement). In principle, our reordered text can be used to improve any Chinese/English SMT system for which Giza++ (or other word aligners) are part of the processing pipeline.

These experiments are a first step in using GLARF-style analyses for MT, potentially improving systems that already perform well with aligned text lacking large gaps in surface alignment. We hypothesize that SMT systems are most likely to benefit from deep analysis for structures where source and target language word order differs the most. We propose using deep analysis to reorder such structures in one language to more closely reflect the word order of the other language. The text would be reordered at two stages in an SMT system: (1) prior to acquiring a translation model; and (2) either prior to translation (if source text is reordered) or after translation (if target text is reordered). Our system moves large constituents (e.g., noun post-modifiers) to bring English word order closer to that of parallel Chinese sentences. This improves word alignment and is likely to improve SMT.

For this work we use two English/Chinese bitext corpora developed by the Linguistic Data Consortium (LDC): the Tides FBIS corpus and the GALE Y1 Q4 Chinese/English Word-Alignment corpus. We used 2300 aligned sentences from FBIS for development purposes. We divided the GALE corpus into into a 3407 sentence development subcorpus (DEV) and a 1505 sentence test subcorpus (TEST). We used the LDC's manual alignments of the FBIS corpus to score these data.

Proceedings of SSST-5, Fifth Workshop on Syntax, Semantics and Structure in Statistical Translation, pages 88–97,
ACL HLT 2011, Portland, Oregon, USA, June 2011.

2 Related Work in SMT

Four papers stand out as closely related to the present study. (Collins et al., 2005; Wang et al., 2007) describe experiments which use manually created parse-tree-based rules to reorder one side of a bitext: German/English in (Collins et al., 2005) and English/Chinese in (Wang et al., 2007). Both achieve BLEU score improvements for SMT: 25.2% to 26.8% for (Collins et al., 2005) and 28.52 to 30.86 for (Wang et al., 2007). (Wang et al., 2007) uses rules very similar to our own as they use the same language pair, although they reorder the Chinese, whereas we reorder the English. The most significant differences between our research and (Collins et al., 2005; Wang et al., 2007) are: (1) our manual rules benefit from a level of representation "deeper" than a surface parse; and (2) In addition to the hand-coded rules, we also use automatic alignment-based rules. (Wu and Fung, 2009) uses PropBank role labels (Palmer et al., 2005) as the basis of a second pass filter over an SMT system to improve the BLEU score from 42.99 to 43.51. The main similarity to the current study is the use of a level of representation that is "deeper" than a surface parse. However, our application of linguistic structure is more like that of (Wang et al., 2007) and our "deep" level connects all predicates and arguments in the sentence, regardless of part of speech, rather than just connecting verbs to their arguments. (Bryl and van Genabith, 2010) describes an open source LFG F-structure alignment tool with an algorithm similar to our previous work. They evaluate their alignment output on 20 manually-aligned German and English F-structures. They leave the impact of their work on MT to future research.

In addition to these papers, there has also been some work on rule-based reordering preprocessors to word alignment based on shallower linguistic information. For example (Crego and Mariño, 2006) reorders based on patterns of POS tags. We hypothesize that this is similar to the above approaches in that patterns of POS tags are likely to simulate parsing or chunking.

3 Preparing the Data

The two stage parsers of previous decades (Hobbs and Grishman, 1976) generated a syntactic representation analogous to the (more accurate) output of current treebank-based parsers (Charniak, 2001) and an additional second stage output that regularized constructions (passive, active, relative clauses) to representations similar to active clauses with no gaps, e.g., *The book was read by Mary* was given a representation similar to that of *Mary read the book*. Treating the active clause as canonical provides a way to reduce variation in language and thus, making it easier to acquire and apply statistical information from corpora–there is more evidence for particular statistical patterns when applications learn patterns and patterns more readily match data.

Two-stage parsers were influenced by linguistic theories (Harris, 1968; Chomsky, 1957; Bresnan and Kaplan, 1982) which distinguish a "surface" and a "deep" level. The deep level neutralizes differences between ways to express the same meaning–a passive like *The cheese was eaten by rats* was analyzed in terms of the active form *Rats ate the cheese*. Currently "semantic parsing" refers to a similar representation, e.g., (Wagner et al., 2007) or our own GLARF (Meyers et al., 2009). However, the term is also used for semantic role labelers (Gildea and Jurafsky, 2002; Xue, 2008), systems which typically label semantic relations between verbs and their arguments and rarely cover arguments of other parts of speech. Second stage semantic parsers like our own, connect all the tokens in the sentence. Aligned text processed in this way can (for example) represent differences in English/Chinese noun modifier order, including relative clauses. In contrast, few role labelers handle noun modifiers and none handle relative clauses. Below, we describe the GLARF framework and our system for generating GLARF representations of English and Chinese sentences.

For each language, we combine several types of information which may include: named entity (NE) tagging, date/number regularization, recognition of multi-word expressions (the preposition *with respect to*, the noun *hand me down* and the verb *ad lib*), role labels for predicates of all parts of speech, regularizing passives and other constructions, error correction, among other processes into a single typed feature structure (TFS) representation. This TFS is converted into a set of 25-tuples representing dependency-style relations between pairs of words in the sentence. Three types of dependencies are

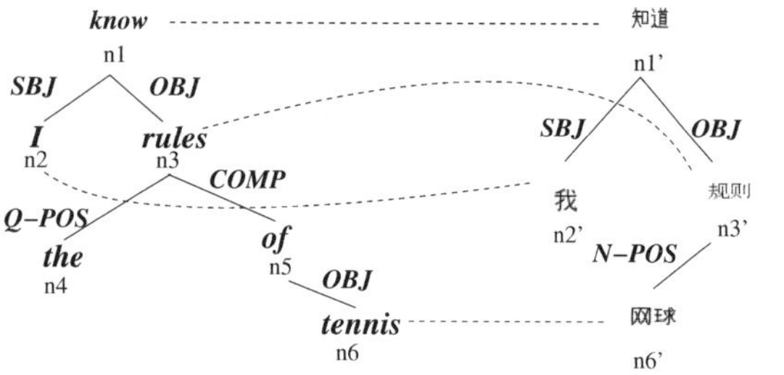

Figure 1: Word-Aligned Logic1 Dependencies

represented: *surface* dependencies (close to the level of the parser), *logic1* dependencies (reflecting various regularizations) and *logic2* dependencies (reflecting the output of a PropBanker, NomBanker and Penn Discourse Treebank transducer).(Palmer et al., 2005; Xue and Palmer, 2003; Meyers et al., 2004; Miltsakaki et al., 2004) The surface dependency graph is a tree; The logic1 dependency graph is an directed acyclic graph; and The logic2 dependency graph is a directed graph with cycles, covering only a subset of the tokens in the sentence. For these experiments, we focus on the logic1 relations, but will sometimes use the surface relations as well. Figure 1 is a simple dependency-based logic1 representation of *I know the rules of tennis* and its Chinese translation. The edge labels name the relations between heads and dependents, e.g., *I* is the SBJ of *know* and the dashed lines indicate word level correspondences. Each node is labeled with both a word and a unique node identifier (n1, n1', etc.)

The English system achieves F-scores for logic1 dependencies on parsed news text in the 80–90% range and the Chinese system achieves F-scores in the 74–84% range, depending on the complexity of the text. The English system has been created over the course of about 9 years, and consequently is more extensive than the Chinese system, which has been created over the past 3 years. The systems are described in more detail in (Meyers et al., 2009).

The GLARF representations are created in a series of steps involving several processors. The English pipeline includes: (1) dividing text into sentences; (2) running the JET NE tagger (Ji and Grishman, 2006); (3) running scripts that clean up data (to prevent parser crashes); (4) running a parser (currently Charniak's 2005 parser based on (Charniak, 2001)); (5) running filters that: (a) correct common parsing errors; (b) merge NE information with the parse, resolving conflicts in constituent boundaries by hand-coded rules; (c) regularize numbers, dates, times and holidays; (d) identify heads and label relations between constituents; (e) regularize text grammatically (filling empty subjects, resolving relative clause and Wh gaps, etc.); (f) mark conjunction scope; (g) identify transparent constituents (e.g., recognizing, that *A variety of different people* has the semantic features of *people* (human), not those of *variety*, the syntactic head of the phrase.); among other aspects. The Chinese pipeline is similar, except that it includes the LDC word segmenter and a PropBanker (Xue, 2008). Also, the regularization routines are not as completely developed, e.g., relative clause gaps and passives are not handled yet. The Chinese system currently uses the Berkeley parser (Petrov and Klein, 2007). Each of these pipelines derives typed feature structure representations, which are then converted into the 25 tuple representation of 3 types of dependencies between pairs of tokens: surface, logic1 and logic2.

To insure that the logic1 graphs are acyclic, we assume that certain edges are surface only and that the resulting directed acyclic graphs can have multiple roots. It turns out that the multiple rooted cases are mostly limited to a few constructions, the most common being parenthetical clauses and relative clauses. A parenthetical clause takes the main clause as an argument. For example, in *The word 'potato', he claimed, is spelled with a final 'e'.*, the verb *claimed*, takes the entire main clause as an argument, we assume that *he claimed* is a dependent on the main verb *(is) spelled* labeled PARENTHETICAL in our surface dependency structure, but that the main verb *(is) spelled* is a dependent of the verb *claimed* in our logic1 structure, labeled COMPLEMENT. Thus the logic1 surface dependency structure have distinct roots. In a relative clause, such as *the book that I read*", we assume that the clause *that I read* is a dependent on the noun *book* in our surface dependency structure with the label RELATIVE, but *book* is a dependent on the verb *read* in our logic1 dependency structure, with the label OBJ. This, means that our logic1 dependency graphs for sentences containing relative clauses are multi-rooted. One of the roots is the same as the root of the surface tree and the other root is the root of the relative clause graph (a relative pronoun or a main verb). Furthermore, there is a surface path connecting the relative clause root to the rest of the graph. Noncyclic graph traversal is possible, provide that: (1) we use the surface path to enter the graph representing the relative clause – otherwise, the traversal would skip the relative clause; and (2) we halt the traversal if we reach this path a second time – this avoids traversing down an endless path. The parenthetical and relative clause are representative of the handful of cases in which naive representations would introduce loops. All cases of which we are aware have the essential properties of one of these two cases: (1) either introducing a different single root of the clause; or (2) introducing an additional root that can be bridged by a surface path.

4 Manual Reordering Rules

We derived manual rules for making the English Word Order more like the Chinese by manually inspecting the data. We inspected the first 100-200 sentences of the DEV corpus by first transliterating the Chinese into English – replaced each Chinese word with the aligned English counterpart. Several patterns emerged which were easy to formalize into rules in the GLARF framework. These patterns were verified and sometimes generalized through discussions with native Chinese speakers and linguists. Our rules, similar to those of (Wang et al., 2007) are as follows (results are discussed in section 6): (1) Front a post-nominal PP headed by a preposition in the list {*of, in, with, about*)}. (2) Front post-nominal relative clause that begins with *that* or does not have any relative pronoun, such that the main predicate is not a copula plus adjective construction. (3) Front post-nominal relative clause that begins with *that* or has no relative pronoun if the main predicate is a copula+adjective construction which is not negated by a word from the set {*no neither nor never not n't*}. (4) Front post-nominal reduced relative in the form of a passive or adjectival phrase. (5) Move adverbials *more than* and *less than* after numbers that they modify. (6) Move PPs that post-modify adjectives to the position before the adjective. (7) Move subordinate conjunctions *before* and *after* to the end of the clause that they introduce. (8) Move an initial one-word-long title (*Mr., Ms., Dr., President*) to the end of the name. (9) Move temporal adverbials (adverb, PP, subordinate clause that is semantically temporal) to pre-verb position.

5 Automatic Node Alignment and its Application for Word Alignment

In this experiment, we automatically derive reorderings of the English sentences from an alignment between nodes in logic1 dependency graphs for the English (source) and Chinese (target) sentences. Source/Target designations are for convenience, since the direction of MT is irrelevant.

We define an alignment as a partial function from the nodes in the source graph and the nodes in the target graph. We, furthermore, assume that this mapping is 1 to 1 for most node pairs, but can be n to 1 (or 1 to n). Furthermore, we allow some nodes, in effect, to represent multiple tokens. These are identified as part of the GLARF analysis of a particular sentence string and reflect language-specific rules. Thus, for our purposes, a mapping between a source and target node, each representing a multi-word expression is 1 to 1, rather than N to N.

We identify the following types of multi-word expressions for this purpose: (a) idiomatic expressions from our monolingual lexicons, (b) dates, (c) times (d) numbers and (e) ACE (Grishman, 2000) NEs. Dates, holidays and times are regularized using ISO-TimeML, e.g., January 3, 1977 becomes 1977-03-01 and numbers are converted to Arabic numbers.

5.1 ALIGN-ALG1

This work uses a modified version of ALIGN-ALG1, a graph alignment algorithm we previously used to align 1990s-style two-stage parser output for MT experiments. ALIGN-ALG1 is an $O(n^2)$ algorithm, n is the maximum number of nodes in the source and target graphs (Meyers et al., 1996; Meyers et al., 1998). Given Source Tree T and Target Tree T', an $alignment(T, T')$ is a partial function from nodes N in T to nodes N' in T'. An exhaustive search of possible alignments would consider all non-intersecting combinations of the $T \times T'$ pairs of source/target nodes – There are at most $T!$ such pairings where $T >= T'$.[1] However, ALIGN-ALG1 assumes that some of these pairings are unlikely, and

[1]This ignores N to 1 matches, which we allow, although relatively rarely.

favors pairings that assume the structure of the trees correspond more closely. In particular, it is assumed that ancestor nodes are more likely to match if most of their descendant nodes match as well.

ALIGN-ALG1 finds the highest scoring alignment, where the score of an alignment is the sum of the scores of the node pairs in the partial function. The score for each node pair (n, n') partially depends on the scores of a mapping from the children of n to the children of n'. While the process of calculating the scores is recursive, it can be made efficient using dynamic programming.

ALIGN-ALG1 assumes that we align r and r', the roots of T and T'. Calculating the scores for r and r', entails calculating the scores of pairs of their children, and by extension all mappings from N to N' that obey the dominance preserving constraint: Given nodes n_1 and n_2 in N and nodes n'_1 and n'_2 in N', where all 4 nodes are part of the alignment, it cannot be the case that: n_1 dominates n_2, but n'_1 does not dominate n'_2. Here, *dominates* means *is an ancestor in the dependency graph.* ALIGN-ALG1 scores each pair of nodes using the formula: $Score(n, n') = Lex(n, n') + ChildVal(n, n')$, where $Lex(n, n')$ is a score based on matching the words labeling nodes n and n', e.g., the score is 1 if the pair is found in a bilingual dictionary and 0 otherwise. Given n has children $c_0, \ldots, c_i$ and n' has children $c'_0, \ldots, c'_j$, to calculate ChildVal: (1) Create Child-Matrix, a $(i + 1) \times (j + 1)$ matrix (2) Fill every position ($1 <= x <= i$, $1 <= x' <= j$) with $Score(x, x')$ (3) Fill every position (i+1, $1 <= x' <= j$) with $Score(n, x')$ minus a penalty (e.g., - .1) for *collapsing an edge*. This treats n' and x' as a single unit, matched to n.[2] (4) Fill every position ($1 <= x <= i$, j+1) with $Score(x, n')$ minus a penalty for *collapsing an edge*. Thus $n + x$ is paired with n'. (5) Set (i+1,j+1) to $-\infty$. Collapsing both source and target edges is not permitted. (6) For all sets of positions in the matrix such that no node or column is repeated, select the set with the highest aggregate score. The aggregate score is the numeric value of $ChildVal(n, n')$. If (n,n') is part of the alignment that is ultimately chosen, this choice of node pairs is also part of the alignment. There are at most $max(i + 1, j + 1)!$ possible pairings. Rather than calculating them all, a greedy heuristic can reduce the calculation time with minimal effect on accuracy: the highest scoring cell in the matrix is chosen first, conflicting cells are eliminated, the next highest scoring cell is chosen, etc.

Consider the example in Figure 1, assuming the dashed lines connect lexical matches (the function LEX returns 1 for these node pairs). Where n1 and n1' are the roots, $Score(n1, n1') = 1 + ChildVal(n1, n1')$. Calculating $ChildVal(n1, n1')$ requires a recursive descent down the pairs of nodes, until the bottom most pair is scored. $Score(n6, n6') = 1$. $Score(n5, n6') = 0 + .9$ (derived by collapsing an edge and subtracting a penalty of .1). $Score(n3, n3') = 1 + .9 = 1.9$. $Score(n2, n2') = 1$. $ChildVal(n1, n1') = 1 + 1.9 = 2.9$. Thus $Score(n1, n1') = 3.9$. The alignment includes: $(n1, n1')$, $(n2, n2')$, $(n3, n3')$, $(n5, n6')$, $(n6, n6')$.

The collapsing of edges helps recognize cases where multiple predicates form substructures, e.g., *take a walk, is angry*, etc. in one tree can map to single verbs in the other tree, allowing outgoing edges from *walk* or *angry* to map to outgoing edges of the corresponding verb, e.g., the agent and goal of *John walked to the store* could map to the agent and goal of *John took a walk to the store*.

In practice, ALIGN-ALG1 falls short because: (1) Our translation dictionary does not have sufficient coverage for the algorithm to perform well; (2) The assumption that the roots of both graphs should be aligned is often false. Parallel text often reflects a dynamic, rather than a literal translation. In one pair of aligned sentences in the FBIS corpus, the English phrase *the above mentioned requests* corresponds to: 陈水扁的这些要求 meaning *these requests of Chen Shui-bian – Chen Shui-bian* has no counterpart in the English. Parts of translations can be omitted due to: (a) the discretion of the translators, (b) the expected world knowledge of particular language communities, (c) the cultural importance of particular information, etc.; (3) Violations of the dominance-preserving constraint exist. The most common type that we have observed consists of sequences of transparent nouns and *of* (e.g., *series of*) in English corresponding to quantifiers in

[2]The slight penalty represents that collapsing edges complicate the analysis and is thus disfavored (Occam's Razor).

Chinese (一系列). Thus the head of the English construction corresponds to the dependent of the Chinese construction and vice versa.

5.2 Lexical Resources

Our primary bilingual Chinese/English dictionary (LEX1) had insufficient coverage for ALIGN-ALG1 to be effective. LEX1 is a merger between: The LDC 2002 Chinese-English Dictionary and HowNet. In addition, we manually added additional translations of units of measure from English. We also used NEDICT, a name translation dictionary (Ji et al., 2009) and AUTODICT, English/Chinese word to word pairs with high similarity scores taken from MT phase tables created as part of the (Zhang et al., 2007) system. The NEDICT was used both for precise matches and partial matches (since, NEs can often be synonymous with substrings of NEs). In addition, we used some WordNet (Fellbaum, 1998) synonyms of English to expand the coverage of all the dictionaries, allowing English words to match Chinese word translations of their synonyms. We allowed additional matches of function words that served similar functions in the two languages including: copulas, pronouns and determiners.

Finally, we use a mutual information (MI) based approach to find further lexical information. We run our alignment program over the corpus two times, the first time, we acquire statistical information useful for generating a MI-based score. This score is used as a lexical score on the second pass for items that do not match any of the dictionaries. On the first pass, we tally the frequency of each pair of source/target words s and t, such that neither s, nor t are matched lexically to any other item in the sentence. We, furthermore, keep track of the number of times each word appears in the corpus and the number of times each word appeared unaligned in the corpus. We tally MI as follows: $\frac{pair-frequency^2}{1+(source-word-frequency \times target-word-frequency)}$ One is added to the denominator as a variation on add-one smoothing (Laplace, 1816), intended to penalize low frequency scores. We calculate this score in two ways: (a) using the global frequencies of the source and target words; and (b) using the frequency these words were unaligned. The larger of the two scores is the one that is actually use.

Different lexicons are given different weights. Matches between words in the hand-coded translation dictionary and NEDICT are given a score of 1.0. Matches in other dictionaries are allotted lower scores to represent that these are based on automatically acquired information, which we assume is less reliable than manually coded information.[3]

5.3 ALIGN-ALG2

With ALIGN-ALG2, we partially address two limitations of ALIGN-ALG1: (1) the assumption that the roots of source and target graph are aligned; and (2) the dominance-preserving constraint. Basically, we assume that structural similarity is favored, but not necessarily at the global level. Thus it is likely that many subparts of corresponding trees correspond closely, but not necessarily the highest nodes in the trees.

We use ALIGN-ALG1 to align every possible pair of S source nodes and T target nodes. Then we look for P, the highest scoring node pair of all SXT pairs. P and all the pairs of descendants that are used to derive this score (the highest scoring pairs of children, grand children, etc.) become the initial output. Then we find all unmatched source and target children, and look up the highest scoring pair of these nodes, and we repeat the process, adding the resulting node pairs to the output. We continue to repeat this process until either all the nodes are included in the output or there is no remaining pair with a score above a threshold score (we leave automatic methods of tuning this score to future work and preliminarily have set this parameter to .3). This means that: 1) some parts of the graphs are left unaligned (the alignment is a partial mapping); 2) the alignment is more resilient to misalignment caused by differences in graph structure, regardless of the reason; and 3) the alignment may be between pair of unconnected graphs, each containing subsets of nodes and edges in the source and target graphs. While more complex than ALIGN-ALG1, ALIGN-ALG2 performs relatively quickly. After one iteration using ALIGN-ALG1, scores are looked up, not recalculated.

[3]Current informal weights of .2 to .6 may be replaced with automatically tuned weights (hill-climbing, etc.) in future work.

5.4 Treating Multiple Tokens as One

In some cases, parsing and segmentation of text can be corrected through minor modifications to our alignment routine. Similarly, we use bilingual lexical information to determine that certain other adjacent tokens should be treated as single words for purposes of alignment.

Given a language for which segmentation is a common source of processing error (Chinese), if a token is unaligned, we check to see whether subdividing the token into two sub-tokens would allow one or both of these sub-tokens to be alignable with unaligned tokens in the other language. We iterate through the string one token at a time, trying all partitions. Given a source token *ABC*, consisting of segments *A*, *B* and *C*, we test the two pairs of subsequences {*A*, *BC*} and {*AB*, *C*}, to see which of the two partitions (if any) could be aligned with unaligned target tokens and we compare the scores of both, selecting the highest score. Unless no partition yields further source/target matches, we then choose the highest scoring partition and add the resulting node pairings to our alignment. In a similar way, if there are a pair of aligned names consisting of source tokens $s_j \dots s_k$ and target tokens $t_j \dots t_k$, we look for adjacent unaligned source nodes (a sequence of nodes ending in s_{j-1} or beginning with s_{k+1}) and/or adjacent target language nodes, such that adding these nodes to the name sequence would produce at least as high a lexical score. The lexicon can also be used to match two adjacent items to the same word. We use a similar routine that checks our lexicons for words that are adjacent to matching words. This is particularly meaningful for the entries automatically acquired by means of MI, as our current method for acquiring MI would not distinguish between 1 to 1 and N to 1 cases. Thus MI scores for adjacent items typically does mean that an N to 1 match is appropriate. For example, the Chinese word 特命全权大使 had high MI with every word in the sequence (except *and*): *ambassador extraordinary and plenipotentiary* (example is from FBIS). This routine was able to cause our procedure to treat this English sequence as a single token.

5.5 Using Node Alignment for Reordering

Given a node alignment, we can attempt to reorder the source language so that words associated with aligned nodes reflect the order of the words labeling the corresponding target nodes. Specifically, we reorder our surface phrase structure-based representation of the source language (English) and then print out all the words yielded from the resulting reordered tree. Reordering takes place in a bottom up fashion as follows: for each phrase P with children $c_0 \dots c_n$, reorder the structure beneath the child nodes first. Then build the new-constituent right to left, one child at a time from $c_n \dots c_0$. Starting with an empty sequence, each item is put in its proper place among the constituents in the sequence so far. At each step, place some c_i after some c_j in $c_{i+1} \dots c_n$, such that c_j $align\_precedes$ c_i and c_j is after every c_k in $c_{i+1} \dots c_n$ such that c_i $align\_precedes$ c_k. If c_j does not exist, c_i is placed at the beginning of the sequence so far.

Definition of X $align\_precedes$ Y, where X and Y are nodes sharing the same parent: (1) Let $pairs_X$ be the set of source/target pairs in the alignment such that some (leaf node) descendant of X is the source node in the pair; (2) Let $pairs_Y$ be the set of pairs in the alignment such that some descendant of Y is the source node in the pair; (3) let X_{tmax} be the last target member of a pair in $pairs_X$, where the order is determined by the word order of the target words labeling the nodes; (4) let Y_{tmin} be the first target member of a pair in $pairs_Y$, where the order is determined the same way; (5) let X_{smin} be the first source member of a pair in $pairs_x$, according to the source sentence word order; (6) let Y_{smax} be the last source word in a pair in $pairs_Y$ ordered the same way. (7) X $align\_precedes$ Y if: X_{tmax} precedes Y_{tmin} and there is no source/target pair Q, R in the alignment such that: (A) R precedes, Y_{tmin}; (B) X_{tmax} precedes R; (C) Q either precedes X_{smin} or follows Y_{smax}; (D) If Q precedes Y_{smax}, then R does not precede Y_{tmin}.

Essentially, the $align\_precedes$ operator provides a conservative way to order the source subtrees S_1 and S_2 by their aligned target sub-tree counterparts T_1 and T_2. The idea is that if T_1 and T_2 are ordered in an opposite manner to S_1 and S_2, the source subtrees should trade places. However,

System	DEV	TEST
BASELINE	53.1%	49.9%
MANUAL	54.0% ($p < .01$)	50.6% (not significant)
ALIGN	53.5% ($p < .05$)	51.1% ($p < .01$)
ALIGN+MI	53.8% ($p < .01$)	51.4% ($p < .01$)

Table 1: F Scores for Reordering Rules

a source/target pair B_s, B_t can block this reordering if doing so would upset the order of the moved constituents relative to B_s and B_t e.g., if before the move, B_s precedes S_2 and B_t precedes T_2, but after the move S_2 would precede B_s. This reordering proceeds from right to left, halting after placing c_0.

6 Results

The results summarized in table 1, provide F-scores (the harmonic mean of precision and recall) of the word alignment resulting from running GIZA++ with and without our reordering rules, using the LDC's manually created word alignments for our DEV and TEST corpora.[4] Giza++ is run with English as source and Chinese as target. Our baseline is the result of running Giza++ on the raw text. The statistical significance of differences from the baseline are provided in parentheses, next to each non-baseline score(rounded to 2 significant digits). We divided both corpora into 20 parts and ran all versions of the program on each section. We compared the system output for each section against the baseline and used the sign test to calculate statistical significance. All system output except one[5] achieved at least $p < .05$ and most systems achieved significance well below $p < .01$.

Informally, we observe that the rules reordering common noun modifiers produce most of the total improvement. However, space limitations prevent a detailed exploration of these differences. The results show that for both DEV and TEST corpora, both reordering approaches improve F-scores of GIZA++ over the baseline. The manual rules (MANUAL) seem to suffer somewhat from overtraining on the DEV corpus, as they were designed based on DEV corpus examples, whereas the alignment based approaches (ALIGN and subsequent entries in the table) seem resilient to these effects. The use of Mutual Information (ALIGN+MI) seems to further improve the F-score.

The two approaches worked for many of the same phenomena, e.g., they fronted many of the same noun post-modifiers. The advantage of the hand-coded rules seems to be that they cover reordering of words which we cannot align. For example, a rule that fronts post-nominal *of* phrases operates regardless of dictionary coverage. Thus the rule-based version fronted the *of* phrase in the NP *the government of the Guangxi Zhuangzu Autonomous Region* in our DEV corpus, due to the absolute application of the rule. However, the alignment-based version did not front the PP because the name was not found in NEDICT. On the other hand, exceptions to this rule were better handled by the alignment-based system. For example, if *series of* aligns with the quantifier 一系列, the PP would be incorrectly fronted by the manual, but not the alignment-based system. Also, the alignment-based method can handle cases not covered by our rules with minimal labor. Thus, the automatic system, but not the manual-rule system fronted the locative PP *in Guangxi* to the position between *been* and *quite* in the sentence: *foreign businessmen have been quite actively investing in Guangxi*. This is closer to the Chinese, but may have been difficult to predict with an automatic rule for several reasons, e.g., it is not clear if all post-verbal locative phrases should front.

We further analyzed the DEV ALIGN+MI run to determine both how often nodes were combined together by our algorithm to produce N to 1 alignments and the number of reorderings undertaken. It turns out that out of the 59,032 pairs of nodes were aligned for 3076 sentence pairs:[6] 55,391 alignments

[4]We used F-scores, which (Fraser and Marcu, 2007) show to correlate well with improvements in BLEU. We weighted precision and recall evenly since we do not currently have BLEU scores for MT that use these alignments and therefore cannot tune the weights. Our results also showed improvements in alignment error rate (AER) (Och and Ney, 2000), which incorporate the "possible" and "sure" portions of the manual alignment into F-score, but do not seem to correlate well with BLEU.

[5]When run on the test corpus, the manual system outperformed the baseline system on only 13 out of 20 sections.

[6]When sentences were misparsed in one language or the other they were not reordered by the program.

were 1 to 1 (93.8% of the total) , 3443 alignments were 2 to 1 (5.8% of the total) and 203 alignments were N to 1, where N is greater than 2 (0.3% of the total). The reordering program moved 1597 single tokens; 2140 blocks 2 or 3 tokens long; 1203 blocks of 4 or 5 tokens; 610 blocks of 6 or 7 tokens, 419 blocks of 8, 9 or 10 tokens, and 383 blocks of more than 10 tokens.

7 Concluding Remarks

We have demonstrated that deep level linguistic analysis can be used to improve word alignment results. It is natural to consider whether or not these reorderings are likely to improve MT results. Both the manual and alignment-based systems moved post-nominal English modifiers to pre-nominal position, to reflect Chinese word order – other movements were much less frequent. In principle, these selective reorderings may help SMT systems identify *phrases* of English that correspond to *phrases* of Chinese, thus improving the quality of the phrase tables, especially when large chunks are moved. We would also expect that the precision of our system to be more important than the recall, since our system would not yield an improvement if it produced too much noise. Further experiments with current MT systems are needed to assess whether this is actually the case. We are considering such tests for future research, using the Moses SMT system (Koehn et al., 2007).

Our representation had several possible advantages over pure parse-based methods. We used semantic features such as temporal, locative and transparent (whether a low-content words inherits its semantics) to help guide our alignment. The regularized structure, also, helped identify long-distance dependency relationships. We are also considering several improvements for our alignment-based rules: (1) using additional dictionary resources such as CATVAR (Habash and Dorr, 2003), so that cross-part-of speech alignments can be more readily recognized; (2) finding more optimal orderings for unaligned source language words. For example, the alignment-based method reordered *a bright star arising from China's policy* to *a bright arising from China 's policy star*, separating *bright* from *star*, even though *bright star* function as a unit; (3) incorporating and using multi-word bilingual dictionary entries.; (4) automatic methods for tuning parameters of our system that are currently hand-coded; (5) training MI on a much larger corpus; (6) investigating possible ways to merge the manual-rules with the alignment-based approach; and (7) performing similar experiments with English/Japanese bitexts.

We would expect both parse-based approaches and our system to handle mismatches that cover large distances better than more shallow approaches to reordering, e.g., (Crego and Mariño, 2006) in the same way that a full-parse handles constituent structure more completely than a chunker. In addition, we would expect our approach to work best in languages where there are large differences in word order, as these are exactly the cases that all predicate-argument structure is designed to handle well (they reduce apparent variation in structure). Towards this end we are currently working on a Japanese/English system. Obviously, the cost of developing GLARF (or similar) systems are high, require linguistic expertise and may not be possible for resource-poor languages. Nevertheless, we maintain that such systems are useful for many purposes and are therefore worth the cost. The GLARF system for English is available for download at `http://nlp.cs.nyu.edu/meyers/GLARF.html`.

Acknowledgments

This work was supported by NSF Grant IIS-0534700 Structure Alignment-based MT.

References

J. Bresnan and R. M. Kaplan. 1982. Syntactic Representation: Lexical-Functional Grammar: A Formal Theory for Grammatical Representation. In J. Bresnan, editor, *The Mental Representation of Grammatical Relations*. The MIT Press, Cambridge.

A. Bryl and J. van Genabith. 2010. f-align: An Open-Source Alignment Tool for LFG f-Structures. In *Proceedings of AMTA 2010*.

E. Charniak. 2001. Immediate-head parsing for language models. In *ACL 2001*, pages 116–123.

N. Chomsky. 1957. *Syntactic Structures*. Mouton, The Hague.

M. Collins, P. Koehn, and I. Kucerova. 2005. Clause Restructuring for Statistical Machine Translation. In *ACL 2005*.

B. A. Cowan. 2008. *A Tree-to-Tree Model for Statistical Machine Translation*. Ph.D. thesis, MIT.

J. M. Crego and J. B. Mariño. 2006. Integration of POS-tag-based source reordering into SMT decoding by an extended search graph. In *AMTA'06*.

C. Fellbaum, editor. 1998. *WordNet: An Electronic Lexical Database*. The MIT Press, Cambridge.

A. Fraser and D. Marcu. 2007. Measuring Word Alignment Quality for Statistical Machine Translation. *Computational Linguistics*, 33:293–303.

D. Gildea and D. Jurafsky. 2002. Automatic Labeling of Semantic Roles. *Computational Linguistics*, 28:245–288.

R. Grishman. 2000. Entity Annotation Guidelines. ftp://jaguar.ncsl.nist.gov/ace/phase1/edt_phase1_v2.2.pdf.

N. Habash and B. Dorr. 2003. CatVar: A Database of Categorial Variations for English. In *Proceedings of the MT Summit*, pages 471–474, New Orleans.

Z. Harris. 1968. *Mathematical Structures of Language*. Wiley-Interscience, New York.

J. R. Hobbs and R. Grishman. 1976. The Automatic Transformational Analysis of English Sentences: An Implementation. *International Journal of Computer Mathematics*, 5:267–283.

H. Ji and R. Grishman. 2006. Analysis and Repair of Name Tagger Errors. In *COLING/ACL 2006*, Sydney, Australia.

H. Ji, R. Grishman, D. Freitag, M. Blume, J. Wang, S. Khadivi, R. Zens, and H. Ney. 2009. Name Translation for Distillation. In *Global Autonomous Language Exploitation*. Springer.

P. Koehn, H. Hoang, A. Birch, C. Callison-Burch, M. Federico, N. Bertoldi, B. Cowan, W. Shen, C. Moran, R. Zens, C. Dyer, O. Bojar, A. Constantin, and E. Herbst. 2007. Moses: Open Source Toolkit for Statistical Machine Translation. In *ACL 2007 Demonstration Session*, Prague.

P. Laplace. 1816. *Essai philosophique sur les probabilits*. Courcier Imprimeur, Paris.

Adam Meyers, Roman Yangarber, and Ralph Grishman. 1996. Alignment of Shared Forests for Bilingual Corpora. In *Proceedings of Coling 1996: The 16th International Conference on Computational Linguistics*, pages 460–465.

Adam Meyers, Roman Yangarber, Ralph Grishman, Catherine Macleod, and Antonio Moreno-Sandoval. 1998. Deriving Transfer Rules from Dominance-Preserving Alignments. In *Proceedings of Coling-ACL98: The 17th International Conference on Computational Linguistics and the 36th Meeting of the Association for Computational Linguistics*.

A. Meyers, R. Reeves, C. Macleod, R. Szekely, V. Zielinska, B. Young, and R. Grishman. 2004. Annotating Noun Argument Structure for NomBank. In *Proceedings of LREC-2004*, Lisbon, Portugal.

A. Meyers, M. Kosaka, N. Xue, H. Ji, A. Sun, S. Liao, and W. Xu. 2009. Automatic Recognition of Logical Relations for English, Chinese and Japanese in the GLARF Framework. In *SEW-2009 at NAACL-HLT-2009*.

E. Miltsakaki, A. Joshi, R. Prasad, and B. Webber. 2004. Annotating discourse connectives and their arguments. In A. Meyers, editor, *NAACL/HLT 2004 Workshop: Frontiers in Corpus Annotation*, pages 9–16, Boston, Massachusetts, USA, May 2 - May 7. Association for Computational Linguistics.

F. J. Och and H. Ney. 2000. Improved Statistical Alignment Models. In *ACL 2000*.

F. J. Och and H. Ney. 2003. A systematic comparison of various statistical alignment models. *Computational Linguistics*, 29(1):19–51.

M. Palmer, D. Gildea, and P. Kingsbury. 2005. The Proposition Bank: An annotated corpus of semantic roles. *Computational Linguistics*, 31(1):71–106.

S. Petrov and D. Klein. 2007. Improved Inference for Unlexicalized Parsing. In *HLT-NAACL 2007*.

L. Shen, J. Xu, and R. Weischedel. 2008. A New String-to-Dependency Machine Translation Algorithm with a Target Dependency Language Model. In *ACL 2008*.

J. Wagner, D. Seddah, J. Foster, and J. van Genabith. 2007. C-Structures and F-Structures for the British National Corpus. In *Proceedings of the Twelfth International Lexical Functional Grammar Conference*, Stanford. CSLI Publications.

C. Wang, M. Collins, and P. Koehn. 2007. Chinese syntactic reordering for statistical machine translation. In *EMNLP-CoNLL 2007*, pages 737–745.

D. Wu and P. Fung. 2009. Semantic roles for smt: A hybrid two-pass model. In *HLT-NAACL-2009*, pages 13–16, Boulder, Colorado, June. Association for Computational Linguistics.

N. Xue and M. Palmer. 2003. Annotating the Propositions in the Penn Chinese Treebank. In *The Proceedings of the 2nd SIGHAN Workshop on Chinese Language Processing*, Sapporo.

N. Xue. 2008. Labeling Chinese Predicates with Semantic roles. *Computational Linguistics*, 34:225–255.

K. Yamada and K. Knight. 2001. A syntax-based statistical translation model. In *ACL*, pages 523–530.

Y. Zhang, R. Zens, and H. Ney. 2007. Chunk-Level Reordering of Source Language Sentences with Automatically Learned Rules for Statistical Machine Translation. In *Proc. of NAACL/HLT 2007*.

M. Zhang, H. Jiang, A. Aw, H. Li, C. L. Tan, and S. Li. 2008. A Tree Sequence Alignment-based Tree-to-Tree Translation Model. In *ACL 2008*.

Automatic Category Label Coarsening for Syntax-Based Machine Translation

Greg Hanneman and **Alon Lavie**
Language Technologies Institute
Carnegie Mellon University
Pittsburgh, PA 15213 USA
{ghannema, alavie}@cs.cmu.edu

Abstract

We consider SCFG-based MT systems that get syntactic category labels from parsing both the source and target sides of parallel training data. The resulting joint nonterminals often lead to needlessly large label sets that are not optimized for an MT scenario. This paper presents a method of iteratively coarsening a label set for a particular language pair and training corpus. We apply this label collapsing on Chinese–English and French–English grammars, obtaining test-set improvements of up to 2.8 BLEU, 5.2 TER, and 0.9 METEOR on Chinese–English translation. An analysis of label collapsing's effect on the grammar and the decoding process is also given.

1 Introduction

A common modeling choice among syntax-based statistical machine translation systems is the use of synchronous context-free grammar (SCFG), where a source-language string and a target-language string are produced simultaneously by applying a series of re-write rules. Given a parallel corpus that has been statistically word-aligned and annotated with constituency structure on one or both sides, SCFG models for MT can be learned via a variety of methods. Parsing may be applied on the source side (Liu et al., 2006), on the target side (Galley et al., 2004), or on both sides of the parallel corpus (Lavie et al., 2008; Zhechev and Way, 2008).

In any of these cases, using the raw label set from source- and/or target-side parsers can be undesirable. Label sets used in statistical parsers are usually inherited directly from monolingual treebank projects, where the inventory of category labels was designed by independent teams of human linguists. These labels sets are not necessarily ideal for statistical parsing, let alone for bilingual syntax-based translation models. Further, the side(s) on which syntax is represented defines the nonterminal label space used by the resulting SCFG. A pair of aligned adjectives, for example, may be labeled ADJ if only source-side syntax is used, JJ if only target-side syntax is used, or ADJ::JJ if syntax from both sides is used in the grammar. Beyond such differences, however, most existing SCFG-based MT systems do not further modify the nonterminal label set in use. Those that do require either specialized decoders or complicated parameter tuning, or the label set may be unsatisfactory from a computational point of view (Section 2).

We believe that representing both source-side and target-side syntax is important. Even assuming two monolingually perfect label sets for the source and target languages, using label information from only one side ignores any meaningful constraints expressed in the labels of the other. On the other hand, using the default node labels from both sides generates a joint nonterminal set of thousands of unique labels, not all of which may be useful. Our real preference is to use a joint nonterminal set adapted to our particular language pair or translation task.

In this paper, we present the first step towards a tailored label set: collapsing syntactic categories to remove the most redundant labels and shrink the overall source–target nonterminal set.[1] There are

[1]The complementary operation, splitting existing labels, is beyond the scope of this paper and is left for future work.

Proceedings of SSST-5, Fifth Workshop on Syntax, Semantics and Structure in Statistical Translation, pages 98–106,
ACL HLT 2011, Portland, Oregon, USA, June 2011. ©2011 Association for Computational Linguistics

two problems with an overly large label set:

First, it encourages labeling ambiguity among rules, a well-known practical problem in SCFG-based MT. Most simply, the same right-hand side may be observed in rule extraction with a variety of left-hand-side labels, each leading to a unique rule in the grammar. The grammar may further contain many rules with the same structure and reordering pattern that differ only with respect to the actual labels in use. Together, these properties can cause an SCFG-based MT system to process a large number of alternative syntactic derivations that use different rules but produce identical output strings. Limiting the possible number of variant labelings cuts down on ambiguous derivations.

Second, a large label set leads to rule sparsity. A rule whose right-hand side can only apply on a very tightly specified set of labels is unlikely to be estimated reliably from a parallel corpus or to apply in all needed cases at test time. However, a coarser version of its application constraints may be more frequently observed in training data and more likely to apply on test data.

We therefore introduce a method for automatically clustering and collapsing category labels, on either one or both sides of SCFG rules, for any language pair and choice of statistical parsers (Section 3). Turning to alignments between source and target parse nodes as an additional source of information, we calculate a distance metric between any two labels in one language based on the difference in alignment probabilities to labels in the other language. We then apply a greedy label collapsing algorithm that repeatedly merges the two labels with the closest distance until some stopping criterion is reached. The resulting coarsened labels are used in the SCFG rules of a syntactic machine translation system in place of the original labels.

In experiments on Chinese–English translation (Section 4), we find significantly improved performance of up to 2.8 BLEU points, 5.2 TER points, and 0.9 METEOR points by applying varying degrees of label collapsing to a baseline syntax-based MT system (Section 5). In our analysis of the results (Section 6), we find that the largest immediate effect of coarsening the label set is to reduce the number of fully abstract hierarchical SCFG rules present in the grammar. These rules' increased permissiveness, in turn, directs the decoder's search into a largely disjoint realm from the search space explored by the baseline system. A full summary and ideas for future work are given in Section 7.

2 Related Work

One example of modifying the SCFG nonterminal set is seen in the Syntax-Augmented MT (SAMT) system of Zollmann and Venugopal (2006). In SAMT rule extraction, rules whose left-hand sides correspond exactly to a target-side parse node t retain that label in the grammar. Additional nonterminal labels of the form $t_1 + t_2$ are created for rules spanning two adjacent parse nodes, while categorial grammar–style nonterminals t_1/t_2 and $t_1 \backslash t_2$ are used for rules spanning a partial t_1 node that is missing a t_2 node to its right or left.

These compound nonterminals in practice lead to a very large label set. Probability estimates for rules with the same structure up to labeling can be combined with the use of a preference grammar (Venugopal et al., 2009), which replaces the variant labelings with a single SCFG rule using generic "X" labels. The generic rule's "preference" over possible labelings is stored as a probability distribution inside the rule for use at decoding time. Preference grammars thus reduce the label set size to one for the purposes of some feature calculations — which avoids the fragmentation of rule scores due to labeling ambiguity — but the original labels persist for specifying which rules may combine with which others.

Chiang (2010) extended SAMT-style labels to both source- and target-side parses, also introducing a mechanism by which SCFG rules may apply at run time even if their labels do not match. Under Chiang's soft matching constraint, a rule headed by a label A::Z may still plug into a substitution site labeled B::Y by paying additional model costs $subst_{B \rightarrow A}$ and $subst_{Y \rightarrow Z}$. This is an on-the-fly method of coarsening the effective label set on a case-by-case basis. Unfortunately, it also requires tuning a separate decoder feature for each pair of source-side and each pair of target-side labels. This tuning can become prohibitively complex when working with standard parser label sets, which typically contain between 30 and 70 labels on each side.

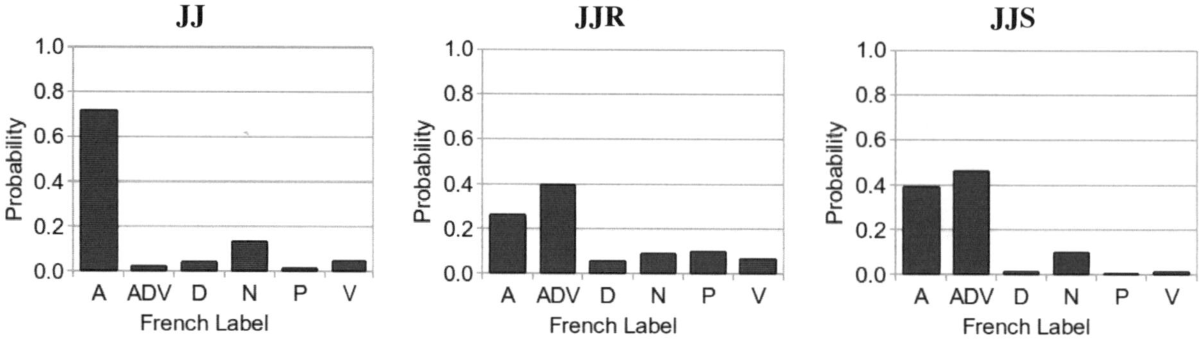

Figure 1: Alignment distributions over French labels for the English adjective labels JJ, JJR, and JJS.

3 Label Collapsing Algorithm

We begin with an initial set of SCFG rules extracted from a parallel parsed corpus, where S denotes the set of labels used on the source side and T denotes the set of labels used on the target side. Each rule has a left-hand side of the form $s :: t$, where $s \in S$ and $t \in T$, meaning that a node labeled s was aligned to a node labeled t in a parallel sentence. From the left-hand sides of all extracted rule instances, we compute label alignment distribution $P(s \mid t)$ by simple counting and normalizing:

$$P(s \mid t) = \frac{\#(s :: t)}{\#(t)} \quad (1)$$

We use an analogous equation to calculate $P(t \mid s)$. For two target-language labels t_1 and t_2, we have an equally simple metric of alignment distribution difference d: the total of the absolute differences in likelihood for each aligned source-language label.

$$d(t_1, t_2) = \sum_{s \in S} |P(s \mid t_1) - P(s \mid t_2)| \quad (2)$$

Again, the calculation for $d(s_1, s_2)$ is analogous.

If t_1 and t_2 are plotted as points in $|S|$-dimensional space such that each point's position in dimension s is equal to $P(s \mid t)$, then this metric is equivalent to the L_1 distance between t_1 and t_2.

Sample alignment distributions into French for three English adjective labels are shown in Figure 1. Bars in the chart represent alignment probabilities between French and English according to Equation 1, with the various French labels as s and JJ, JJR, or JJS as t. To compute an L_1 alignment distribution difference between a pair of English adjective tags, we sum the absolute differences in bar heights for each column of two graphs, as in Equation 2. It is already visually clear from Figure 1 that all three English labels are somewhat related in terms of distribution, but it appears that JJR and JJS are more closely related to each other than either is to JJ. This is reflected in the actual L_1 distances: $d(\text{JJ}, \text{JJR}) = 0.9941$ and $d(\text{JJ}, \text{JJS}) = 0.8730$, but $d(\text{JJR}, \text{JJS}) = 0.3996$.

Given the above method for computing an alignment distribution difference for any pair of labels, we develop an iterative greedy method for label collapsing. At each step, we compute the L_1 distance between all pairs of labels, then collapse the pair with the smallest distance into a single label. Then L_1 distances are recomputed over the new, smaller label set, and again the label pair with the smallest distance is collapsed. This process continues until some stopping criterion is reached. Label pairs being considered for collapsing may be only source-side labels, only target-side labels, or both. In general, we choose to allow label collapsing to apply on either side during each iteration of our algorithm.

In the limit, label collapsing can be applied iteratively until all syntactic categories on both the source and target sides have been collapsed into a single label. In Section 5, we explore several earlier and more meaningful stopping points.

4 Experimental Setup

Experiments are conducted on Chinese-to-English translation using approximately 300,000 sentence pairs from the FBIS corpus. To obtain parse trees over both sides of each parallel corpus, we used the English and Chinese grammars of the Berkeley parser (Petrov and Klein, 2007).

Given a parsed and word-aligned parallel sentence, we extract SCFG rules from it following the procedure of Lavie et al. (2008). The method first identifies node alignments between the two parse trees according to support from the word alignments. A node in the source parse tree will be aligned to a node in the target parse tree if all the words in the yield of the source node are either all aligned to words within the yield of the target node or have no alignments at all. Then SCFG rules can be extracted from adjacent levels of aligned nodes, which specify points at which the tree pair can be decomposed into minimal SCFG rules. In addition to producing a minimal rule, each decomposition point also produces a phrase pair rule with the node pair's yields as the right-hand side, as long as the length of the yield is less than a specified threshold.

Following grammar extraction, labels are optionally clustered and collapsed according to the algorithm in Section 3. The grammar is re-written with the modified nonterminals, then scored as usual according to our translation model features. Feature weights themselves are learned via minimum error rate training as implemented in Z-MERT (Zaidan, 2009) with the BLEU metric (Papineni et al., 2002). Decoding is carried out with Joshua (Li et al., 2009), an open-source platform for SCFG-based MT.

Due to engineering limitations in decoding with a large grammar, we apply three additional error-correction and filtering steps to every system. First, we observed that the syntactic parsers were most likely to make labeling errors for cardinal numbers in English and punctuation marks in all languages. We thus post-process the parses of our training data to tag all English cardinal numbers as CD and to overwrite the labels of various punctuation marks with the correct labels as defined by each language's label set. Second, after rule extraction, we compute the distribution of left-hand-side labels for each unique labeled right-hand side in the grammar, and we remove the labels in the least frequent 10% of the distribution. This puts a general-purpose limit on labeling ambiguity. Third, we filter and prune the final scored grammar to each individual development and test set before decoding: all matching phrase pairs are retained, along with the most frequent 10,000 hierarchical grammar rules.

5 Experiments and Results

In our first set of experiments, we sought to explore the effect of increasing degrees of label collapsing on a baseline system and to determine a reasonable stopping point. Starting with the baseline grammar, we ran the label collapsing algorithm of Section 3 until all the constituent labels on each side had been collapsed into a single category. We next examined the L_1 distances between the label pairs that had been merged in each iteration of the algorithm. This data is shown in Figure 2 as a plot of L_1 distance versus iteration number. The distances between the successive labels merged in the first 29 iterations of the algorithm are nearly monotonically increasing, followed by a much larger discontinuity at iteration 30. Similar patterns emerge for iterations 30 to 45 and for iterations 46 to 60. The next regions of the graph, from iterations 61 to 81 and from iterations 82 to 99, show an increasing prevalence of discontinuities. Finally, from iterations 100 to 123, the successive L_1 distances entirely alternate between very high and very low values.

Discontinuities are merely the result of a label pair in one language suddenly scoring much lower on the distribution difference metric than previously, thanks to some change that has occurred in the label set of the other language. Looking back to Figure 1, for example, we could bring the distributions for JJ and JJS much closer together by merging A and ADV on the French side. Although such sudden drops in distribution difference value are expected, they may provide an indication of when the label collapsing algorithm has progressed too far, since we have so reduced the label set that categories previously very different have become much less distinguishable. On the other hand, further reduction of the label set may have a variety of pratical benefits.

We tested this trade-off empirically by building five Chinese–English MT systems, each exhibiting an increasing degree of label collapsing compared to the original label set, which serves as our baseline. The degree of label collapsing in each of the five systems corresponds to one of the major discontinuity features highlighted in the right-hand side Figure 2. The systems were tuned on the NIST MT 2006 data set, and we evaluated performance on the NIST MT 2003 and 2008 sets. (All data sets have four

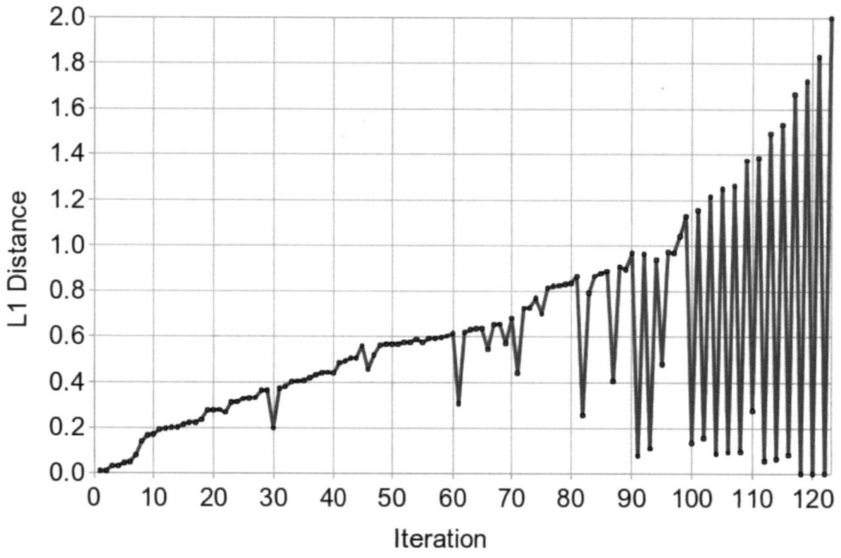

Iter.	L_1 Dist.
29	0.3646
45	0.5607
60	0.6155
81	0.8665
99	1.1303

Figure 2: Observed L_1 distance values for the labels merged in each iteration of our algorithm on a Chinese–English SCFG. We divide the graph into six distinct regions using the cutoffs at right.

Chinese–English System	MT 2003 Test Set METEOR	MT 2003 Test Set BLEU	MT 2003 Test Set TER	MT 2008 Test Set METEOR	MT 2008 Test Set BLEU	MT 2008 Test Set TER
Baseline	54.35	24.39	68.01	45.68	18.27	69.18
Collapsed, 29 iterations	**55.24**	27.03	63.77	46.25	19.78	65.88
Collapsed, 45 iterations	54.65	26.69	**62.76**	46.02	19.60	**64.88**
Collapsed, 60 iterations	55.11	**27.23**	63.06	**46.30**	20.19	65.18
Collapsed, 81 iterations	54.87	26.87	64.92	45.70	**20.48**	66.75
Collapsed, 99 iterations	54.86	26.16	64.17	45.87	19.52	65.61

Table 1: Results of applying increasing degrees of label collapsing on our Chinese–English baseline system. Bold figures indicate the best score in each column.

references.) Table 1 reports automatic metric results for version 1.0 of METEOR (Lavie and Denkowski, 2009) using the default settings, uncased IBM-style BLEU (Papineni et al., 2002), and uncased TER version 0.7 (Snover et al., 2006).

No matter the degree of label collapsing, we find significant improvements in BLEU and TER scores on both test sets. On the MT 2003 set, label-collapsed systems score 1.77 to 2.84 BLEU points and 3.09 to 5.25 TER points better than the baseline. On MT 2008, improvements range from 1.25 to 2.21 points on BLEU and from 2.43 to 4.30 points on TER. Improvements on both sets according to METEOR, though smaller, are still noticable (up to 0.89 points). In the case of BLEU, we verified the significance of the improvements by conducting paired bootstrap resampling (Koehn, 2004) on the MT 2003 output. With $n = 1000$ and $p < 0.05$, all five label-collapsed systems were statistically significant improvements over the baseline, and all other collapsed systems were significant improvements over the 99-iteration system.

Thus, though the system that provides the highest score changes across metrics and test sets, the overall pattern of scores suggests that over-collapsing labels may start to weaken results. A more moderate stopping point is thus preferable, but beyond that we suspect the best result is determined more by the test set, automatic metric choice, and MERT instability than systematic changes in the label set.

6 Analysis

Table 1 showed a strong practical benefit to running the label collapsing algorithm. In this section, we seek to further understand where this benefit comes from, tracing the effects of label collapsing via its modification of labels themselves, the differences in the resulting grammars, and collapsing's effect on decoding and output.

6.1 Labels Selected for Collapsing

Our first concern is for the size of the grammar's overall nonterminal set. The baseline system uses a total of 55 labels on the Chinese side and 71 on the English side, leading to an observed joint nonterminal set of 1556 unique labels. After 29 iterations of label collapsing, this is reduced to 46 Chinese, 51 English, and 1035 joint labels — a reduction of 33%. In the grammar of our most collapsed grammar variant (99 iterations), the nonterminal set is reduced to 14 English and 14 Chinese labels, for a total of 106 joint labels and a reduction of 93% from the baseline grammar. This demonstrates one facet of our introductory claim from Section 1: since we have improved translation results by removing the vast majority of our grammar nonterminals, most of the initial joint Chinese–English syntactic categories were not necessary for Chinese–English translation.

We identify three broad trends in the sets of labels that are collapsed:

- **Full Subtype Collapsing.** The Chinese-side parses include six phrase-level tags for various types of verb compounds. As label collapsing progresses, these labels are all combined with each other at relatively low L_1 distances.

- **Partial Subtype Collapsing.** In English, three of the four noun labels (NN, NNS, and NNPS) form a cohesive cluster early on in Chinese–English collapsing. However, the fourth tag (NNP, for singular proper nouns) remains separate, then later joins a cluster for more adjective-like labels.

- **Combination by Syntactic Function.** In French–English label collapsing (see below), we find the creation of a combined label in English for reduced relative clauses (RRC), adjective phrases headed by a *wh*-adjective (WHADJP), and interjections (INTJ). Even though these tags are unrelated in surface form, at some level they all represent parenthetical insertions or explanatory phrases.

The formulation of the L_1 distance metric in Section 3 means that our label collapsing algorithm will naturally produce different label clusters for different input grammars — any change in the Viterbi word alignments, underlying parallel corpus, initial label set, or choice of automatic parser will necessarily change the label alignment distributions on which the collapsing algorithm is based. In particular, the label clusters formed in one language are likely to be markedly different depending on which other language it is paired with. We examine these differences in more detail for the case of English when paired with either Chinese or with French. Our 29-iteration run of label collapsing for Chinese–English merged labels on the English side 19 times. For an exact comparison, we run iterations of label collapsing on a large-scale French–English grammar, extracted in the same way as the Chinese–English grammar, until the same number of English-side merges have been carried out, then examine the results.

Table 2 shows the English label clusters created from the Chinese–English and French–English grammars, arranged by broad syntactic categories. The differences in English label clusters hint at differences in the source-side label sets, as well as structural divergences relevant for translating Chinese versus French into English.

For example, Table 2 shows partial subtype collapsing of the English verb tags when paired with French. The French Berkeley parser has a single tag, V, to represent all verbs, and most English verb tags as well as the tag for modals very consistently align to it. The exception is VBG, for present-progressive or gerundive verb forms, which is more easily conflatable in French–English translation with a noun or an adjective. In translation from Chinese, however, it is VBG that is combined early on with a smaller selection of English verb labels that correspond most strongly to a basic Chinese verb. Other English verb tags are more likely to align to Chinese copulas, existential verbs, and nouns; they are not combined with the group for more "typical" verbs until iteration 67. The adverb series presents another example of translational divergence between language pairs.

Cluster	Chinese–English	French–English
Nouns	NN NNS NNPS #	NN NNS $
Verbs	VB VBG VBN	VB VBD VBN VBP VBZ MD
Adverbs	RB RBR	RBR RBS
Punctuation	LRB RRB “ ” , .	“ ”
Prepositions		IN TO SYM
Determiners		DT PRP$
Noun phrases	NP NX QP UCP NAC	NP WHNP NX WHADVP NAC
Adjective phrases	ADJP WHADJP	
Adverb phrases	ADVP WHADVP	
Prepositional phrases		PP WHPP
Sentences	S SINV SBARQ FRAG	S SQ SBARQ

Table 2: English-side label clusters created after partial label collapsing of a Chinese–English and a French–English grammar. In each case, the algorithm has been run until merges have occurred 19 times on the English side.

6.2 Effect on the Grammar

With a smaller label set, we also expect a reduction in the overall size of our various label-collapsed grammars as labeling ambiguity is removed. In the aggregate, however, even 99 iterations of Chinese–English label collapsing has a minimal effect on the total number of unique rules in the resulting SCFG. A clearer picture emerges when we separate rules according to their form. Figure 3 partitions the grammar into three parts: one for phrase pairs, where the rules' right-hand sides are made up entirely of terminals ("P-type" rules); one for hierarchical rules whose right-hand sides are made up entirely of nonterminals (abstract or "A-type" rules); and one for hierarchical rules whose right-hand sides include a mix of terminals and nonterminals (remaining grammar or "G-type" rules).

This separation reveals two interesting facts. First, although the size of the label set continues to shrink considerably between iterations 29 and 81, the number of unique rules in the grammar remains relatively unchanged. Second, the reduction in the size of the grammar is largely due to a reduction in the number of fully abstract grammar rules, rather than phrase pairs or partially lexicalized grammar rules. From these observations, we infer that the major practical benefit of label collapsing is a reduction in rule sparsity rather than a reduction in left-hand-side labeling ambiguity. Many highly ambiguous rules have had their possible left-hand-side labels effectively pruned down by the pre-processing steps we described in Section 4, which in preliminary experiments had a larger effect on the overall size of the grammar than label collapsing. As a more complementary technique, increasing the applicability of the fully abstract rules via label collapsing is important for performance. Such rules make up 49% to 59% of the hierarchical rules retained at decoding time, and they account for 76% to 87% of the rule application instances on the MT 2003 test set.

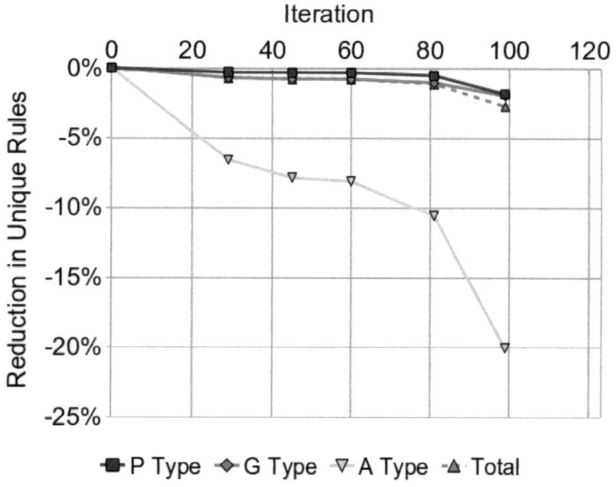

Figure 3: The effect of label collapsing on the number of unique phrase pairs, partially lexicalized grammar rules, and fully abstract grammar rules.

6.3 Effect on Decoding and Output

Interestingly, the label collapsing algorithm does not owe its success at decoding time to a significant increase in the number of rule applications. Among our systems, both the 45-iteration and the

60-iteration collapsed versions scored highly according to automatic metrics. Nevertheless, the 45-iteration system used 32% and 38% more rule applications than the baseline on the MT 2003 and MT 2008 test sets, respectively, while the 60-iteration system used 15% and 11% fewer. The number of unique rule types and the number of reordering rules applied on a test set may also go up or down.

Instead, the practical effect of making the grammar more permissive seems to be a significant change in the search space explored during decoding. This can be seen superficially via an examination of output n-best lists. On both test sets combined (2276 sentences), the 60-iteration label-collapsed system's top-best output appears in the baseline's 100-best list in only 81 sentences. When it does appear in the baseline, the improved system's translation is ranked fairly highly — always 30th place or higher. Conversely, the baseline's top-best output tends to be ranked lower in the improved system's n-best list: among the 114 times it appears, it is placed as low as 87th.

We ran a small follow-up analysis on the translation fragments explored during decoding. Using a modified version of the Joshua decoder, we dumped lists of hypergraph entries that were explored by cube pruning during Joshua's lazy generation of a 100-best list. These entries represent the decoder's approximative search through the larger space of translations licenced by the grammar for each test sentence. We then compared the hypergraph entries, excluding glue rules, produced on the first 100 sentences of the MT 2003 test set by both the baseline and the 60-iteration label-collapsed system.

A full 90% of the entries produced by the label-collapsed system had no analogue in the baseline system. The average length of the entries that do match is 2.3 source words, compared with an average of 6.2 words for the non-matched entries. We believe that the increased permissiveness of the hierarchical grammar rules is again the root cause of these results. Low-level constituents are more likely to be matched in both the baseline and the label-collapsed system, but different applications of the grammar rules, perhaps combined with retuned feature weights, leads the search for larger translation fragments into new areas.

7 Conclusions and Future Work

This paper has presented a language-specific method for automatically coarsening the label set used in an SCFG-based MT system. Our motivation for collapsing labels comes from the intuition that the full cross-product of joint source–target labels, as produced by statistical parsers, is too large and not specifically created for bilingual MT modeling. The greedy collapsing algorithm we developed is based on iterative merging of the two single-language labels whose alignment distributions are most similar according to a simple L_1 distance metric.

In applying varying degrees of label collapsing to a baseline MT system, we found significantly improved automatic metric results even when the size of the joint label set had been reduced by 93%. The best results, however, were obtained with more moderate coarsening. The coarser labels that our method produces are syntactically meaningful and represent specific cross-language behaviors of the language pair involved. At the grammar level, label collapsing primarily caused a reduction in the number of rules whose right-hand sides are made up entirely of nonterminals. The coarser labels made the grammar more permissive, cutting down on the problem of rule sparsity. Labeling ambiguity, on the other hand, was more effectively addressed by pre-processing we applied to the grammar beforehand. At run time, the more permissive collapsed grammar allowed the decoder to search a markedly different region of the allowable translation space than in the baseline system, generally leading to improved output.

One shortcoming of our current algorithm is that it is based entirely on label alignment distribution without regard to the different contexts in which labels occur. It thus cannot distinguish between two labels that align similarly but appear in very different rules. For example, singular common nouns (NN) and plural proper nouns (NNPS) in English both most frequently align to French nouns (N) and are thus strong candidates for label collapsing under our algorithm. However, when building noun phrases, an N::NNPS will more likely require a rule to delete a French-side determiner, while an N::NN will typically require a determiner in both French and English. Thus, collapsing NN and NNPS may lead to additional ambiguity or incorrect choices when applying larger rules.

Another dimension to be explored is the trade-off between greedy collapsing and other methods that cluster all labels at once. K-means clustering could be a reasonable contrast in this respect; its downside would be that all labels in one language must be assigned to clusters without knowledge of what clusters are being formed in the other language.

Finally, label collapsing is only the first step in a broader exploration of SCFG labeling for MT. We also plan to investigate methods for refining existing category labels in order to find finer-grained subtypes that are useful for translating a particular language pair. By running label collapsing and refining together, our end goal is to be able to adapt standard parser labels to individual translation scenarios.

Acknowledgments

This research was supported in part by U.S. National Science Foundation grants IIS-0713402 and IIS-0915327 and by the DARPA GALE program. Thanks to Chris Dyer for providing the word-aligned and preprocessed FBIS corpus we used in our Chinese–English experiments, and to Jon Clark for suggesting and setting up the hypergraph comparison analysis. We also thank Yahoo! for the use of the M45 research computing cluster, where we ran many steps of our experimental pipeline.

References

David Chiang. 2010. Learning to translate with source and target syntax. In *Proceedings of the 48th Annual Meeting of the Association for Computational Linguistics*, pages 1443–1452, Uppsala, Sweden, July.

Michel Galley, Mark Hopkins, Kevin Knight, and Daniel Marcu. 2004. What's in a translation rule? In *HLT-NAACL 2004: Main Proceedings*, pages 273–280, Boston, MA, May.

Philipp Koehn. 2004. Statistical significance tests for machine translation evaluation. In *Proceedings of EMNLP 2004*, pages 388–395, Barcelona, Spain, July.

Alon Lavie and Michael J. Denkowski. 2009. The METEOR metric for automatic evaluation of machine translation. *Machine Translation*, 23(2–3):105–115.

Alon Lavie, Alok Parlikar, and Vamshi Ambati. 2008. Syntax-driven learning of sub-sentential translation equivalents and translation rules from parsed parallel corpora. In *Proceedings of the Second ACL Workshop on Syntax and Structure in Statistical Translation*, pages 87–95, Columbus, OH, June.

Zhifei Li, Chris Callison-Burch, Chris Dyer, Juri Ganitkevitch, Sanjeev Khudanpur, Lane Schwartz, Wren N.G. Thornton, Jonathan Weese, and Omar F. Zaidan. 2009. Joshua: An open source toolkit for parsing-based machine translation. In *Proceedings of the Fourth Workshop on Statistical Machine Translation*, pages 135–139, Athens, Greece, March.

Yang Liu, Qun Liu, and Shouxun Lin. 2006. Tree-to-string alignment template for statistical machine translation. In *Proceedings of the 21st International Conference on Computational Linguistics and 44th Annual Meeting of the ACL*, pages 609–616, Sydney, Australia, July.

Kishore Papineni, Salim Roukos, Todd Ward, and Wei-Jing Zhu. 2002. BLEU: A method for automatic evalution of machine translation. In *Proceedings of the 40th Annual Meeting of the Association for Computational Linguistics*, pages 311–318, Philadelphia, PA, July.

Slav Petrov and Dan Klein. 2007. Improved inference for unlexicalized parsing. In *Proceedings of NAACL HLT 2007*, pages 404–411, Rochester, NY, April.

Matthew Snover, Bonnie Dorr, Richard Schwartz, Linnea Micciulla, and John Makhoul. 2006. A study of translation edit rate with targeted human annotation. In *Proceedings of the Seventh Conference of the Association for Machine Translation in the Americas*, pages 223–231, Cambridge, MA, August.

Ashish Venugopal, Andreas Zollmann, Noah A. Smith, and Stephan Vogel. 2009. Preference grammars: Softening syntactic constraints to improve statistical machine translation. In *Human Language Technologies: The 2009 Annual Conference of the North American Chapter of the ACL*, pages 236–244, Boulder, CO, June.

Omar F. Zaidan. 2009. Z-MERT: A fully configurable open source tool for minimum error rate training of machine translation systems. *The Prague Bulletin of Mathematical Linguistics*, 91:79–88.

Ventsislav Zhechev and Andy Way. 2008. Automatic generation of parallel treebanks. In *Proceedings of the 22nd International Conference on Computational Linguistics*, pages 1105–1112, Manchester, England, August.

Andreas Zollmann and Ashish Venugopal. 2006. Syntax augmented machine translation via chart parsing. In *Proceedings of the Workshop on Statistical Machine Translation*, pages 138–141, New York, NY, June.

Utilizing Target-Side Semantic Role Labels to Assist Hierarchical Phrase-based Machine Translation

Qin Gao and **Stephan Vogel**
Language Technologies Institute, Carnegie Mellon University
5000 Forbes Avenue
Pittsburgh, PA 15213
{qing, stephan.vogel}@cs.cmu.edu

Abstract

In this paper we present a novel approach of utilizing Semantic Role Labeling (SRL) information to improve Hierarchical Phrase-based Machine Translation. We propose an algorithm to extract SRL-aware Synchronous Context-Free Grammar (SCFG) rules. Conventional Hiero-style SCFG rules will also be extracted in the same framework. Special conversion rules are applied to ensure that when SRL-aware SCFG rules are used in derivation, the decoder only generates hypotheses with complete semantic structures. We perform machine translation experiments using 9 different Chinese-English test-sets. Our approach achieved an average BLEU score improvement of 0.49 as well as 1.21 point reduction in TER.

1 Introduction

Syntax-based Machine Translation methods have achieved comparable performance to Phrase-based systems. Hierarchical Phrase-based Machine Translation, proposed by Chiang (Chiang, 2007), uses a general non-terminal label X but does not use linguistic information from the source or the target language. There have been efforts to include linguistic information into machine translation. Liu et al (2006) experimented with tree-to-string translation models that utilize source side parse trees, and later improved the method by using the Packed Forest data structure to reduce the impact of parsing errors (Liu and Huang, 2010). The string-to-tree (Galley et al, 2006) and tree-to-tree (Chiang, 2010) methods have also been the subject of experimentation, as well as other formalisms such as Dependency Trees (Shen et al., 2008).

One problem that arises by using full syntactic labels is that they require an exact match of the constituents in extracted phrases, so it faces the risk of losing coverage of the rules. SAMT (Zollmann and Venugopal, 2006) and Tree Sequence Alignment (Zhang et al., 2008) are proposed to amend this problem by allowing non-constituent phrases to be extracted. The reported results show that while utilizing linguistic information helps, the *coverage* is more important (Chiang, 2010). When dealing with formalisms such as semantic role labeling, the coverage problem is also critical. In this paper we follow Chiang's observation and use SRL labels to augment the extraction of SCFG rules. I.e., the formalism provides additional information and more rules instead of restrictions that remove existing rules. This preserves the coverage of rules.

Recently there has been increased attention to use semantic information in machine translation. Liu and Gildea (2008; 2010) proposed using Semantic Role Labels (SRL) in their tree-to-string machine translation system and demonstrated improvement over conventional tree-to-string methods. Wu and Fung (2009) developed a framework to reorder the output using information from both the source and the target SRL labels. In this paper, we explore an approach of using the target side SRL information in addition to a Hierarchical Phrase-based Machine Translation framework. The proposed method extracts initial phrases with two different heuristics: The first heuristic is used to extract rules that have a general left-hand-side (LHS) non-terminal tag X,

Proceedings of SSST-5, Fifth Workshop on Syntax, Semantics and Structure in Statistical Translation, pages 107–115,
ACL HLT 2011, Portland, Oregon, USA, June 2011.

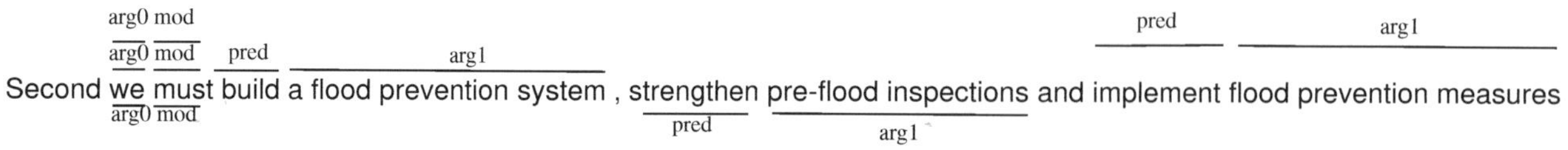

Figure 1: Example of predicate-argument structure in a sentence

i.e., Hiero rules. The second will extract phrases that contain information of SRL structures. The predicate and arguments that the phrase covers will be represented in the LHS non-terminal tags. After that, we obtain rules from the initial phrases in the same way as the Hiero extraction algorithm, which replaces nesting phrases with their corresponding non-terminals.

By applying this scheme, we will obtain rules that contain SRL information, without sacrificing the coverage of rules. In this paper, we call such rules SRL-aware SCFG rules. During decoding, both the conventional Hiero-style SCFG rules with general tag X and SRL-aware SCFG rules are used in a synchronous Chart Parsing algorithm. Special conversion rules are introduced to ensure that whenever SRL-aware SCFG rules are used in the derivation, a complete predicate-argument structure is built.

The main contributions are:

1. an algorithm to extract SRL-aware SCFG rules using target side SRL information.

2. an approach to use Hiero rules side-by-side with information-rich SRL-aware SCFG rules, which improves the quality of translation results.

In section 2 we briefly review SCFG-based machine translation and SRL. In section 3, we describe the SRL-aware SCFG rules. Section 4 provides the detail of the rule extraction algorithm. Section 5 presents two alternative methods how to utilize the SRL information. The experimental results are given in Section 6, followed by analysis and conclusion in Section 7.

2 Background

2.1 Hierarchical Phrase-based Machine Translation

Proposed by Chiang (2005), the Hierarchical Phrase-based Machine Translation model (commonly known as the Hiero model) has achieved results comparable, if not superior, to conventional Phrase-based approaches. The basic idea is to treat the translation as a synchronous parsing problem. Using the source side terminals as input, the decoder tries to build a parse tree and synchronously generate target side terminals. The rules that generates such synchronous parse trees are in the following form:

$$X \rightarrow (f_1\ X_1\ f_2\ X_2\ f_3, e_1\ X_2\ e_2\ X_1\ e_3)$$

where X_1 and X_2 are non-terminals, and the subscripts represents the correspondence between the non-terminals. In Chiang's Hiero model all non-terminals will have the same tag, i.e. X. The formalism, known as Synchronous Context-Free Grammar (SCFG) does not require the non-terminals to have a unique tag name. Instead, they may have tags with syntactic or semantic meanings, such as NP or VP.

2.2 Semantic Role Labeling and Machine Translation

The task of semantic role labeling is to label the semantic relationships between predicates and arguments. This relationship can be treated as a dependency structure called "Predicate-Argument Structure" (PA structure for short). Figure 1 depicts examples of multiple PA structures in a sentence. The lines indicate the span of the predicates and arguments of each PA structure, and the tags attached to these lines show their role labels.

Despite the similarity between PA structure and dependency trees, SRL offers a structure that posses better granularity. Instead of trying to analyze all links between words in the sentences, PA structure only deals with the relationships between verbs and constituents that are arguments of the predicates. This information is useful in preserving the meaning of the sentence during the translation process.

However, using semantic role representation in machine translation has its own set of problems.

First, we face the coverage problem. Some sentences might not have semantic structure at all, if, for instance they consist of single noun phrases or contain only rare predicates that are not covered by the semantic role labeler. Moreover, the PA structures are not guaranteed to cover the whole sentence. This is especially true when two or more predicates are presented in a coordinated structure. In this case, the arguments of other predicates will not be covered in the PA structure of the predicate.

The second problem is that the SRL labels are only on the constituents of predicate and arguments. There is no analysis conducted inside the augments. That is different from syntactic parsing or dependency parsing, which both provide a complete tree from the sentence to every individual word. As we can see in Figure 1, words such as "Second" and "and" are not covered. Inside the NPs such as "a flood prevention system", SRL will not provide more information. Therefore it is hard to build a self-contained formalization based only on SRL labels. Most work on SRL labels is built upon or assisted by other formalisms. For instance, Liu and Gildea (2010) integrated SRL label into a tree-to-string translation system. Wu and Fung (2009) used SRL labels for reordering the n-best output of phrase-based translation systems. Similarly, in our work we also adopt the methodology of using SRL information to assist existing formalism. The difference of our method from Wu and Fung is that we embed the SRL information directly into the decode, instead of doing two-pass decoding. Also, our method is different from Liu and Gildea (2010) that we utilize target side SRL information instead of the source side.

As we will see in section 3, we define a mapping function from the SRL structures that a phrase covers to a non-terminal tag before extracting the SCFG rules. The tags will restrict the derivation of the target side parse tree to accept only SRL structures we have seen in the training corpus. The mapping from SRL structures to non-terminal tags can be defined according to the SRL annotation set.

In this paper we adopt the PropBank (Palmer et al., 2005) annotation set of semantic labels, because the annotation set is relatively simple and easy to parse. The small set of argument tags also makes the number of LHS non-terminal tags small, which alleviates the problem of data scarcity. However the methodology of this paper is not limited to PropBank tags. By defining appropriate mapping, it is also possible to use other annotation sets, such as FrameNet (Baker et al., 2002).

3 SRL-aware SCFG Rules

The SRL-aware SCFG rules are SCFG rules. They contain at least one non-terminal label with information about the PA structure that is covered by the non-terminal. The labels are called SRL-aware labels, and the non-terminal itself is called SRL-aware non-terminal. The non-terminal can be on the left hand side or right hand side or the rule, and we do not require all the non-terminals in the rules be SRL-aware, thus, the general tag X can also be used. In this paper, we assign SRL-aware labels based on the SRL structure they cover. The label contains the following components:

1. The predicate frame; that is the predicate whose predicate argument structure belongs to the SRL-aware non-terminal.
2. The set of complete arguments the SRL-aware non-terminal covers.

In practice, the predicates are stemmed. For example, if we have a target side phrase: *She beats eggs today*, where *She* will be labeled as *ARG0* of the predicate *beat*, and *eggs* will be labeled as *ARG1*, *today* will be labeled as *ARG-TMP*, respectively. The SRL-aware label that covers this phrase is:

$$\#beat/0\_1\_TMP$$

There are two notes for the definition. Firstly, the order of arguments is not important in the label. $\#beat/0\_1\_TMP$ is treated identically to $\#beat/0\_TMP\_1$. Secondly, as we always require the predicate to be represented, an SRL-aware non-terminal should always cover the predicate. This property will be re-emphasized when we discuss the rule extraction algorithm in Section 3. Figure 2 shows some examples of the SRL-aware SCFG rules.

When the RHS non-terminal is an SRL-aware non-terminal, we define the rule as a conversion rule. A conversion rule is only generated when the right

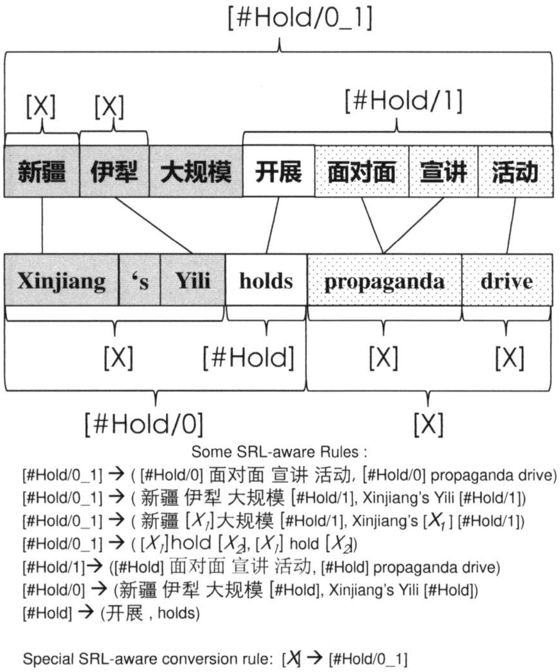

Figure 2: Example SRL structure with word alignment

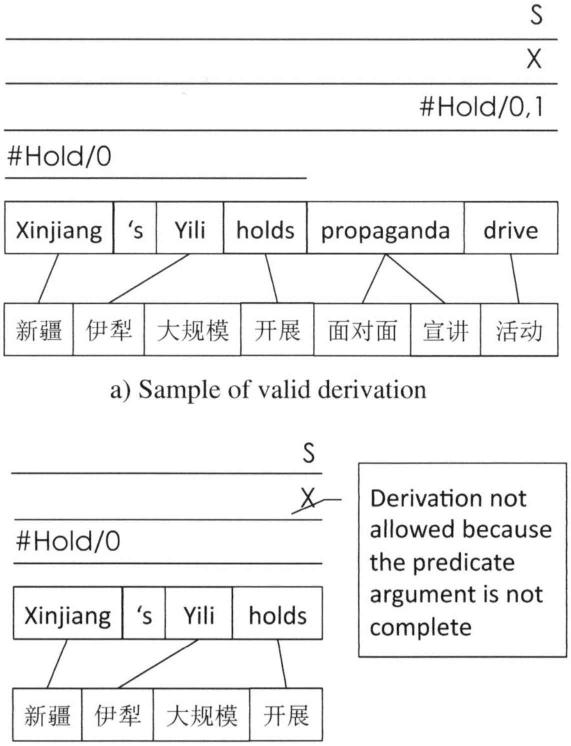

a) Sample of valid derivation

b) Sample of invalid derivation

Figure 3: Example of a derivations of sentence

hand side is a complete SRL structure. For example, $\#hold/0$ is not a complete SRL structure in Figure 2, because it lacks of a required argument, while $\#hold/0\_1$ is a complete SRL structure. In this case, the conversion rule $X \rightarrow \#hold/0\_1$ will be extracted from the example shown in Figure 2, but not the other. Together with the *glue rules* that commonly used in Hiero decoder, i.e. $S \rightarrow (S\ X_1, S\ X_1)$ and $S \rightarrow (X_1, X_1)$, the conversion rules ensures that whenever SRL-aware SCFG rules are used in parsing, the output parse tree contains only complete SRL structures. This is because only complete SRL structures that we have observed in the training data can be converted back to the general tag X.

After we have extracted the SRL-aware SCFG rules, derivation can be done on the input of source sentence. For example, the sentence 新疆 大规模 开展 面对面 宣讲 活动 [1] can generate the parse tree and translation in Figure 3a) using the rules shown in Figure 2. Also, we can see in Figure 3b) that incomplete SRL structures cannot be generated due to the absence of a proper conversion rule.

We can see from the example in Figure 3a), that the SRL-aware SCFG rules fit perfectly in the SCFG framework. Therefore no modification need to be made on a decoder, such as MosesChart decoder,for instance (Hoang and Koehn, 2008). The main problem is how to extract the SRL-aware SCFG rules from the corpus and estimate the feature values so that it works together with the conventional Hiero rules. In the next two sections we will present the rule extraction algorithm and two alternative methods for comparison.

4 Rule Extraction Algorithm

The Hiero rule extraction algorithm uses the following steps:

1. Extract the initial phrases with the commonly used alignment template heuristics. To reduce the number of phrases extracted, an additional restriction is applied that the boundary words must be aligned on both sides. Also, the maximum length of initial phrases is fixed, and usually set to 10.

[1] The translation is *Xinjiang's Yili holds propaganda drive* and the Pinyin transliteration is *Xinjiang daguimo kaizhan mianduimian xuanjiang huodong*

2. If an initial phrase pair contains another phrase pair, then we can replace the embedded phrase pairs with non-terminal X. Restrictions also apply in this stage. Firstly the source side phrase can only contain two or less non-terminals. Secondly, two source side non-terminals must not be next to each other. And finally, after the substitution, at least one remaining terminal in the source side should have alignment links to the target side terminals.

It is easy to see this scheme is not able to handle the extraction of SRL-aware SCFG rules. The length of initial phrases is limited and it may not be able to cover a complete predicate-argument structure. In the meantime, the restrictions on unaligned words on the boundaries will cause a large number of SRL-aware SCFG rules to be excluded. Therefore, a modified algorithm is proposed to handle extraction of SRL-aware SCFG rules.

One sentence may have multiple verbs and, therefore, multiple PA structures. Different PA structures may be nested within each other. However we do not want to complicate the representation by attempting to build a tree structure from multiple structures. Instead, we treat them independently.

For each word-aligned sentence pair, if there is no PA structure given, we run the general Hiero extraction algorithm. Otherwise, for each PA structure, we apply the algorithm for SRL-aware rule extraction, which takes two steps, extracting the initial SRL-aware phrases and extracting the SRL-aware SCFG rules.

4.1 Extraction of Initial SRL-aware Phrases

First, a different heuristics is used to extract initial SRL-aware phrases. These phrases have the following properties:

1. On the target side, the phrase covers at least one complete constituent in the PA structure, which must include the predicate. The phrase pair can include words that are not part of any argument; however it cannot include partial arguments. In Figure 4b), the phrase pair is not included in the initial SRL-aware phrases because it includes a word A from argument $ARG2$. However, in Figure 4a), inclusion of the first target word A, which is not part of any argument, is allowed.

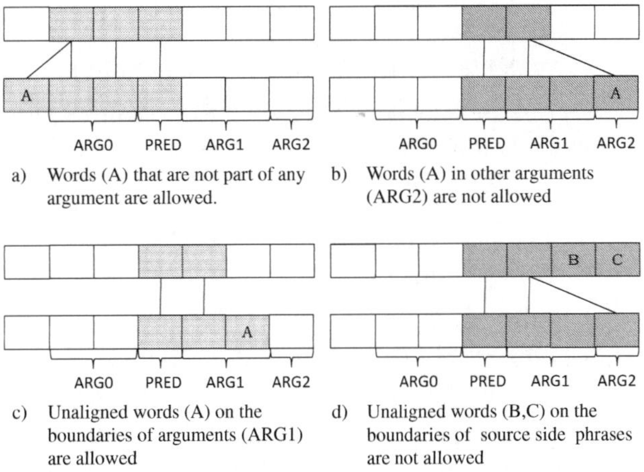

Figure 4: Demonstration of restrictions of whether or not a rule is included in initial SRL-aware phrases. The sub-figures a) and c) show two cases that unaligned words or words not in any arguments are allowed in extracted phrases and sub-figures b) and d) show two cases that the phrases are excluded from the phrase table. The shaded blocks indicate the range of candidate phrases.

2. At least one word pair between the source and the target side phrase is aligned, and no words in the source or the target side phrase align to words outside the phrase pair. These are the standard heuristics used in the hierarchical phrase extraction algorithm.

3. For the target side, unaligned words on the boundaries are allowed only if the word is found inside one of the arguments. On the source side, however, unaligned words are not allowed on the boundaries. The idea is demonstrated in Figure 4c) and 4d). In Figure 4c), the unaligned boundary word A is included in the target side phrase because it is part of an argument. In Figure 4d), unaligned words B and C are not allowed to be included in the proposed phrase.

Given a PA structure of the sentence, we applied following algorithm:

1. Extract all possible target side phrases that contain **the predicate** and **any number of arguments**.

2. For each of the extracted target side phrases T, find the minimum span of the source side phrase S that contains all the words aligned to

the target side phrase. This can be done by simply calculating the minimum and maximum index of the source side words aligned to the target side phrase.

3. Find the minimum span of target side phrase T_1 that are aligned to the source side phrase S. If the minimum span is already covered by the target side phrase extracted in the previous step, i.e. $T_1 = T$, we add the phrase pair (S, T) to the pool of initial phrases. If the newly obtained target side phrase is larger than the original one, then we need to decide whether the new span contains a word in another arguments. If so, then we do not add the phrase pair, return to step 2 and continue with the next target side phrase. Otherwise, we update $T := T_1$ and go back to step 2.

The readers may notice that although in several steps we need to determine whether there are links outside the phrase pairs, the information is easy to compute. We only need to keep track of the maximum and minimum indices of words that each source and target word aligns to. With the indices pre-computed, in the worst case scenario we only need to calculate M times for the maximum and minimum indices, where M is the total number of words in the source and the target side, before we can determine the validity of the largest target side SRL-aware phrase. The worst case complexity of the algorithm is $O(N * M)$, where N is the number of arguments in the segmentation. This is only a rough upper bound for the time complexity; the average case will be much better.

4.2 Extracting SRL-aware SCFG Rules

Before we generate rules from the extracted initial phrases, we first need to assign non-terminal labels to the initial SRL-aware phrases. We define a map from the SRL structures to non-terminal tags of SCFG rules. An SRL-aware non-terminal label is a combination of the predicate label and the argument labels. The predicate label is the stemmed predicate. We can eliminate the morphology to alleviate the problem of the data scarcity. In addition, the argument labels represent all the arguments that the current SRL-aware rule covers. The mapping is trivial given the initial SRL-aware phrase extraction algorithm, and it can be determined directly in the first step.

The initial phrases already are SCFG rules. To extract rules with non-terminals we will replace the sub-phrases with non-terminals if the sub-phrase is embedded in another phrase pair. The algorithm is similar to that described by Chiang (2005). However we apply new restrictions because we now have two sets of different initial phrases. If the outer rule is SRL-aware, we allow both sets of the initial phrases to be candidates of embedded phrases. However if the outer rule is X, we do not allow a replacement of SRL-aware SCFG rules within it. Therefore we will have rules where LHS non-terminals are SRL-aware, and some RHS non-terminals are X, but not vice versa. The reason for the restriction is to prevent the conversion of incomplete predicate-argument structures back to X. As we mentioned before, one of the design goals of our algorithm is to ensure that once SRL-aware SCFG rules are used in the derivation, a complete PA structure must be generated before it can be converted back. The only way of converting SRL-aware tags back to X is through special conversion rules, whose LHS is the X and the RHS is a complete SRL-aware tag. Extracting such conversion rules is trivial given the SRL labels.

The extracted rules are subject to filtering by the same restrictions as conventional Hiero rules. The filtering criteria include:

1. Two non-terminals on the source side should not be adjacent.

2. We allow up to two non-terminals on the RHS.

3. The source side rule contains no more than five tokens including terminals and non-terminals.

5 Decoder Integration

The extracted SCFG rules, both SRL-aware and X, will go through the feature estimation process to produce the rule table. Integrated with the conversion rules, most chart-based decoders such as MosesChart (Hoang and Koehn, 2008), cdec (Dyer et al, 2010) and Joshua (Li et al, 2009) can use these rules in decoding. We applied MosesChart for tuning and decoding.

While the SRL-aware SCFG rules are used to constrain the search space and derivation, we do not in-

		mt02	mt03	mt04	mt05	mt08	bl-nw	bl-wb	dv-nw	dv-wb	avg
	BLEU	29.56	27.02	30.28	26.80	21.16	21.96	20.10	24.26	20.13	n/a
Baseline	TER	68.87	70.19	67.18	70.60	69.93	64.44	64.74	63.21	66.61	n/a
	(T-B)/2	19.66	21.59	18.45	21.90	24.39	21.24	22.32	19.48	23.24	n/a
	BLEU	+0.33	−0.50	+0.20	+0.47	−0.16	+1.24	+1.13	+0.39	+1.35	+0.49
SRL	TER	−1.58	−1.77	−1.93	−1.68	−0.71	−0.29	−0.22	−1.36	−1.34	−1.21
	(T-B)/2	−0.95	−0.63	−1.07	−1.08	−0.28	−0.76	−0.68	−0.88	−1.35	−0.85

Table 1: Experiment results on Chinese-English translation tasks, bl-nw and bl-wb are newswire and weblog parts for DEV07-blind, dv-nw and dv-wb are newswire and weblog parts for DEV07-dev. We present the BLEU scores, TER scores and (TER-BLEU)/2.

troduce new features into the system. The features we used in the decoder are commonly used, including source and target rule translation probabilities, the lexical translation probabilities, and the language model probability. The feature values are calculated by MLE estimation.

Besides the expanded rule table and conversion rules, the decoder does not need to be modified. We incorporate MERT to tune the feature weights. The minimum modifications for the decoder make the proposed method an easy replacement for Hiero rule extractors.

6 Experiments and discussion

We performed experiments on Chinese to English translation tasks. The data set we used in the experiments is a subset of the FBIS corpus. We filter the corpus with maximum sentence length be 30. The corpus has 2.5 million words in Chinese side and 3.1 million on English side.

We adopted the ASSERT semantic role labeler (Pradhan et al., 2004) to label the English side sentences. The parallel sentences are aligned using MGIZA++ (Gao and Vogel, 2008) and then the proposed rule extraction algorithm was used in extracting the SRL-aware SCFG rules. We used the MosesChart decoder (Hoang and Koehn, 2008) and the Moses toolkit (Koehn et al, 2007) for tuning and decoding. The language model is a trigram language model trained on English GIGAWord corpus (V1-V3) using the SRILM toolkit.

We used the NIST MT06 test set for tuning, and experimented with an additional 9 test sets, including MT02, 03, 04, 05, 08, and GALE test sets DEV07-dev and DEV07-blind. DEV07-dev and DEV07-blind are further divided into newswire and weblog parts.

We experimented with the proposed method and the alternative methods presented in section 4, and the results of nine test sets are listed in Table 1. As we can observe from the results, the largest improvement we discovered from our proposed method is more than 1 BLEU point, and a significant drop is only observed on one test set, MT03, where we lose 0.5 BLEU points. Averaged across all the test sets, the improvement is 0.49 BLEU points on the small training set. When TER is also taken into account, all of the nine test sets showed consistent improvement. The (TER-BLEU)/2 score, which we used as the primary evaluation metric, improved by 0.85 across nine test sets.

As we expected, the coverage of SRL-aware SCFG rules is not as good as the Hiero rules. We analyzed the top-best derivation of the results. Only 1836 out of 7235 sentences in the test sets used SRL-aware SCFG rules. However, the BLEU scores on the 1836 sentences improved from 27.98 in the baseline system to 28.80, while the remaining 5399 sentences only improved from 30.13 to 30.22. The observation suggests the potential for further improvement if we can increase the coverage by using more data or by modifying the mapping from tags to the structures to make rules more general.

We display the hypothesis of a sentence in Figure 5 to demonstrate a concrete example of improvements obtained by using the method,. As this figure demonstrate, the SRL-aware SCFG rules enable the system to pick the correct structure and reordering for the verbs *trigger* and *enter*.

Given the results presented in the paper, the question arises as to whether it is prudent to integrate multiple formalisms or labeling systems, such as

Source	乌克兰 因 总统 选举 引发 的 混乱 进入 第三 周
SRLTag	Ukraine because of the chaos **triggered** by the presidential election has **entered** the third week
Baseline	Ukraine today because of the chaos **triggered in** the third week of the presidential election
References	The chaos **caused** by Ukraine's presidential election has **entered** its third week. The turmoil in Ukraine **triggered** by the presidential election **entered** the third week The chaos **sparked** off by the presidential election in Ukraine has **entered** its third week. Ukraine **heads** into a third week of turmoil **caused** by the presidential election

Figure 5: An example of improvement caused by better attachment of verbs and its arguments

syntactic parsing or SRL labeling. Hierarchical phrase-based machine translation is often criticized for not explicitly incorporating linguistic knowledge. On the other hand, fully syntactic-based machine translation suffers from low coverage of rules. The methodology in this paper, in contrast, introduces linguistic information to assist a formalism that does not incorporate linguistic information. The merits of doing so are obvious. While most parts of the system are not changed, a portion of the system is considerably improved. Also, the system encodes the information in the non-terminal tags, which is widely used in other methods such as SAMT. However, it is not necessary an optimal solution. Huang et al in a very recent work (Huang et al., 2010) proposed using vector space to represent similarity between the syntactic structures. This is also an interesting possible direction to explore in the near future.

7 Conclusion and future work

In this paper we presented a method of utilizing the target side predicate-argument structure to assist Hierarchical Phrase-based Machine Translation. With a hybrid rule extraction algorithm, we can extract SRL-aware SCFG rules together with conventional Hiero rules. Additional conversion rules ensure the generated predicate-argument structures are complete when SRL-aware SCFG rules are used in the decoding procedure. Experimental results showed improvement on BLEU and TER metrics with 9 test sets, and even larger improvements are observed when only considering the sentences in which SRL-aware SCFG rules are used for the top-best derivation.

We are currently following three directions for the future work. The first focuses on improving the quality of the rules and feature estimation. We are investigating different labeling systems other than the relatively simple PropBank labeling system, and plan to experiment with different methods of mapping structure to the SRL-aware labels.

Recent advances in vector space representations on the syntactic structures, which may be able to work with, or replace the SRL-aware non-terminal labels, inspire the second direction.

Finally, the third direction is to incorporate source side semantic role labeling information into the framework. Currently our method can only use target side SRL information, but the source side information is also valuable. Exploring how to build models to represent SRL information from both sides into one complete framework is a promising research direction to follow.

References

Collin F. Baker, Charles J. Fillmore, and Beau Cronin. 2002. The structure of the framenet database. *International Journal of Lexicography*, 16(3):281–296.

David Chiang. 2005. A hierachical phrase-based model for statistical machine translation. In *Proceedings of the 43rd Annual Meeting of Association for Computational Linguistics*, pages 263–270.

David Chiang. 2007. Hierarchical phrase-based translation. *Computational Linguistics*, 33(2):201–228.

David Chiang. 2010. Learning to translate with source and target syntax. In *Proceedings of the 48th Annual Meeting of the Association for Computational Linguistics*, pages 1443–1452.

Chris Dyer et al. 2010. cdec: A decoder, alignment, and learning framework for finite-state and context-free translation models. In *Proceedings of the ACL 2010 System Demonstrations*, ACLDemos '10, pages 7–12.

Michel Galley et al. 2006. Scalable inference and training of context-rich syntactic translation models. In *Proceedings of the 21st International Conference on Computational Linguistics and the 44th annual meeting of the Association for Computational Linguistics*, pages 961–968.

Qin Gao and Stephan Vogel. 2008. Parallel implementations of word alignment tool. In *Software Engineering, Testing, and Quality Assurance for Natural Language Processing*, pages 49–57, Columbus, Ohio, June. Association for Computational Linguistics.

Hieu Hoang and Philipp Koehn. 2008. Design of the moses decoder for statistical machine translation. In *Software Engineering, Testing, and Quality Assurance for Natural Language Processing*, SETQA-NLP '08, pages 58–65, Morristown, NJ, USA. Association for Computational Linguistics.

Zhongqiang Huang, Martin Cmejrek, and Bowen Zhou. 2010. Soft syntactic constraints for hierarchical phrase-based translation using latent syntactic distributions. In *Proceedings of the 2010 Conference on Empirical Methods in Natural Language Processing*, pages 138–147, Cambridge, MA, October. Association for Computational Linguistics.

Philipp Koehn et al. 2007. Moses: Open source toolkit for statistical machine translation. In *Proceedings of the 45th Annual Meeting of the Association for Computational Linguistics Companion Volume Proceedings of the Demo and Poster Sessions*, pages 177–180, Prague, Czech Republic, June. Association for Computational Linguistics.

Zhifei Li et al. 2009. Joshua: an open source toolkit for parsing-based machine translation. In *Proceedings of the Fourth Workshop on Statistical Machine Translation*, StatMT '09, pages 135–139.

Ding Liu and Daniel Gildea. 2008. Improved tree-to-string transducers for machine translation. In *ACL Workshop on Statistical Machine Translation (ACL08-SMT)*, pages 62–69.

Ding Liu and Daniel Gildea. 2010. Semantic role features for machine translation. In *Proceedings of the 23rd International Conference on Computational Linguistics (COLING-10)*.

Yang Liu and Liang Huang. 2010. Tree-based and forest-based translation. In *Tutorial Abstracts of ACL 2010*, page 2, Uppsala, Sweden, July. Association for Computational Linguistics.

Yang Liu, Qun Liu, and Shouxun Lin. 2006. Tree-to-string alignment template for statistical machine translation. In *Proceedings of the 21st International Conference on Computational Linguistics and the 44th annual meeting of the Association for Computational Linguistics*, pages 609–616.

Martha Palmer, Daniel Gildea, and Paul Kingsbury. 2005. The proposition bank: An annotated corpus of semantic roles. *Computational Linguistics*, 31(1):71–106, Mar.

Sameer S. Pradhan, Wayne Ward, Kadri Hacioglu, James H. Martin, and Daniel Jurafsky. 2004. Shallow semantic parsing using support vector machines. In *Proceedings of the Human Language Technology Conference/North American chapter of the Association for Computational Linguistics annual meeting (HLT/NAACL-2004)*.

Libin Shen, Jinxi Xu, and Ralph Weischedel. 2008. A new string-to-dependency machine translation algorithm with a target dependency language model. In *Proceedings of ACL-08: HLT*, pages 577–585, Columbus, Ohio, June. Association for Computational Linguistics.

Dekai Wu and Pascale Fung. 2009. Semantic roles for smt: a hybrid two-pass model. In *Proceedings of The 2009 Annual Conference of the North American Chapter of the Association for Computational Linguistics, Companion Volume: Short Papers*, pages 13–16.

Min Zhang, Hongfei Jiang, Aiti Aw, Haizhou Li, Chew Lim Tang, and Sheng Li. 2008. A tree sequence alignment-based tree-to-tree translation model. In *Proceedings of the 46th Annual Meeting of the Association for Computational Linguistics (ACL-08 HLT)*, pages 559–567.

Andreas Zollmann and Ashish Venugopal. 2006. Syntax augmented machine translation via chart parsing. In *Proceedings of the Workshop on Statistical Machine Translation*, pages 138–141.

Combining statistical and semantic approaches to the translation of ontologies and taxonomies

John McCrae
AG Semantic Computing
Universität Bielefeld
Bielefeld, Germany
jmccrae@cit-ec.uni-bielefeld.de

Mauricio Espinoza
Universidad de Cuenca
Cuenca, Ecuador
mauricio.espinoza@ucuenca.edu.ec

Elena Montiel-Ponsoda, Guadalupe Aguado-de-Cea
Ontology Engineering Group
Universidad Politécnica de Madrid
Madrid, Spain
{emontiel, lupe}@fi.upm.es

Philipp Cimiano
AG Semantic Computing
Universität Bielefeld
Bielefeld, Germany
cimiano@cit-ec.uni-bielefeld.de

Abstract

Ontologies and taxonomies are widely used to organize concepts providing the basis for activities such as indexing, and as background knowledge for NLP tasks. As such, translation of these resources would prove useful to adapt these systems to new languages. However, we show that the nature of these resources is significantly different from the "free-text" paradigm used to train most statistical machine translation systems. In particular, we see significant differences in the linguistic nature of these resources and such resources have rich additional semantics. We demonstrate that as a result of these linguistic differences, standard SMT methods, in particular evaluation metrics, can produce poor performance. We then look to the task of leveraging these semantics for translation, which we approach in three ways: by adapting the translation system to the domain of the resource; by examining if semantics can help to predict the syntactic structure used in translation; and by evaluating if we can use existing translated taxonomies to disambiguate translations. We present some early results from these experiments, which shed light on the degree of success we may have with each approach.

1 Introduction

Taxonomies and ontologies are data structures that organise conceptual information by establishing relations among concepts, hierarchical and partitive relations being the most important ones. Nowadays, ontologies have a wide range of uses in many domains, for example, finance (International Accounting Standards Board, 2007), bio-medicine (Collier et al., 2008) (Ashburner et al., 2000) and libraries (Mischo, 1982). These resources normally attach labels in natural language to the concepts and relations that define their structure, and these labels can be used for a number of purposes, such as providing user interface localization (McCrae et al., 2010), multilingual data access (Declerck et al., 2010), information extraction (Müller et al., 2004) and natural language generation (Bontcheva, 2005). It seems natural that for applications that use such ontologies and taxonomies, translation of the natural language descriptions associated with them is required in order to adapt these methods to new languages. Currently, there has been some work on this in the context of ontology localisation, such as Espinoza et al. (2008) and (2009), Cimiano et al. (2010), Fu et al. (2010) and Navigli and Penzetto (2010). However, this work has focused on the case in which exact or partial translations are found in other similar resources such as bilingual lexica. Instead, in this paper we look at how we may gain an adequate translation using statistical machine translation approaches that also utilise the semantic information beyond the label or term describing the concept, that is relations among the concepts in the ontology, as well as the attributes or properties that describe concepts, as will be explained in more detail in section 2.

Current work in machine translation has shown that word sense disambiguation can play an important role by using the surrounding words as context to disambiguate terms (Carpuat and Wu, 2007) (Apidianaki, 2009). Such techniques have

Proceedings of SSST-5, Fifth Workshop on Syntax, Semantics and Structure in Statistical Translation, pages 116–125,
ACL HLT 2011, Portland, Oregon, USA, June 2011.

been extrapolated to the translation of taxonomies and ontologies, in which the "context" of a taxonomy or ontology label corresponds to the *ontology structure* that surrounds the label in question. This structure, which is made up of the lexical information provided by labels and the semantic information provided by the ontology structure, defines the sense of the concept and can be exploited in the disambiguation process (Espinoza et al., 2008).

2 Definition of Taxonomy and Ontology Translation

2.1 Formal Definition

We define a taxonomy as a set of concepts, C, with equivalence (synonymy) links, S, subsumption (hypernymy) links, H, and a labelling function l that maps each concept to a single label from a language Σ^*. Formally we define a taxonomy, T, as a set of tuples (C, S, H, l) such that $S \subseteq \mathcal{P}(C \times C)$ and $H \subseteq \mathcal{P}(C \times C)$ and l is a function in $C \rightarrow \Sigma^*$. We also require that S is a transitive, symmetric and reflexive relation, and H is transitive. While we note here that this abstraction does not come close to capturing the full expressive power of many ontologies (or even taxonomies), it is sufficient for this paper to focus on the use of only equivalence and subsumption relationships for translation.

2.2 Analysis of ontology labels

Another important issue to note here is that the kind of language used within ontologies and taxonomies is significantly different from that found within free text. In particular, we observe that the terms used to designate concepts are frequently just noun phrases and are significantly shorter than a usual sentence. In the case of the relations between concepts (dubbed *object properties*) and attributes of concepts (*data type properties*), these are occasionally labelled by means of verbal phrases. We demonstrate this by looking at three widely used ontologies/taxonomies.

1. **Friend of a friend**: The Friend of a Friend (FOAF) ontology is used to describe social networks on the Semantic Web (Brickley and Miller, 2010). It is a small taxonomy with very short labels. Labels for concepts are compound words made up of up to three words.

2. **Gene Ontology**: The Gene Ontology (Ashburner et al., 2000) is a very large database of terminology related to genetics. We note that while some of the terms are technical and do not require translation, e.g., *ESCRT-I*, the majority do, e.g., *cytokinesis by cell plate formation*.

3. **IFRS 2009**: The IFRS taxonomy (International Accounting Standards Board, 2007) is used for providing electronic financial reports for auditing. The terms contained within this taxonomy are frequently long and are entirely noun phrases.

We applied tokenization and manual phrase analysis to the labels in these resources and the results are summarized in table 1. As can be observed, the variety of types of labels we may come across when linguistically analysing and translating ontology and taxonomy labels is quite large. We can identify the two following properties that may influence the translation process of taxonomy and ontology labels. Firstly, the length of terms ranges from single words to highly complex compound phrases, but is still generally shorter than a sentence. Secondly, terms are frequently about highly specialized domains of knowledge.

For properties in the ontology we also identify terms which consist of:

- Noun phrases identifying concepts.
- Verbal phrases that are only made up of the verb with an optional preposition.
- Complex verbal phrases that include the predicate.
- Noun phrases that indicate possession of a particular characteristic (e.g., *interest* meaning *X has an interest in Y*).

3 Creation of a corpus for taxonomy and ontology translation

For the purpose of training systems to work on the translation of ontologies and taxonomies, it is necessary to create a corpus that has similar linguistic structure to that found in ontologies and taxonomies. We used the titles of Wikipedia[1] for the following

[1] http://www.wikipedia.org

	Size	Mean tokens per label	Noun Phrases	Verb Phrases
FOAF	79	1.57	94.9%	8.9%
Gene Ontology	33795	4.45	100.0%	0.0%
IFRS 2009	2757	8.39	100.0%	0.0%

Table 1: Lexical Analysis of labels

	Link	Direct	Fragment	Broken
German	487372	484314	1735	1323
Spanish	347953	346941	330	682

Table 2: Number of translation for pages in Wikipedia

reasons:

- Links to articles in different languages can be viewed as translations of the page titles.
- The titles of articles have similar properties to the ontologies labels mentioned above with an average of 2.46 tokens.
- There are a very large number of labels. In fact we found that there were 5,941,890[2] articles of which 3,515,640 were content pages (i.e., not special pages such as category pages)

We included non-content pages (in particular, category pages) in the corpus as they were generally useful for translation, especially the titles of category pages. In table 2 we see the number of translations, which we further grouped according to whether they actually corresponded to pages in the other languages, as it is also possible that the translations links pointed to subsections of an article or to missing pages.

Wikipedia also includes redirect links that allow for alternative titles to be mapped to a given concept. These can be useful as they contain synonyms, but also introduce a lot more noise into the corpus as they also include misspelled and foreign terms. To evaluate the effectiveness of including these data for creating a machine translation corpus, we took a random sample of 100 pages which at least one page redirects to (there are 1,244,647 of these pages in total). We found that these pages had a total of 242 extra titles from the redirect page of which 204 (84.3%) where true synonyms, 19 (7.9%) were misspellings, 8 (3.3%) were foreign names for concepts (e.g., the French name for "Zeebrugge"), and 11 (4.5%) were unrelated. As such, we conclude that these extra titles were useful for constructing the corpus, increasing the size of the corpus by approximately 50% across all languages. There are several advantages to deriving a corpus from Wikipedia, for example it is possible to provide some hierarchical links by the use of the category that a page belongs to, such as has been performed by the DBpedia project (Auer et al., 2007).

[2]All statistics are based on the dump on 17th March 2011

4 Evaluation metrics for taxonomy and ontology translation

Given the linguistic differences in taxonomy and ontology labels, it seems necessary to investigate the effectiveness of various metrics for the evaluation of translation quality. There are a number of metrics that are widely used for evaluating translation. Here we will focus on some of the most widely used, namely BLEU (Papineni et al., 2002), NIST (Doddington, 2002), METEOR (Banerjee and Lavie, 2005) and WER (McCowan et al., 2004). However, it is not clear which of these methods correlate best with human evaluation, particularly for the ontologies with short labels. To evaluate this we collected a mixture of ontologies with short labels on the topics of human diseases, agriculture, geometry and project management, producing 437 labels. These were translated with web translation services from English to Spanish, in particular Google Translate[3], Yahoo! BabelFish[4] and SDL FreeTranslation[5]. Having obtained translations for each label in the ontology we calculated the evaluation scores using the four metrics mentioned above. We found that the source ontologies had an average

[3]http://translate.google.com
[4]http://babelfish.yahoo.com
[5]http://www.freetranslation.com

	BLEU	NIST	METEOR	WER
Evaluator 1, Fluency	0.108	0.036	0.134	0.122
Evaluator 1, Adequacy	0.209	0.214	0.303	0.169
Evaluator 2, Fluency	0.183	0.062	0.266	0.164
Evaluator 2, Adequacy	0.177	0.111	0.251	0.194
Evaluator 3, Fluency	0.151	0.067	0.210	0.204
Evaluator 3, Adequacy	0.143	0.129	0.221	0.120

Table 3: Correlation between manual evaluation results and automatic evaluation scores

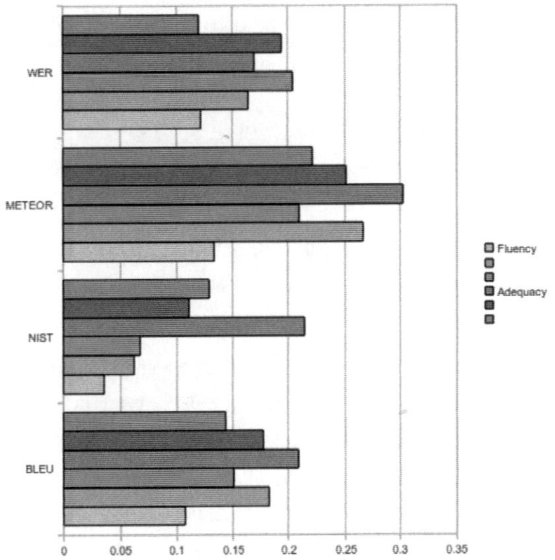

Figure 1: Correlation between manual evaluation results and automatic evaluation scores

label length of 2.45 tokens and the translations generated had an average length of 2.16 tokens. We then created a data set by mixing the translations from the web translation services with a number of translations from the source ontologies, to act as a control. We then gave these translations to 3 evaluators, who scored them for adequacy and fluency as described in Koehn (2010). Finally, we calculated the Pearson correlation coefficient between the automatic scores and the manual scores obtained. These are presented in table 3 and figure 1.

As we can see from these results, one metric, namely METEOR, seems to perform best in evaluating the quality of the translations. In fact this is not surprising as there is a clear mathematical deficiency that both NIST and BLEU have for evaluating translations for very short labels like the ones we have here. To illustrate this, we recall the formulation of BLEU as given in (Papineni et al., 2002):

$$\text{BLEU} = BP \cdot \exp\left(\sum_{n=1}^{N} w_n \log p_n\right)$$

Where BP is a brevity penalty, w_n a weight value and p_n represents the n-gram precision, indicating how many times a particular n-gram in the source text is found among the target translations. We note, however, that for very short labels it is highly likely that p_n will be zero. This creates a significant issue, as from the equation above, if any of the values of p_n are zero, the overall score, BLEU, will also be zero.

For the results above we chose $N = 2$, and corrected for single-word labels. However, the scores were still significantly worse, similar problems affect the NIST metric. As such, for the taxonomy and ontology translation task we do not recommend using BLEU or NIST as an evaluation metric. We note that METEOR is a more sophisticated method than WER and, as expected, performs better.

5 Approaches for taxonomy and ontology translation

5.1 Domain adaptation

It is generally the case that many ontologies and taxonomies focus on only a very specific domain, thus it seems likely that adaptation of translation systems by use of an in-domain corpus may improve translation quality. This is particularly valid in the case of ontologies which frequently contain "subject" annotations[6] for not only the whole data structure but often individual elements. To demonstrate this we tried to translate the IFRS 2009 taxonomy using the Moses Decoder (Koehn et al., 2007), which we trained on the EuroParl corpus (Koehn, 2005), translating from Spanish to English. As the IFRS taxonomy is on the topic of finance and accounting, we

[6] For example from the Dublin Core vocabulary: see `http://dublincore.org/`

	Baseline	With domain adaptation
WER*	0.135	0.138
METEOR	0.324	0.335
NIST	1.229	1.278
BLEU	0.090	0.116

Table 4: Results of domain-adapted translation. *Lower WER scores are better

	$P(syn\|s)$	$P(syn\|p)$	$P(syn\|n)$
English	0.147	0.012	0.001
Dutch	0.137	0.011	0.001
German	0.125	0.007	0.001
Spanish	0.126	0.012	0.001

Table 5: Probability of syntactic relationship given a semantic relationship in IFRS labels

chose all terms from our Wikipedia corpus which belonged to categories containing the words: "finance", "financial", "accounting", "accountancy", "bank", "banking", "economy", "economic", "investment", "insurance"and "actuarial" and as such we had a domain corpus of approximately 5000 terms. We then proceeded to recompute the phrase table using the methodology as described in Wu et al, (2008), computing the probabilities as follows for some weighting factor $0 < \lambda < 1$:

$$p(e|f) = \lambda p_1(e|f) + (1 - \lambda)p_d(e|f)$$

Where p_1 is the EuroParl trained probability and p_d the scores on our domain subset. The evaluation for these metrics is given in table 4. As can be seen with the exception of the WER metric, the domain adaption does seem to help in translation, which corroborates the results obtained by other authors.

5.2 Syntactic Analysis

One key question to figure out is: if we have a semantic model can this be used to predict the syntactic structure of the translation to a significant degree? As an example of this we consider the taxonomic term "statement", which is translated by Google Translate[7] to German as "Erklärung", whereas the term "annual statement" is translated as "Jahresabschluss". However, if the taxonomy contains a subsumption (hypernymy) relationship between these terms we can deduce that the translation "Erklärung" is not correct and the translation "Abschluss" should be preferred. We chose to evaluate this idea on the IFRS taxonomy as the labels it contains are much longer and more structured than some of the other resources. Furthermore, in this taxonomy the original English labels have been translated into ten languages, so that it is already a multilingual resource that can be used as gold standard. Regarding the syntax of labels, it is often the case that one term is derived from another by addition of a complementary phrase. For example the following terms all exist in the taxonomy:

1. Minimum finance lease payments receivable
2. Minimum finance lease payments receivable, at present value
3. Minimum finance lease payments receivable, at present value, end of period not later than one year
4. Minimum finance lease payments receivable, at present value, end of period later than one year and not later than five years

A high-quality translation of these terms would ideally preserve this same syntactic structure in the target language.We attempt to answer how useful ontological structure is by trying to deduce if there is a semantic relationship between terms then is it more likely that there is a syntactic relationship. We started by simplifying the idea of syntactic dependency to the following: we say that two terms are syntactically related if one label is a sub-string of another, so that in the example above the first label is syntactically related to the other three and the second is related to the last two. For English, we found that there were 3744 syntactically related terms according to this criteria, corresponding to 0.1% of all label pairs within the taxonomy, for all languages. For ontology structure we used the number of relations indicated in the taxonomy, of which there are 1070 indicating a subsumption relationship and 987 indicating a partitive relationship[8]. This means that

[7]Translations results obtained 8th March 2011

[8]IFRS includes links for calculating certain values, i.e., that "Total Assets" is a sum of values such as "Total Assets in Prop-

$e \to f$	$P(syn_f \mid syn_e, s)$	$P(syn_f \mid syn_e, p)$	$P(syn_f \mid syn_e, n)$
English $\to$ Spanish	0.813 ± 0.059	0.750 ± 0.205	0.835 ± 0.013
English $\to$ German	0.835 ± 0.062	0.417 ± 0.212	0.790 ± 0.013
English $\to$ Dutch	0.875 ± 0.063	0.833 ± 0.226	0.898 ± 0.013
Average	0.841 ± 0.035	0.665 ± 0.101	0.841 ± 0.008

Table 6: Probability of cross-lingual preservation of syntax given semantic relationship in IFRS. Note here s refers to the source language and t to the target language. Error values are 95% of standard deviation.

0.08% of label pairs were semantically related. We then examined if the semantic relation could predict whether there was a syntactic relationship between the terms in a single language. We define N_s as the number of label pairs with a subsumption relationship and similarly define N_p, N_n and N_{syn} for partitive, semantically unrelated and syntactically related pairs. We also define $N_{s \wedge syn}$, $N_{p \wedge syn}$ and $N_{n \wedge syn}$ for label pairs with both subsumption, partitive or no semantic relation and a syntactic relationships. As such we define the following values

$$P(syn|s) = \frac{N_{s \wedge syn}}{N_s}$$

Similarly we define $P(syn|p)$ and $P(syn|n)$ and present these values in table 5 for four languages.

As we can see from these results, it seems that both subsumption and partitive relationships are strongly indicative of syntactic relationships as we might expect. The second question is: is it more likely that we see a syntactic dependency in translation if we have a semantic relationship, i.e., is the syntax more likely to be preserved if these terms are semantically related. We define N_{syn_e} as the value of N_{syn} for a language e, e.g., $N_{syn_{en}}$ is the number of syntactically related English label pairs in the taxonomy. As each label has exactly one translation we can also define $N_{syn_e \wedge syn_f \wedge s}$ as the number of concepts whose labels are syntactically related in both language e and f and are semantically related by a subsumption relationship; similarly we define $N_{syn_e \wedge syn_f \wedge p}$ and $N_{syn_e \wedge syn_f \wedge n}$. Hence we can define

$$P(syn_f|syn_e, s) = \frac{N_{syn_f \wedge syn_e \wedge s}}{N_{syn_e \wedge s}}$$

erty, Plant and Equipment", we view such a relationship as semantically indicative that one term is part of another, i.e., as partitive or meronymic

And similarly define $P(syn_f|syn_e, p)$ and $P(syn_f|syn_e, n)$. We calculated these values on the IFRS taxonomies, the results of which are represented in table 6.

The partitive data was very sparse, due to the fact that only 15 concepts in the source taxonomy had a partitive relationship and were syntactically related, so we cannot draw any strong conclusions from it. For the subsumption relationship we have a clearer result and in fact averaged across all language pairs we found that the likelihood of the syntax being preserved in the translation was nearly exactly the same for semantically related and semantically unrelated concepts. From this result we can conclude that the probability of syntax given either subsumptive or partitive relationship is not very large, at least from the reduced syntactic model we used here. While our model reduces syntax to n-gram overlap, we believe that if there was a stronger correlation using a more sophisticated syntactic model, we would still see some noticable effect here as we did mono-lingually. We also note that we applied this to only one taxonomy and it is possible that the result may be different in a different resource. Furthermore, we note there is a strong relationship between semantics and syntax in a mono-lingual context and as such adaption of a language model to incorporate this bias may improve the translation of ontologies and taxonomies.

5.3 Comparison of ontology structure

Our third intuition in approaching ontology translation is that the comparison of ontology or taxonomy structures containing source and target labels may help in the disambiguation process of translation candidates. A prerequisite in this sense is the availability of equivalent (or similar) ontology structures to be compared.

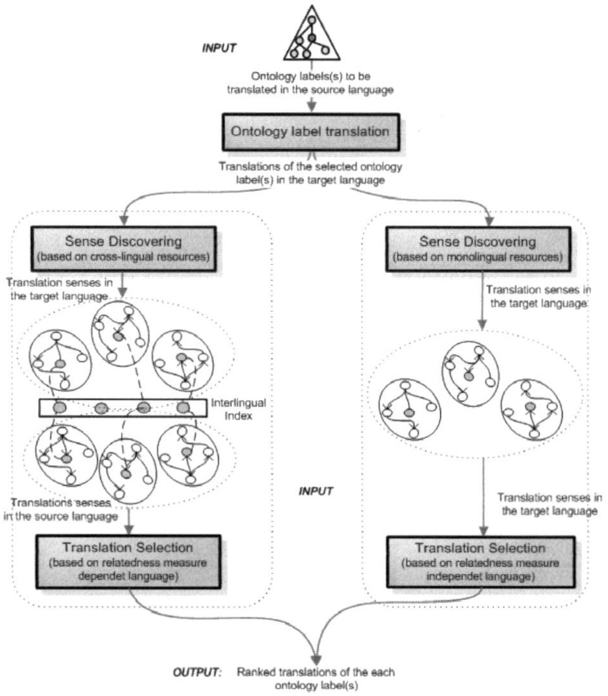

Figure 2: Two approaches to translate ontology labels.

From a technical point of view, we consider the translation task as a word sense disambiguation task. We identify two methods for comparing ontology structures, which are illustrated in Figure 2.

The first method relies on a multilingual resource, i.e., a multilingual ontology or taxonomy. The ontology represented on the left-hand side of the figure consists of several monolingual conceptualizations related to each other by means of an interlingual index, as is the case in the EuroWordNet lexicon (Vossen, 1999). For example, if the original label is *chair* for seat in English, several translations for it are obtained in Spanish such as: *silla* (for seat), *cátedra* (for university position), *presidente* (for person leading a meeting). Each of these correspond to a sense in the English WordNet, and hence each translation selects a hierachical structure with English labels. The next step is to compare the input structure of the original ontology containing *chair* against the three different structures in English representing the several senses of chair and obtain the corresponding label in Spanish.

The second method relies on a monolingual resource, i.e., on monolingual ontologies in the target language, which means that we need to compare structures documented with labels in different languages. As such we obtain a separate translated ontologies for each combination of label translations suggested by the baseline system. Selecting the correct translations is then clearly a hard optimization problem.

For the time being, we have only experimented with the first approach using EuroWordNet. Several solutions have been proposed in the context of ontology matching in a monolingual scenario (see (Shvaiko and Euzenat, 2005) or (Giunchiglia et al., 2006)). The ranking method we use to compare structures relies on an *equivalence probability measure* between two candidate structures, as proposed in (Trillo et al., 2007).

We assume that we have a taxonomy or ontology entity o_1 and we wish to deduce if it is similar to another taxonomy or ontology entity o_2 from a reference taxonomy or ontology (i.e., EuroWordNet) in the same language. We shall make a simplifying assumption that each ontology entity is associated with a unique label, e.g., l_{o_1}. As such we wish to deduce if o_1 represents the same concept as o_2 and hence if l_{o_2} is a translation for l_{o_1}. Our model relies on the Vector Space Model (Raghavan and Wong, 1986) to calculate the similarity between different labels, which essentially involves calculating a vector from the bag of words contained within each labels and then calculating the cosine similarity between these vectors. We shall denotes this as $v(o_1, o_2)$. We then use four main features in the calculation of the similarity

- The VSM-similarity between the labels of entities, o_1, o_2.
- The VSM-similarity between any glosses (descriptions) that may exist in the source or reference taxonomy/ontology.
- The hypernym similarity given to a fixed depth d, given that set of hypernyms of an entity o_i is given as a set

$$h^O(o_i) = \{h|(o_i, h) \in H\}$$

Then we calculate the similarity for $d > 1$ recursively as

$$s_h(o_1, o_2, d) = \frac{\sum_{h_1 \in h^O(o_1), h_2 \in h^O(o_2)} \sigma(h_1, h_2, d)}{|h^O(o_1)||h^O(o_2)|}$$

$$\sigma(h_1, h_2, d) = \alpha v(h_1, h_2) + (1 - \alpha) s_h(h_1, h_2, d - 1)$$

And for $d = 1$ it is given as

$$s_h(o_1, o_2, 1) = \frac{\sum_{h_1 \in h^O(o_1), h_2 \in h^O(o_2)} v(h_1, h_2)}{|h^O(o_1)||h^O(o_2)|}$$

- The hyponym similarity, calculated as the hypernym similarity but using the hyponym set given by

$$H^O(o_i) = \{h | (h, o_i) \in H\}$$

We then incorporate these factors into a vector $\mathbf{x}$ and calculate the similarity of two entities as

$$s(o_1, o_2) = \mathbf{w}^T \mathbf{x}$$

Where $\mathbf{w}$ is a weight vector of non-negative reals and satisfies $||\mathbf{w}|| = 1$, which we set manually.

We then applied this to the FOAF ontology (Brickley and Miller, 2010), which was manually translated to give us a reference translation. After that, we collected a set of candidate translations obtained by using the web translation resources referenced in section 3, along with additional candidates found in our multilingual resource. Finally, we used EuroWordNet (Vossen, 1999) as the reference taxonomy and ranked the translations according to the score given by the metric above. In table 7, we present the results where our system selected the candidate translation with the highest similarity to our source ontology entity. In the case that we could not find a reference translation we split the label into tokens and found the translation by selecting the best token. We compared these results to a baseline method that selected one of the reference translations at random.

These results are in all cases significantly stronger than the baseline results showing that by comparing the structure of ontology elements it is possible to significantly improve the quality of translation. These results are encouraging and we believe that more research is needed in this sense. In particular, we would like to investigate the benefits of performing a cross-lingual ontology alignment in which we measure the semantic similarity of terms in different languages.

	Baseline	Best Translation
WER*	0.725	0.617
METEOR	0.089	0.157
NIST	0.070	0.139
BLEU	0.103	0.187

Table 7: Results of selecting translation by structural comparison. *Lower WER scores are better

6 Conclusion

In this paper we presented the problem of ontology and taxonomy translation as a special case of machine translation that has certain extra characteristics. Our examination of the problem showed that the main two differences are the presence of structured semantics and shorter, hence more ambiguous, labels. We demonstrated that as a result of this linguistic nature, some machine translation metrics do not perform as well as they do in free-text translations. We then presented the results of early investigations into how we may use the special features of taxonomy and ontology translation to improve quality of translation. The first of these was domain adaptation, which in line with other authors is useful for texts in a particular domain. We also investigated the possibility of using the link between syntactic similarity and semantic similarity to help, however although we find that mono-lingually there was a strong correspondence between syntax and semantics, this result did not seem to extend well to a cross-lingual setting. As such we believe there may only be slight benefits of using techniques, however further investigation is needed. Finally, we looked at using word sense disambiguation by comparing the structure of the input ontology to that of an already translated reference ontology. We found this method to be very effective in choosing the best translations. However it is dependent on the existence of a multilingual resource that already has such terms. As such, we view the topic of taxonomy and ontology translation as an interesting sub-problem of machine translation and believe there is still much fruitful work to be done to obtain a system that can correctly leverage the semantics present in these data structures in a way that improves translation quality.

References

Marianna Apidianaki. 2009. Data-driven semantic analysis for multilingual WSD and lexical selection in translation. In *Proceedings of the 12th Conference of the European Chapter of the Association for Computational Linguistics (EACL)*.

Michael Ashburner, Catherine Ball, Judith Blake, David Botstein, Heather Butler, J. Michael Cherry, Allan Davis, et al. 2000. Gene ontology: tool for the unification of biology. The Gene Ontology Consortium. *Nature genetics*, 25(1):25–29.

Sören Auer, Christian Bizer, Georgi Kobilarov, Jens Lehmann, Richard Cyganiak, and Zachary Ives. 2007. Dbpedia: A nucleus for a web of open data. *The Semantic Web*, 4825:722–735.

Satanjeev Banerjee and Alon Lavie. 2005. METEOR: An automatic metric for MT evaluation with improved correlation with human judgments. *Intrinsic and Extrinsic Evaluation Measures for Machine Translation and/or Summarization*, page 65.

Kalina Bontcheva. 2005. Generating tailored textual summaries from ontologies. In *The Semantic Web: Research and Applications*, pages 531–545. Springer.

Dan Brickley and Libby Miller, 2010. *FOAF Vocabulary Specification 0.98.* Accessed 3 December 2010.

Marine Carpuat and Dekai Wu. 2007. Improving Statistical Machine Translation using Word Sense Disambiguation. In *Proceedings of the 2007 Joint Conference on Empirical Methods in Natural Language Processing and Computational Natural Language Learning (EMNLP-CoNLL 2007)*.

Philipp Cimiano, Elena Montiel-Ponsoda, Paul Buitelaar, Mauricio Espinoza, and Asunción Gómez-Pérez. 2010. A note on ontology localization. *Journal of Applied Ontology (JAO)*, 5:127–137.

Nigel Collier, Son Doan, Ai Kawazoe, Reiko Matsuda Goodwin, Mike Conway, Yoshio Tateno, Quoc-Hung Ngo, Dinh Dien, Asanee Kawtrakul, Koichi Takeuchi, Mika Shigematsu, and Kiyosu Taniguchi. 2008. BioCaster: detecting public health rumors with a Web-based text mining system. *Oxford Bioinformatics*, 24(24):2940–2941.

Thierry Declerck, Hans-Ullrich Krieger, Susan Marie Thomas, Paul Buitelaar, Sean O'Riain, Tobias Wunner, Gilles Maguet, John McCrae, Dennis Spohr, and Elena Montiel-Ponsoda. 2010. Ontology-based Multilingual Access to Financial Reports for Sharing Business Knowledge across Europe. In József Roóz and János Ivanyos, editors, *Internal Financial Control Assessment Applying Multilingual Ontology Framework*, pages 67–76. HVG Press Kft.

George Doddington. 2002. Automatic evaluation of machine translation quality using n-gram co-occurrence statistics. In *Proceedings of the second international conference on Human Language Technology Research*, pages 138–145. Morgan Kaufmann Publishers Inc.

Mauricio Espinoza, Asunción Gómez-Pérez, and Eduardo Mena. 2008. Enriching an Ontology with Multilingual Information. In *Proceedings of the 5th Annual of the European Semantic Web Conference (ESWC08)*, pages 333–347.

Mauricio Espinoza, Elena Montiel-Ponsoda, and Asunción Gómez-Pérez. 2009. Ontology Localization. In *Proceedings of the 5th International Conference on Knowledge Capture (KCAP09)*, pages 33–40.

Bo Fu, Rob Brennan, and Declan O'Sullivan. 2010. Cross-Lingual Ontology Mapping and Its Use on the Multilingual Semantic Web. In *Proceedings of the 1st Workshop on the Multilingual Semantic Web, at the 19th International World Wide Web Conference (WWW 2010)*.

Fausto Giunchiglia, Pavel Shvaiko, and Mikalai Yatskevich. 2006. Discovering missing background knowledge in ontology matching. In *Proceeding of the 17th European Conference on Artificial Intelligence*, pages 382–386.

International Accounting Standards Board, 2007. *International Financial Reporting Standards 2007 (including International Accounting Standards (IAS) and Interpretations as at 1 January 2007)*.

Philipp Koehn, Hieu Hoang, Alexandra Birch, Chris Callison-Burch, Marcello Federico, Nicola Bertoldi, Brooke Cowan, Wade Shen, Christine Moran, Richard Zens, et al. 2007. Moses: Open source toolkit for statistical machine translation. In *Proceedings of the 45th Annual Meeting of the ACL on Interactive Poster and Demonstration Sessions*, pages 177–180.

Philipp Koehn. 2005. Europarl: A parallel corpus for statistical machine translation. In *Proceedings of the Tenth Machine Translation Summit*.

Philipp Koehn. 2010. *Statistical Machine Translation*. Cambridge University Press.

Iain McCowan, Darren Moore, John Dines, Daniel Gatica-Perez, Mike Flynn, Pierre Wellner, and Hervé Bourlard. 2004. On the use of information retrieval measures for speech recognition evaluation. Technical report, IDIAP.

John McCrae, Jesús Campana, and Philipp Cimiano. 2010. CLOVA: An Architecture for Cross-Language Semantic Data Querying. In *Proceedings of the First Mutlilingual Semantic Web Workshop*.

William Mischo. 1982. Library of Congress Subject Headings. *Cataloging & Classification Quarterly*, 1(2):105–124.

Hans-Michael Müller, Eimear E Kenny, and Paul W Sternberg. 2004. Textpresso: An ontology-based information retrieval and extraction system for biological literature. *PLoS Biol*, 2(11):e309.

Roberto Navigli and Simone Paolo Ponzetto. 2010. Babelnet: Building a very large multilingual semantic network. In *Proceedings of the 48th Annual Meeting of the Association for Computational Linguistics*, pages 216–225.

Kishore Papineni, Salim Roukos, Todd Ward, and Wei-Jing Zhu. 2002. BLEU: a method for automatic evaluation of machine translation. In *Proceedings of the 40th annual meeting on association for computational linguistics*, pages 311–318. Association for Computational Linguistics.

V.Vijay Raghavan and S.K.M. Wong. 1986. A critical analysis of vector space model for information retrieval. *Journal of the American Society for Information Science*, 37(5):279–287.

Pavel Shvaiko and Jerome Euzenat. 2005. A survey of schema-based matching approaches. *Journal on Data Semantics IV*, pages 146–171.

Fabian Suchanek, Gjergji Kasneci, and Gerhard Weikum. 2007. Yago: a core of semantic knowledge. In *Proceedings of the 16th international conference on World Wide Web*, pages 697–706.

Raquel Trillo, Jorge Gracia, Mauricio Espinoza, and Eduardo Mena. 2007. Discovering the semantics of user keywords. *Journal of Universal Computer Science*, 13(12):1908–1935.

Piek Vossen. 1999. EuroWordNet a multilingual database with lexical semantic networks. *Computational Linguistics*, 25(4).

Hua Wu, Haifeng Wang, and Chengqing Zong. 2008. Domain adaptation for statistical machine translation with domain dictionary and monolingual corpora. In *Proceedings of the 22nd International Conference on Computational Linguistics-Volume 1*, pages 993–1000. Association for Computational Linguistics.

A Semantic Feature for Statistical Machine Translation

Rafael E. Banchs
Institute for Infocomm Research
1 Fusionopolis Way, 21-01, Singapore 138632
rembanchs@i2r.a-star.edu.sg

Marta R. Costa-jussà
Barcelona Media Innovation Centre
Av. Diagonal 177, planta 9, 08018 Barcelona
marta.ruiz@barcelonamedia.org

Abstract

A semantic feature for statistical machine translation, based on Latent Semantic Indexing, is proposed and evaluated. The objective of the proposed feature is to account for the degree of similarity between a given input sentence and each individual sentence in the training dataset. This similarity is computed in a reduced vector-space constructed by means of the Latent Semantic Indexing decomposition. The computed similarity values are used as an additional feature in the log-linear model combination approach to statistical machine translation. In our implementation, the proposed feature is dynamically adjusted for each translation unit in the translation table according to the current input sentence to be translated. This model aims at favoring those translation units that were extracted from training sentences that are semantically related to the current input sentence being translated. Experimental results on a Spanish-to-English translation task on the Bible corpus demonstrate a significant improvement on translation quality with respect to a baseline system.

1 Introduction

In recent years, the statistical approach to machine translation has gained a lot of attention from both the scientific and the commercial perspective. This has basically been a consequence of the increasing availability of bilingual training material as well as the increasing storage and processing capabilities of current computational systems, which have allowed for the construction of machine translation systems with general-public acceptance quality.

For several reasons, the most prominent statistical machine translation paradigm currently used is the phrase-based approach (Koehn *et al.*, 2003), which has been derived from the IBM's word-based approach originally proposed in the early 90's (Brown *et al.*, 1993). This original approach was heavily rooted on the noisy-channel model framework, which, in our view, continues to play an important role in the fundamental conception of current statistical machine translation.

While one of the major assumptions of the noisy-channel model approach is the independence between decoding and source language probabilities, there exists strong evidence on the important role played by source language structure and context within the task of human translation (Padilla & Bajo, 1998). In this sense, the inability of mainstream statistical machine translation to tackle with source-context information in a reliable way has been already recognized as a major drawback of the statistical approach, whereas the use of source-context information has been proven to be effective in the case of example-based machine translation (Carl & Way, 2003). In this regard, attempts for incorporating source-context information into the phrase-based machine translation framework have been already reported (Carpuat & Wu, 2007; Carpuat & Wu, 2008; Haque *et al.*, 2009; España-Bonet *et al.*, 2009; Haque *et al.*, 2010; Costa-jussà & Banchs, 2010). However, as far as we know, no transcendental improvements in performance have been achieved or, at least, reported yet.

In this work, we elaborate deeper on the ideas we have recently presented and discussed in Costa-jussà & Banchs (2010), where we used a similarity metric between the source sentence to be translated and all the sentences in the training set as an addi-

Proceedings of SSST-5, Fifth Workshop on Syntax, Semantics and Structure in Statistical Translation, pages 126–134,
ACL HLT 2011, Portland, Oregon, USA, June 2011.

tional feature in the log-linear combination (Och & Ney, 2002) of models of a phrase-based translation system. Such a feature, which is dynamic in the sense that depends on the input sentence to be translated, is intended to favor those translation units which were extracted from training sentences that are similar to the current input sentence over those translation units which were extracted from different or unrelated sentences. Different from our original methodology, where sentence similarities were assessed over a term-document matrix representation for words and statistical classes of words, here we compute sentence similarities in a low-dimensional vector space constructed by means of Latent Semantic Indexing (Landauer *et al.*, 1998).

The rest of the paper is organized as follows. Section 2 presents an overview of some recent approaches attempting to introduce source-context information into the statistical machine translation framework. Then, section 3 introduces the methodology that is proposed and evaluated in this work, and section 4 focuses on some implementation issues. Section 5 describes the experimental settings and results. Section 6 presents a manual evaluation of a selected sample of system translations and discusses the most relevant findings and observations. Finally, section 7 presents the most relevant conclusions of this work and provides guidelines for further research in this area.

2 Related Work

Several attempts for incorporating source-context information into the statistical machine translation framework have been reported in the literature during the last few years. Without attempting to be comprehensive, we provide a brief overlook of some of the most sounded recent works within this area which are relevant to the phrase-based statistical machine translation approach. For a more comprehensive review of the state-of-the-art, the reader can refer to Haque *et al.* (2010).

On the one hand, there are some semantic approaches. In Carpuat & Wu (2007), for instance, word sense disambiguation techniques are introduced into statistical machine translation; and in Carpuat & Wu (2008), dynamically-built context-dependant phrasal translation lexicons are shown to be more useful for phrase-based machine translation than conventional static phrasal translation lexicons, which ignore all contextual information.

On the other hand, there are approaches which use machine learning techniques. In Haque *et al.* (2009), different syntactic and lexical features are proposed for incorporating information about the neighbouring words; and in España-Bonet *et al.* (2009), local classifiers are trained, using linguistic and context information, to translate a phrase.

Finally, our recent approach, which is inspired on information retrieval techniques for measuring the source-context similarity between the input sentence to be translated and the original training material, was presented in Costa-jussà & Banchs (2010). As our present methodology is closely related to this approach, more details are provided in the following section.

3 Proposed Methodology

As already mentioned, the methodology proposed and evaluated in this work is based on the source-context similarity approach we presented in Costa-jussà & Banchs (2010). Different from that work, here we introduce the use Latent Semantic Indexing (Landauer *et al.*, 1998) to construct a vector-space model representation of the data collection in a reduced-dimensionality space before computing source sentence similarities. First, in subsection 3.1, we review the source-context similarity approach. Then, in subsection 3.2 we present the basics of Latent Semantic Indexing.

3.1 The Source-Context Similarity Approach

The method we proposed in Costa-jussà & Banchs (2010) introduces and extended concept of translation unit or phrase by defining a tuple of three elements: phrase-source-side, phrase-target-side, and source-context:

$$TU = \{PSS \,|||\, PTS \,|||\, SC\}\ . \qquad (1)$$

In the most simplistic approach, the source-context element of a given translation unit can be approximated by the complete source sentence the translation unit was originally extracted from. To illustrate this point, consider the following conventional translation unit {*vino*|||*wine*} which has been extracted from the training sentence *sus ojos están brillantes por el vino y sus dientes blancos por la leche* (his eyes shall be red with wine and his teeth white with milk). According to (1), the extended translation unit *TU* is defined as {*vino*|||*wine*|||*sus ojos están brillantes por el vino y sus dientes blancos por la leche*}. Notice that, from this definition, identical source-target phrase pairs that have been extracted from different training sentences are regarded as different translation units!

According to this definition, the relatedness of contexts between any translation unit and an input sentence to be translated can be computed by means of some distance or similarity metric over a semantic space representation for sentences. This idea is implemented in practice by means of the following dynamic feature function:

$$F(TU,IN) = SIM(TU,IN) = SIM(SC,IN)\ , \tag{2}$$

where *TU* refers to a given translation unit, *IN* refers to the input sentence to be translated, *SC* refers to the source-context component of translation unit *TU* (which in our implementation is the source training sentence which the translation unit was extracted from), and *SIM* is a similarity metric over a given model space.

As implied in (2), the source-context feature to be implemented consists of a similarity measurement between the input sentence to be translated *IN* and the source-context component *SC* of the available translation units.

In Costa-jussà & Banchs (2010), we used the cosine of the angle between vectors in a term-sentence matrix representation (Salton *et al.*, 1975) for computing the source-context similarity feature described in (2). In this work, we use Latent Semantic Indexing (Landauer *et al.*, 1998) for projecting the term-sentence matrix representation into a low-dimensional space and use the cosine of the angle between vectors in the resulting reduced space for computing the source-context similarity feature. With this, we expect to reduce the noise resulting from data sparseness problems in the original full-dimensional representation.

To better illustrate the concepts discussed here, let us consider the Spanish word *vino* and the corresponding English translations for its two senses: *wine* and *came*. Both translations can be automatically inferred from training data; and Table 1 illustrates the resulting probability values derived for both senses of the Spanish word *vino* from the actual training dataset used in this work (a detailed description of the dataset is given in section 5).

Notice from the table, how in general the most probable sense of *vino* in our considered dataset is *wine*. This actually happens because the English word *wine* is always related to the Spanish word *vino*, whereas the English word *came* can refer to many different inflections of the same Spanish word: *vine*, *viniste*, *vino*, *vinimos*, *vinieron*, etc.

phrase	$\phi(f\|e)$	$lex(f\|e)$	$\phi(e\|f)$	$lex(e\|f)$
{*vino*|||*wine*}	0.665198	0.721612	0.273551	0.329431
{*vino*|||*came*}	0.253568	0.131398	0.418478	0.446488

Table 1: Actual probability values for the two possible translations of the Spanish word *vino*.

The idea of the proposed source-context feature is to use the contextual similarity between the input sentence to be translated and the sentences in the training dataset as an additional source of information that should be helpful during decoding.

Consider for instance the following two sentences corresponding to the *wine* sense of *vino*:

SC1: No habéis comido pan ni tomado **vino** ni licor , para que sepáis que yo soy Jehovah vuestro Dios . (Ye have not eaten bread , neither have ye drunk **wine** or strong drink : that ye might know that I am the Lord your God .)

SC2: Cuando fue divulgada esta orden , los hijos de Israel dieron muchas primicias de grano , **vino** nuevo , aceite , miel y de todos los frutos de la tierra . (And as soon as the commandment came abroad , the children of Israel brought in abundance the firstfruits of corn , **wine** , and oil , and honey , and of all the increase of the field .)

and the following two sentences corresponding to the *came* sense of *vino*:

SC3: Al tercer día **vino** Jeroboam con todo el pueblo a Roboam , como el rey había hablado diciendo : Volved a mí al tercer día . (So Jeroboam and all the people **came** to Rehoboam the third day , as the king had appointed , saying , Come to me again the third day .)

SC4: Ella **vino** y ha estado desde la mañana hasta ahora . No ha vuelto a casa ni por un momento . (She **came** , and hath continued even from the morning until now , that she tarried a little in the house .)

As the context for a given word is generally determined by its surrounding words, we should be able to infer the correct sense for the word *vino* in a new Spanish sentence by considering its similarity to sentences SC1, SC2, SC3 and SC4. Now, suppose we want to translate the following two input sentences into English:

IN1: Hasta que yo venga y os lleve a una tierra como la vuestra , tierra de grano y de **vino** , tierra de pan y de viñas , tierra de aceite de olivo y de miel . (Until I come and take you away to a land like your own land , a land of corn and **wine** , a land of bread and vineyards , a land of oil olive and of honey .)

IN2: Cuando amanecía , la mujer **vino** y cayó delante de la puerta de la casa de aquel hombre donde estaba su señor , hasta que fue de día . (Then **came** the woman in the dawning of the day , and fell down at the door of the man 's house where her lord was , till it was light .)

We can select the appropriate sense for *vino* in each case by considering the sentence similarity between each of these two sentences and "training" sentences SC1, SC2, SC3 and SC4. The actual similarity values are presented in Table 2.

	SC1	SC2	SC3	SC4
sense	{*vino*|||*wine*}		{*vino*|||*came*}	
IN1	0.0636	**0.2666**	0.0351	0.0310
IN2	0.0023	0.0513	**0.0888**	0.0774

Table 2: Actual similarity values between input and training sentences containing the word *vino*.

As seen from the table, the source-context similarity feature is actually giving preference to the phrase pair {*vino*|||*wine*} in the case of input sentence IN1 and to {*vino*|||*came*} in the case of IN2. Notice that more than one similarity value is generally available for each phrase pair. In our proposed implementation, the largest similarity value is the one that is retained. More details on how we compute these sentence similarities are given in the following subsection.

3.2 Latent Semantic Indexing

Latent Semantic Indexing (Landauer *et al.*, 1998) can be regarded as the text mining equivalent of Principal Component Analysis (Pearson, 1901). Both methods are based on the singular value decomposition (SVD) of a matrix (Golub & Kahan, 1965), according to which a rectangular matrix **X** of dimensions *MxN* can be factorized as follows:

$$\mathbf{X} = \mathbf{U}\,\mathbf{\Sigma}\,\mathbf{V}^{\mathrm{T}}, \qquad (3)$$

where **U** and **V** are unitary matrices of dimensions *MxM* and *NxN*, respectively, and **Σ** is a diagonal matrix containing the singular values associated to the decomposition.

According to Landauer *et al.* (1998), a low-dimensional representation of a given document vector $\boldsymbol{x}$ can be obtained by means of the SVD decomposition depicted in (3) as follows:

$$\boldsymbol{y}^{\mathrm{T}} = \boldsymbol{x}^{\mathrm{T}}\,\mathbf{U}_{\mathbf{MxL}}, \qquad (4)$$

where $\boldsymbol{y}$ is the *L*-dimensional document vector corresponding to the projection of an *M*-dimensional document vector $\boldsymbol{x}$, and $\mathbf{U}_{\mathbf{MxL}}$ is a matrix containing the *L* first column vectors of the unitary matrix **U** obtained from (3).

Finally, the feature *F(TU,IN)* described in (2) is implemented as the internal product between normalized versions of the vector projections obtained in (4). In our case, a vector-space model representation is constructed for sentences, instead of documents, and the source-context similarity values between translation units and input sentences are computed accordingly:

$$F\,(TU,\,IN) = \left\langle \boldsymbol{sc}^{\mathrm{T}}\,\mathbf{U}_{\mathbf{MxL}} / |\boldsymbol{sc}^{\mathrm{T}}\mathbf{U}_{\mathbf{MxL}}|\,,\ \boldsymbol{in}^{\mathrm{T}}\,\mathbf{U}_{\mathbf{MxL}} / |\boldsymbol{in}^{\mathrm{T}}\mathbf{U}_{\mathbf{MxL}}| \right\rangle \qquad (5)$$

While the value of *M* is given by the vocabulary size in the data collection under consideration, several implementation questions arise regarding the most appropriate values for *N* (amount of sentences to be used for estimating the projection operator **U**) and *L* (the dimensionality of the reduced space). These and other implementation issues are discussed in detail in the following section.

4 Implementation Issues

This section discusses some important implementation issues that have to be dealt with in order to implement and evaluate the proposed approach. First, in subsection 4.1, the problem of implementing a dynamic feature in a standard phrase-based machine translation framework is discussed. Then, in subsections 4.2 and 4.3, the problems of determining the amount of data required for estimating the Latent Semantic Indexing projection operator and the most appropriate dimensionality size for the reduced space representation are discussed.

4.1 Implementing a Dynamic Feature

As defined in (2), the value of the proposed source-context similarity feature depends on each individual input sentence to be translated by the system. This definition implies a major difference between this feature and other conventional phrase-based translation features: it is a dynamic feature in the sense that it cannot be computed in advance before the input sentences to be translated are known.

This on-the-fly requirement, along with the extended translation unit definition presented in (1), makes it not possible to directly implement the proposed methodology within a standard phrase-based machine translation framework such as MOSES (Koehn *et al.*, 2007). As it is not our intention to develop a customized decoding tool for implementing and testing our proposed feature, we followed or previous implementation of an off-line version of the proposed methodology (Costa-jussà & Banchs, 2010), which, although very inefficient in the practice, allows us to evaluate the impact of the source-context feature on a state-of-the-art phrase-based translation system.

According to this, our practical implementation is a follows:

- Two sentence similarity matrices are computed: one between sentences in the development and training sets, and the other between sentences in the test and training datasets.
- Each matrix entry m_{ij} should contain the similarity score between the ith sentence in the training set and the jth sentence in the development (or test) set.
- For each sentence s in the test and development sets, a phrase list L_S of all potential phrases that can be used during decoding is extracted from the aligned training set.
- The corresponding source-context similarity values are assigned to each phrase in lists L_S according to values in the corresponding similarity matrices.
- Each phrase list L_S is collapsed into a phrase table T_S by removing repetitions (when removing repeated entries in the list, the largest value of the source-context similarity feature is retained).
- Each phrase table is completed by adding standard feature values (which are computed in the standard manner).
- MOSES is used on a sentence-per-sentence basis, using a different translation table for each development (or test) sentence.

4.2 Dataset for Latent Semantic Indexing

Another important implementation issue that requires attention is the computation of the Singular Value Decomposition described in (3). Ideally, the term-sentence matrix **X** to be decomposed should include all available data, i.e. training, development and test sentences; however, in the practice, this is not possible because of two reasons. First, the sizes of typical datasets and vocabularies used in statistical machine translation systems are large enough to make Singular Value Decomposition unfeasible from a computational point of view[1]. Second, in a practical application system, the "test set" is actually unknown during the system construction and training phases. In this way, a realistic implementation should be able to work with previously unseen data.

In order to overcome the problem of applying the Singular Value Decomposition described in (3) to the full term-sentence matrix of all available data, we implemented an approximated procedure. In our approximation, we compute the similarity matrix between two set of sentences as the average of several similarity matrices that are computed over reduced space projections estimated with different random samples of the training data sentences. In this way, our source-context similarity feature, previously defined in (5), becomes:

$$F\,(TU,\,IN) \approx \frac{1}{K} \Sigma_k \left\langle \boldsymbol{sc}^T \mathbf{U}^k_{MxL} / |\boldsymbol{sc}^T \mathbf{U}^k_{MxL}|\,,\ \boldsymbol{in}^T \mathbf{U}^k_{MxL} / |\boldsymbol{in}^T \mathbf{U}^k_{MxL}| \right\rangle \qquad (6)$$

where $\mathbf{U}^k_{MxL}$ refers to a projection operator that has been computed by means of the Singular Valued Decomposition of a term-sentence matrix $\mathbf{X}^k$ constructed with a random sample of N sentences. Note that a total of K different similarity scores are averaged in (6).

In order to evaluate the variability of the similarity values estimated by this approximation, several experiments were conducted for different values of N and L, where the variance of the estimates over $K=10$ different realizations were computed. Figure 1 shows the resulting standard deviations for similarity values estimated for different values of L when varying N (upper panel), and for different values of N when varying L (lower panel).

As seen from the figure, the range $500<N<1000$ seems to constitute a good compromise between the size of selected random sentence sets and the observed variability for similarity value estimates, as it provides a significant reduction in the computed standard deviations with respect to $N=100$, and not important improvement is observed when

[1] Even in the case of a small dataset such as the one considered here (see details in section 5) the Singular Value Decomposition of the full term-sentence matrix can take several weeks to be completed in and standard Linux-based server.

N>1000. According to this, we selected *N=1000* for our proposed approximation described in (6).

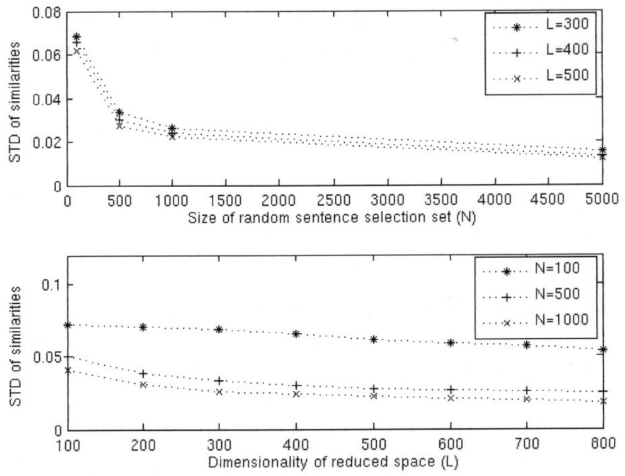

Figure 1: Standard deviations (STD) for similarity values between development and test datasets (described in section 5) estimated for different values of L when varying N (upper panel), and for different values of N when varying L (lower panel). In all cases K=10.

4.3 Reduced Space Dimensionality

The third and final implementation issue to be discussed is the selection of the reduced space dimensionality. It have been reported in the literature that dimensionality reduction, by means of Latent Semantic Indexing, into the range between *100* and *1000* provides good space representations for word and sentence association applications (Landauer *et al.*, 1998). Although it is reasonable to assume this condition to be valid also for the application under consideration, we conducted a more detailed exploratory analysis for selecting the dimensionality *L* to be used in our experiments.

First, we studied the distributions of context-similarity values computed according to (6) over the available data. Figure 2 shows the average distributions of similarities between sentences in the development and training datasets (see data description in section 5) at different dimensionality values. As can be seen from the figure, a dimensionality value of *L=100* exhibits a very nice distribution of similarity values; however, according to the results depicted in Figure 1 (lower panel), the variability of estimates for such a low dimensionality is relatively high. On the other hand, notice again from Figure 2, how a much larger dimensionality value such as *L=5000* already starts to exhibit a distribution of similarities that is heavily biased towards the low similarity region. According to this result, and taking also into account the results in Figure 1, we finally decided setting the dimensionality of the reduced space to *L=500*.

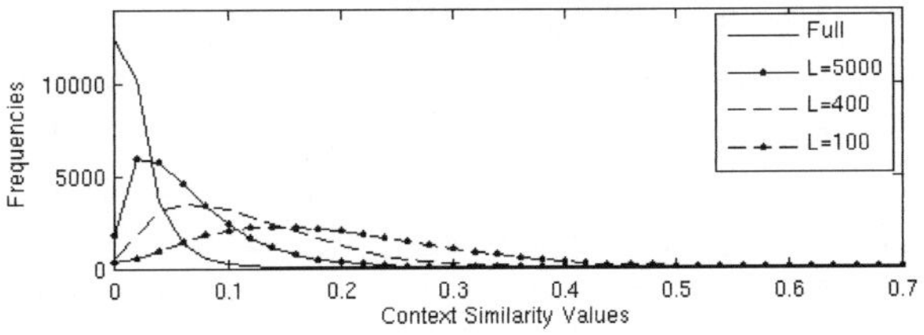

Figure 2: Average distributions of similarity values between development and training sentences computed at different dimensionality values. For all cases presented here N=500 and K=10.

5 Experimental Work

This section describes the experimental work conducted to evaluate the incidence of the proposed source-context similarity feature on translation quality for a state-of-the-art phrase-based statistical machine translation. First, subsection 5.1 describes the dataset and experimental setting. Then, subsection 5.2 presents and discusses the results.

5.1 Experimental Setting

The proposed methodology is evaluated on the Bible dataset (Chew *et al.*, 2006) Spanish-to-English translation task, using the MOSES framework as baseline phrase-based statistical machine translation system (Koehn *et al.*, 2007). Table 3 presents the main statistics of the bilingual corpus used.

dataset	lang.	sentences	tokens	vocab	av. lenght
Train	Spa	28,887	781,113	28,178	27
Train	Eng	28,887	848,776	13,126	29
Test	Spa	500	13,312	2,879	27
Test	Eng	500	14,562	2,156	29
Dev	Spa	500	13,170	2,862	26
Dev	Eng	500	14,537	2,095	29

Table 3: Main statistics of the bilingual corpus under consideration (number of sentences, tokens, vocabulary, and average sentence length)

Regarding the baseline system, we used the default parameters of MOSES, which include the grow-final-diagonal alignment symmetrisation, the lexicalized reordering, a 5-gram language model using Kneser-Ney smoothing, and phrases up to length 10, among others. The optimization was done using the standard MERT procedure (Och & Ney, 2002).

5.2 Experimental Results

Table 4 presents the translation BLEU, measured over the development and test sets, for three different system implementations: the baseline system, a second system implementing the source-context similarity feature over the full-dimensional vector space (FVS), just as we implemented it in Costa-jussà & Banchs (2010), and a third system implementing the source-context similarity feature based on Latent Semantic Indexing (LSI).

	Development	Test
Baseline	39.92	38.92
Source-context (FVS)	40.61	39.43
Source-context (LSI)	**40.80**	**39.86**

Table 4: BLEU scores over development and test datasets corresponding to three system implementations: baseline, and source-context similarity feature at full-dimensional vector space (FVS) and by means of Latent Semantic Indexing (LSI).

As seen from the table, the system implementing the Latent Semantic Indexing based source-context similarity feature outperforms the baseline system by almost one absolute BLEU point, and the full-dimensional vector space system by some less than a half absolute BLEU point. An analysis of significance (Koehn, 2004) showed that the differences among the systems are statistically significant.

A more comprehensive manual analysis of both the baseline and source-context LSI system outputs was required to better asses the incidence of the implemented source-context similarity feature on the generated translations. The result of this analysis is presented in the following section.

6 Manual Evaluation

This section presents and discusses the results of a manual evaluation that was conducted over a sample set of translations. Previous to the manual evaluation, we performed a sentence-based automatic evaluation using BLEU for the *500* sentences in the test dataset. We obtained that our proposed approach is better than the baseline system in *208* sentences, while the baseline is better than our system in *173* sentences and the remaining *119* had the same BLEU scores.

Some output sentences were randomly selected, regardless of which system performed better, for conducting a manual inspection. From these sentences, we have extracted some segments that illustrate specific cases in which our proposed source-context feature is actually helping to select a better translation unit according to the context of the input sentence being translated. Five of these segments are presented in Table 5, where the relevant fragments within the segments are shown in bold.

Example 1	
source	No des sueño a **tus ojos** ni dejes dormitar tus párpados .
reference	Give not sleep to **thine eyes** , nor slumber to thine eyelids .
baseline	Not sleep in **thy sight** , Let neither slumber thy eyelids .
LSI-context	Give not sleep to **thine eyes** neither slumber , Let thine eyelids .
Example 2	
source	Entonces ellos se acercaron , **echaron mano a** Jesús y le prendieron ...
reference	Then came they , and **laid hands on** Jesus , and took him ...
baseline	And they came near , and **cast hand to** Jesus , and took him ...
LSI-context	And they came near , and **laid hands on** Jesus , and took him ...
Example 3	
source	Y al tercer día , he aquí que un hombre **vino** del campamento de Saúl ...
reference	It came even to pass on the third day , that , behold , a man **came** out of the camp from Saul ...
baseline	And the third day , behold , a man **wine** of the camp of Saul ...
LSI-context	And the third day , behold , there **came** a man of the camp of Saul ...
Example 4	
source	... **sed** confortados ; **sed** de un mismo sentir ...
reference	... **be** of good comfort , **be** of one mind ...
baseline	... **thirst** confortados ; **thirst** of one mind 's sake ...
LSI-context	... **be** ye confortados : **be** ye of one mind 's sake ...
Example 5	
source	... según sus familias , según sus idiomas , en **sus territorios** y en sus naciones .
reference	... after their families , after their tongues , in **their countries** , and in their nations .
baseline	... according to their families , after their tongues , in **their coasts** , and in their nations .
LSI-context	... after their families , after their tongues , in **their lands** , and in their nations .

Table 5: Sample segments where the LSI-based source-context feature has helped to accomplish better translation unit selections.

As seen from the table, the LSI-based source-context system is clearly accomplishing more appropriate unit selections. However, in most of the cases this does not imply either a better overall translation or a closer match to the available reference translation. This can explain the relative low BLEU gain achieved by the method.

Similarly, we also extracted some segments that illustrate specific cases in which our proposed source-context feature fails in helping to select a better translation unit. Table 6 presents four of these cases.

Example 1	
source	… yo he sido enviado con **malas noticias** para ti .
reference	… for I am sent to thee with **heavy tidings** .
baseline	… for I have sent with **evil tidings** unto thee .
LSI-context	… I am sent with **evil tidings** unto thee .
Example 2	
source	… heredad de Jehovah son los hijos ; recompensa es el **fruto del vientre** .
reference	… children are an heritage of the Lord : and the **fruit of the womb** is his reward .
baseline	… the inheritance of the Lord , are the children ; reward is the **fruit of the belly** .
LSI-context	… the inheritance of the Lord are the children , and reward is the **fruit of the belly** .
Example 3	
source	… y que **había enaltecido su reino** por amor a su pueblo Israel .
reference	… and that **he had exalted his kingdom** for his people Israel 's sake .
baseline	… and for **his kingdom was lifted up** his people Israel .
LSI-context	… and for **his kingdom was lifted up** unto his people Israel .
Example 4	
source	Y sucederá que a causa de la **abundancia de leche** , comerá leche cuajada …
reference	And it shall come to pass , for the **abundance of milk** that he shall eat butter …
baseline	And it shall come to pass , that by reason of the **multitude of milk** , shall eat with milk cuajada …
LSI-context	And it shall come to pass by reason of the **multitude of milk** , and shall eat with milk cuajada …

Table 6: Sample segments where the LSI-based source-context feature has failed to accomplish better translation unit selections.

In the latter examples in Table 6, the proposed source-context feature is clearly failing to provide better lexical selections. In some cases, this seems to be due to the lack of enough source-context information in the input sentence to be translated. However, in other cases, it is because the source-context feature alone is not able to compensate the system's bias towards more frequent translations.

7 Conclusions and Future Work

A new semantically-motivated feature for statistical machine translation based on Latent Semantic Indexing has been proposed and evaluated. The objective of the proposed feature is to account for the degree of similarity between a given input sentence and each individual sentence in the training dataset. This similarity is computed in a reduced vector-space constructed by means of the Latent Semantic Indexing decomposition.

The computed similarity values are used as an additional feature in the log-linear model combination approach to statistical machine translation. In our implementation, the proposed feature is dynamically adjusted for each translation unit in the translation table according to the current input sentence to be translated.

Experimental results on a Spanish-to-English translation task on the Bible corpus showed significant improvements of almost *1* and *0.5* absolute BLEU points with respect to a baseline system and a similar system evaluating sentence similarity at the full-dimensional vector space, respectively. A manual evaluation revealed that the proposed feature is actually helping the translation system to perform a better selection of translation units on a semantic basis.

As future work, we intend to evaluate different association and distance metrics, as well as to extend the current notion of source-context from the input sentence to be translated to any other kind of available information beyond the input sentence limits. Similarly, different paradigms of semantic space representations, including those statistically motivated, will be studied and evaluated.

Implementation issues are also to be revisited for better evaluating the impact of both the amount of training data and the dimensionality of the reduced space on the method's performance. Finally, an on-line version of the method must be implemented in order to be able to evaluate the proposed methodology over larger data collections.

Acknowledgments

The authors would like to thank the Institute for Infocomm Research, as well as Barcelona Media Innovation Centre and the Juan de la Cierva fellowship program, for their support and permission to publish this work.

References

Brown, P., Della-Pietra, S., Della-Pietra, V., Mercer, R. (1993) The Mathematics of Statistical Machine Translation: Computational Linguistics 19(2), 263--311

Carl, M., Way, A. (2003) Recent Advances in Example-Based Machine Translation. Kluwer Academic

Carpuat, M., Wu, D. (2007) How Phrase Sense Disambiguation Outperforms Word Sense Disambiguation for Statistical Machine Translation. In: 11th International Conference on Theoretical and Methodological Issues in Machine Translation. Skovde

Carpuat, M., Wu, D. (2008) Evaluation of Context-Dependent Phrasal Translation Lexicons for Statistical Machine Translation. In: 6th International Conference on Language Resources and Evaluation (LREC). Marrakech

Chew, P. A., Verzi, S. J., Bauer, T. L., McClain, J. T. (2006) Evaluation of the Bible as a Resource for Cross-Language Information Retrieval. In: Workshop on Multilingual Language Resources and Interoperability, pp. 68--74, Sydney

Costa-jussà, M. R., Banchs, R.E. (2010) A Vector-Space Dynamic Feature for Phrase-Based Statistical Machine Translation. Journal of Intelligent Information Systems

España-Bonet, C., Gimenez, J., Marquez, L. (2009) Discriminative Phrase-Based Models for Arabic Machine Translation. ACM Transactions on Asian Language Information Processing Journal (Special Issue on Arabic Natural Language Processing)

Golub, G. H., Kahan, W. (1965) Calculating the Singular Values and Pseudo-Inverse of a Matrix. Journal of the Society for Industrial and Applied Mathematics: Numerical Analysis 2(2), 205--224

Haque, R., Naskar, S. K., Ma, Y., Way, A. (2009) Using Supertags as Source Language Context in SMT. In: 13th Annual Conference of the European Association for Machine Translation, pp. 234--241. Barcelona

Haque, R., Naskar, S. K., van den Bosh, A., Way, A. (2010) Supertags as Source Language Context in Hierarchical Phrase-Based SMT. In: 9th Conference of the Association for Machine Translation in the Americas (AMTA)

Koehn, P., Och, F. J., Marcu, D. (2003) Statistical Phrase-Based Translation. In: Human Language Technology Conference and Conference on Empirical Methods in Natural Language Processing (HLT-EMNLP), pp. 48--54. Edmonton

Koehn, P. (2004) Statistical Significance Test for Machine Translation Evaluation. In: Conference on Empirical Methods in Natural Language Processing (EMNLP)

Koehn, P., Hoang, H., Birch, A., Callison-Burch, C., Federico, M., Bertoldi, N., Cowan, B., Shen, W., Moran, C., Zens, R., Dyer, C., Bojar, O., Constantin, A., Herbst, E. (2007) Moses: Open Source Toolkit for Statistical Machine Translation. In: 45th Annual Metting of the Association for Computational Linguistics, pp. 177--180. Prague

Landauer, T. K., Laham, D., Foltz, P. (1998) Learning Human-Like Knowledge by Singular Value Decomposition: A Progress Report. In: Conference on Advances in Neural Information Processing Systems, pp. 45--51. Denver

Landauer, T. K., Foltz, P.W., Laham, D. (1998) Introduction to Latent Semantic Analysis. Discourse Processes 25, 259--284

Och, F. J., Ney, H. (2002) Discriminative Training and Maximum Entropy Models for Statistical Machine Translation. In: 40th Annual Meeting of the Association for Computational Linguistics, pp. 295--302

Padilla, P., Bajo, T. (1998) Hacia un Modelo de Memoria y Atención en la Interpretación Simultánea. Quaderns: Revista de Traducció 2, 107--117

Pearson, K. (1901) On Lines and Planes of Closest Fit to Systems of Points in Space. Philosophical Magazine 2(6), 559--572

Salton, G., Wong, A., Yang, C. S. (1975) A Vector Space Model for Automatic Indexing. Communications of the ACM 18(11), 613--620

A General-Purpose Rule Extractor for SCFG-Based Machine Translation

Greg Hanneman and **Michelle Burroughs** and **Alon Lavie**
Language Technologies Institute
Carnegie Mellon University
Pittsburgh, PA 15213 USA
{ghannema, mburroug, alavie}@cs.cmu.edu

Abstract

We present a rule extractor for SCFG-based MT that generalizes many of the contraints present in existing SCFG extraction algorithms. Our method's increased rule coverage comes from allowing multiple alignments, virtual nodes, and multiple tree decompositions in the extraction process. At decoding time, we improve automatic metric scores by significantly increasing the number of phrase pairs that match a given test set, while our experiments with hierarchical grammar filtering indicate that more intelligent filtering schemes will also provide a key to future gains.

1 Introduction

Syntax-based machine translation systems, regardless of the underlying formalism they use, depend on a method for acquiring bilingual rules in that formalism to build the system's translation model. In modern syntax-based MT, this formalism is often synchronous context-free grammar (SCFG), and the SCFG rules are obtained automatically from parallel data through a large variety of methods.

Some SCFG rule extraction techniques require only Viterbi word alignment links between the source and target sides of the input corpus (Chiang, 2005), while methods based on linguistic constituency structure require the source and/or target side of the input to be parsed. Among such techniques, most retain the dependency on Viterbi word alignments for each sentence (Galley et al., 2004; Zollmann and Venugopal, 2006; Lavie et al., 2008; Chiang, 2010) while others make use of a general, corpus-level statistical lexicon instead of individual alignment links (Zhechev and Way, 2008). Each method may also place constraints on the size, format, or structure of the rules it returns.

This paper describes a new, general-purpose rule extractor intended for cases in which two parse trees and Viterbi word alignment links are provided for each sentence, although compatibility with single-parse-tree extraction methods can be achieved by supplying a flat "dummy" parse for the missing tree. Our framework for rule extraction is thus most similar to the Stat-XFER system (Lavie et al., 2008; Ambati et al., 2009) and the tree-to-tree situation considered by Chiang (2010). However, we significantly broaden the scope of allowable rules compared to the Stat-XFER heuristics, and our approach differs from Chiang's system in its respect of the linguistic constituency constraints expressed in the input tree structure. In summary, we attempt to extract the greatest possible number of syntactically motivated rules while not allowing them to violate explicit constituent boundaries on either the source or target side. This is achieved by allowing creation of virtual nodes, by allowing multiple decompositions of the same tree pair, and by allowing extraction of SCFG rules beyond the minimial set required to regenerate the tree pair.

After describing our extraction method and comparing it to a number of existing SCFG extraction techniques, we present a series of experiments examining the number of rules that may be produced from an input corpus. We also describe experiments on Chinese-to-English translation that suggest that filtering a very large extracted grammar to a more

Proceedings of SSST-5, Fifth Workshop on Syntax, Semantics and Structure in Statistical Translation, pages 135–144,
ACL HLT 2011, Portland, Oregon, USA, June 2011.

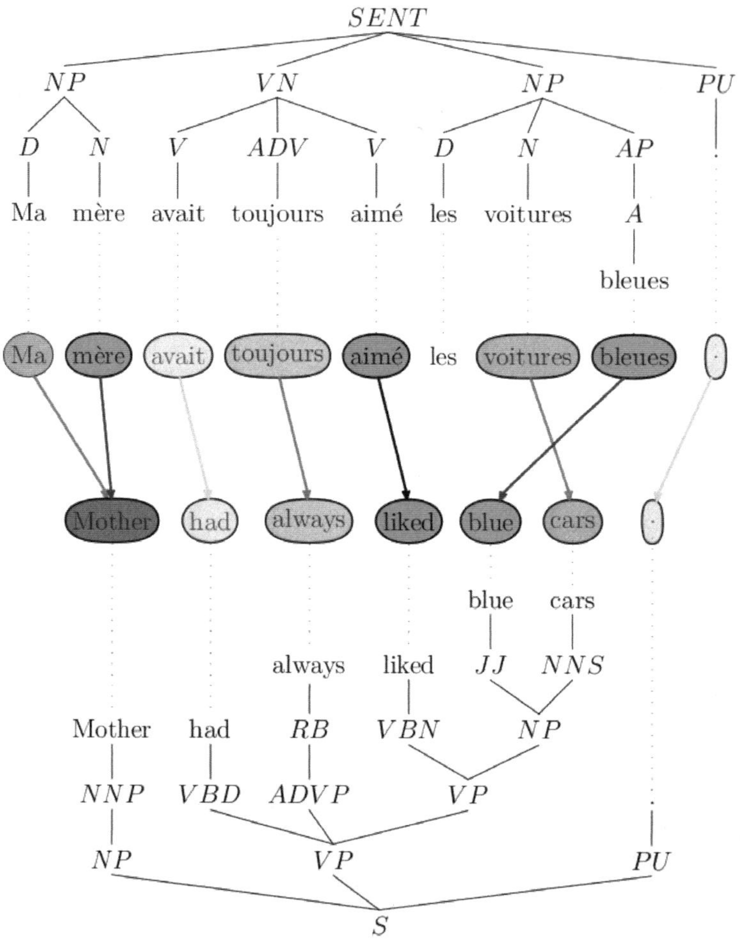

Figure 1: Sample input for our rule extraction algorithm. It consists of a source-side parse tree (French) and a target-side parse tree (English) connected by a Viterbi word alignment.

moderate-sized translation model is an important consideration for obtaining strong results. Finally, this paper concludes with some suggestions for future work.

2 Rule Extraction Algorithm

We begin with a parallel sentence consisting of a source-side parse tree S, a target-side parse tree T, and a Viterbi word alignment between the trees' leaves. A sample sentence of this type is shown in Figure 1. Our goal is to extract a number of SCFG rules that are licensed by this input.

2.1 Node Alignment

Our algorithm first computes a node alignment between the parallel trees. A node s in tree S is aligned to a node t in tree T if the following constraints are met. First, all words in the yield of s must either be aligned to words within the yield of t, or they must be unaligned. Second, the reverse must also hold: all words in the yield of t must be aligned to words within the yield of s or again be unaligned. This is analogous to the word-alignment consistency constraint of phrase-based SMT phrase extraction (Koehn et al., 2003). In Figure 1, for example, the NP dominating the French words *les voitures bleues* is aligned to the equivalent English NP node dominating *blue cars*.

As in phrase-based SMT, where a phrase in one language may be consistent with multiple possible phrases in the other language, we allow parse nodes in both trees to have multiple node alignments. This is in contrast to one-derivation rule extractors such as that of Lavie et al. (2008), in which each node in S may only be aligned to a single node in T and vice versa. The French NP node *Ma mère*, for example, aligns to both the NNP and NP nodes in English producing *Mother*.

Besides aligning existing nodes in both parse trees to the extent possible, we also permit the introduction of "virtual" nodes into either tree. Virtual nodes are created when two or more contiguous children of an existing node are aligned consistently to a node or a similar set of two or more contiguous children of a node in the opposite parse tree. Virtual nodes may be aligned to "original" nodes in the opposite tree or to other virtual nodes.

In Figure 1, the existing English NP node *blue cars* can be aligned to a new virtual node in French that dominates the N node *voitures* and the AP node *bleues*. The virtual node is inserted as the parent of N and AP, and as the child of the NP node directly above. In conjunction with node alignments between existing nodes, this means that the English NP *blue cars* is now aligned twice: once to the original French NP node and once to the virtual node N+AP. We thus replicate the behavior of "growing into the gaps" from phrase-based SMT in the presence of unaligned words. As another example, a virtual node in French covering the V node *avait* and the ADV node *toujours* could be created to align consistently with a virtual node in English covering the VBD node *had* and the ADVP node *always*.

Since virtual nodes are always created out of children of the same node, they are always consistent with the existing syntactic structure of the tree. Within the constraints of the existing tree structure and word alignments, however, all possible virtual nodes are considered. This is in keeping with our philosophy of allowing multiple alignments without violating constituent boundaries. Near the top of the trees in Figure 1, for example, French virtual nodes NP+VN+NP (aligned to English NP+VP) and VN+NP+PU (aligned to VP+PU) both exist, even though they overlap. In our procedure, we do allow a limit to be placed the number of child nodes that can be combined into a virtual node. Setting this limit to two, for instance, will constrain node alignment to the space of possible synchronous binarizations consistent with the Viterbi word alignments.

2.2 Grammar Extraction

Given the final set of node alignments between the source tree and the target tree, SCFG rules are obtained via a grammar extraction step. Rule extraction proceeds in a depth-first manner, such that rules are extracted and cached for all descendents of a source node s before rules in which s is the left-hand side are considered. Extracting rules where source node s is the left-hand side consists of two phases: decomposition and combination.

The first phase is decomposition of node s into all distinct sets $D = \{d_1, d_2, \ldots, d_n\}$ of descendent nodes such that D spans the entire yield of node s, where $d_i \in D$ is node-aligned or is an unaligned terminal for all i, and d_i has no ancestor a where a is a descendent of s and a is node-aligned. Each D thus represents the right-hand side of a minimal SCFG rule rooted at s. Due to the introduction of overlapping virtual nodes, the decomposition step may involve finding multiple sets of decomposition points when there are multiple nodes with the same span at the same level of the tree.

The second phase involves composition of all rules derived from each element of D subject to certain constraints. Rules are constructed using s, the set of nodes $T_s = \{t \mid s \text{ is aligned to } t\}$, and each decomposed node set D. The set of left-hand sides is $\{s\} \times T_s$, but there may be many right-hand sides for a given t and D. Define $rhs(d)$ as the set of right-hand sides of rules that are derived from d, plus all alignments of d to its aligned set T_d. If d is a terminal, word alignments are used in the place of node alignments. To create a set of right-hand sides, we generate the set $R = rhs(d_1) \times \ldots \times rhs(d_n)$. For each $r \in R$, we execute a $combine$ operation such that $combine(r)$ creates a new right-hand side by combining the component right-hand sides and recalculating co-indexes between the source- and target-side nonterminals. Finally, we insert any unaligned terminals on either side.

We work through a small example of grammar extraction using Figure 2, which replicates a fragment of Figure 1 with virtual nodes included. The English node JJ is aligned to the French nodes A and AP, the English node NNS is aligned to the French node N and the virtual node D+N, and the English node NP is aligned to the French node NP and the

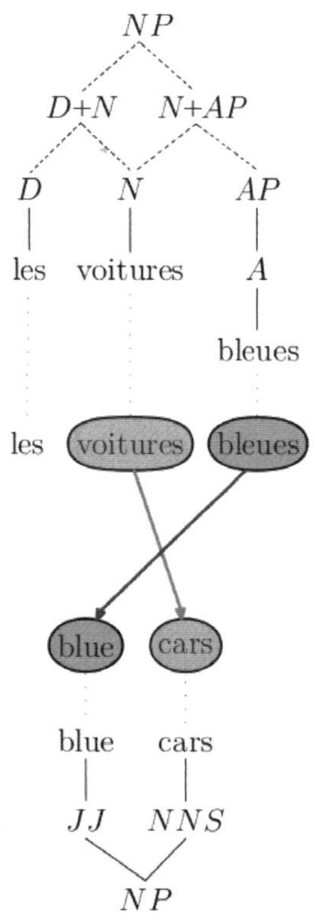

Figure 2: A fragment of Figure 1 with virtual nodes (symbolized by dashed lines) added on the French side. Nodes D, N, and AP are all original children of the French NP.

virtual node N+AP. To extract rules from the French node NP, we consider two potential decompositions: $D_1 = \{\text{D+N}, \text{AP}\}$ and $D_2 = \{\text{les}, \text{N+AP}\}$. Since the French NP is aligned only to the English NP, the set of left-hand sides is {NP::NP}, where we use the symbol "::" to separate the source and target sides of joint nonterminal label or a rule.

In the next step, we use cached rules and alignments to generate all potential right-hand-side pieces from these top-level nodes:

$$rhs(\text{D+N}) = \left\{ \begin{array}{l} [\text{D+N}^1] :: [\text{NNS}^1], \\ [\text{les voitures}] :: [\text{cars}] \end{array} \right\}$$

$$rhs(\text{AP}) = \left\{ \begin{array}{l} [\text{AP}^1] :: [\text{JJ}^1], \\ [\text{A}^1] :: [\text{JJ}^1], \\ [\text{bleues}] :: [\text{blue}] \end{array} \right\}$$

$$rhs(\text{les}) = \emptyset$$

$$rhs(\text{N+AP}) = \left\{ \begin{array}{l} [\text{N+AP}^1] :: [\text{NP}^1], \\ [\text{N}^1\ \text{AP}^2] :: [\text{JJ}^2\ \text{NNS}^1], \\ [\text{N}^1\ \text{A}^2] :: [\text{JJ}^2\ \text{NNS}^1], \\ [\text{voitures AP}^1] :: [\text{JJ}^1\ \text{cars}], \\ [\text{voitures A}^1] :: [\text{JJ}^1\ \text{cars}], \\ [\text{N}^1\ \text{bleues}] :: [\text{blue NNS}^1], \\ [\text{voitures bleues}] :: [\text{blue cars}] \end{array} \right\}$$

Next we must combine these pieces. For example, from D_1 we derive the full right-hand sides

1. *combine*([les voitures]::[cars], [bleues]::[blue]) = [les voitures bleues]::[blue cars]
2. *combine*([les voitures]::[cars], [A^1]::[JJ^1]) = [les voitures A^1]::[JJ^1 cars]
3. *combine*([les voitures]::[cars], [AP^1]::[JJ^1]) = [les voitures AP^1]::[JJ^1 cars]
4. *combine*([D+N^1]::[NNS^1], [bleues]::[blue]) = [D+N^1 bleues]::[blue NNS^1]
5. *combine*([D+N^1]::[NNS^1], [A^1]::[JJ^1]) = [D+N^1 A^2]::[JJ^2 NNS^1]
6. *combine*([D+N^1]::[NNS^1], [AP^1]::[JJ^1]) = [D+N^1 AP^2]::[JJ^2 NNS^1]

Similarly, we derive seven full right-hand sides from D_2. Since $rhs(\text{les})$ is empty, rules derived have right-hand sides equivalent to $rhs(\text{N+AP})$ with the unaligned *les* added on the source side to complete the span of the French NP. For example, *combine*([N+AP^1]::[NP^1]) = [les N+AP^1]::[NP^1].

In the final step, the left-hand side is added to each full right-hand side. Thus,

$$\text{NP} :: \text{NP} \rightarrow [\text{les voitures A}^1] :: [\text{JJ}^1\ \text{cars}]$$

is one example rule extracted from this tree.

The number of rules can grow rapidly: if the parse tree has a branching factor of b and a depth of h, there are potentially $O(2^{b^h})$ rules extracted. To control this, we allow certain constraints on the rules extracted that can short-circuit right-hand-side formation. We allow separate restrictions on the number of items that may appear on the right-hand side of phrase pair rules (max_p) and hierarchical grammar rules (max_g). We also optionally allow the exclusion of parallel unary rules — that is, rules whose right-hand sides consist solely of a pair of aligned nonterminals.

System	Tree Constraints	Multiple Alignments	Virtual Nodes	Multiple Derivations
Hiero	No	—	—	Yes
Stat-XFER	Yes	No	Some	No
GHKM	Yes	No	No	Yes
SAMT	No	No	Yes	Yes
Chiang (2010)	No	No	Yes	Yes
This work	Yes	Yes	Yes	Yes

Table 1: Comparisons between the rule extractor described in this paper and other SCFG rule extraction methods.

3 Comparison to Other Methods

Table 1 compares the rule extractor described in Section 2 to other SCFG extraction methods described in the literature. We include comparisons of our work against the Hiero system (Chiang, 2005), the Stat-XFER system rule learner most recently described by Ambati et al. (2009), the composed version of GHKM rule extraction (Galley et al., 2006), the so-called Syntax-Augmented MT (SAMT) system (Zollmann and Venugopal, 2006), and a Hiero–SAMT extension with source- and target-side syntax described by Chiang (2010). Note that some of these methods make use of only target-side parse trees — or no parse trees at all, in the case of Hiero — but our primary interest in comparison is the constraints placed on the rule extraction process rather than the final output form of the rules themselves. We highlight four specific dimensions along these lines.

Tree Constraints. As we mentioned in this paper's introduction, we do not allow any part of our extracted rules to violate constituent boundaries in the input parse trees. This is in contrast to Hiero-derived techniques, which focus on expanding grammar coverage by extracting rules for all spans in the input sentence pair that are consistently word-aligned, regardless of their correspondence to linguistic constituents. Practitioners of both phrase-based and syntax-based SMT have reported severe grammar coverage issues when rules are required to exactly match parse constituents (Koehn et al., 2003; Chiang, 2010). In our work, we attempt to improve the coverage of the grammar by allowing multiple node alignments, virtual nodes, and multiple tree decompositions rather than ignoring structure constraints.

Multiple Alignments. In contrast to all other extraction methods in Table 1, ours allows a node in one parse tree to be aligned with multiple nodes in the other tree, as long as the word-alignment and structure constraints are satisfied. However, we do not allow a node to have multiple simultaneous alignments — a single node alignment must be chosen for extracting an individual rule. In practice, this prevents extraction of "triangle" rules where the same node appears on both the left- and right-hand side of the same rule.[1]

Virtual Nodes. In keeping with our philosophy of representing multiple alignments, our use of multiple and overlapping virtual nodes is less restrictive than the single-alignment constraint of Stat-XFER. Another key difference is that Stat-XFER requires all virtual nodes to be aligned to original nodes in the other language, while we permit virtual–virtual node alignments. In respecting existing tree structure constraints, our virtual node placement is more restrictive than SAMT or Chiang, where extracted nodes may cross existing constituent boundaries.

Multiple Derivations. Galley et al. (2006) argued that breaking a single tree pair into multiple decompositions is important for correct probability modeling. We agree, and we base our rule extractor's acquisition of multiple derivations per tree pair on techniques from both GHKM and Hiero. More specifically, we borrow from Hiero the idea of creating hierarchical rules by subtracting and abstracting all possible subsets of smaller phrases (aligned nodes in our case) from larger phrases. Like GHKM,

[1] Figure 2 includes a potential triangle rule, D+N :: NNS $\rightarrow$ [les N^1] :: [NNS^1], where the English NNS node appears on both sides of the rule. It is simultaneously aligned to the French D+N and N nodes.

we do this exhaustively within some limit, although in our case we use a rank limit on a rule's right-hand side rather than a limit on the depth of the subnode subtractions. Our constraint achieves the goal of controlling the size of the rule set while remaining flexibile in terms of depth depending on the shape of the parse trees.

4 Experiments

We conducted experiments with our rule extractor on the FBIS corpus, made up of approximately 302,000 Chinese–English sentence pairs. We parsed the corpus with the Chinese and English grammars of the Berkeley parser (Petrov and Klein, 2007) and word-aligned it with GIZA++ (Och and Ney, 2003). The parsed and word-aligned FBIS corpus served as the input to our rule extractor, which we ran with a number of different settings.

First, we acquired a baseline rule extraction ("xfer-orig") from our corpus using an implementation of the basic Stat-XFER rule learner (Lavie et al., 2008), which decomposes each input tree pair into a single set of minimal SCFG rules[2] using only original nodes in the parse trees. Next, we tested the effect of allowing multiple decompositions by running our own rule learner, but restricting its rules to also only make use of original nodes ("compatible"). Finally, we investigated the total number of extractable rules by allowing the creation of virtual nodes from up to four adjacent sibling nodes and placing two different limits on the length of the right-hand side ("full-short" and "full-long"). These configurations are summarized in Table 2.

Rule Set	max_p	max_g	**Virtual**	**Unary**
xfer-orig	10	∞	No	Yes
compatible	10	5	No	Yes
full-short	5	5	Yes	No
full-long	7	7	Yes	No

Table 2: Rule sets considered by a Stat-XFER baseline ("xfer-orig") and our own rule extractor.

[2]In practice, some Stat-XFER aligned nodes produce two rules instead of one: a minimal hierarchical SCFG rule is always produced, and a phrase pair rule will also be produced for node yields within the max_p cutoff.

4.1 Rules Extracted

As expected, we find that allowing multiple decompositions of each tree pair has a significant effect on the number of extracted rules. Table 3 breaks the extracted rules for each configuration down into phrase pairs (all terminals on the right-hand side) and hierarchical rules (containing at least one nonterminal on the right-hand side). We also count the number of extracted rule instances (tokens) against the number of unique rules (types). The results show that multiple decomposition leads to a four-fold increase in the number of extracted grammar rules, even when the length of the Stat-XFER baseline rules is unbounded. The number of extracted phrase pairs shows a smaller increase, but this is expected: the number of possible phrase pairs is proportional to the square of the sentence length, while the number of possible hierarchical rules is exponential, so there is more room for coverage improvement in the hierarchical grammar.

With virtual nodes included, there is again a large jump in both the number of extracted rule tokens and types, even at relatively short length limits. When both max_p and max_g are set to 7, our rule extractor produces 1.5 times as many unique phrase pairs and 20.5 times as many unique hierarchical rules as the baseline Stat-XFER system, and nearly twice the number of hierarchical rules as when using length limits of 5. Ambati et al. (2009) showed the usefulness of extending rule extraction from exact original–original node alignments to cases in which original–virtual and virtual–original alignments were also permitted. Our experiments confirm this, as only 60% (full-short) and 54% (full-long) of our extracted rule types are made up of only original–original node alignments. Further, we find a contribution from the new virtual–virtual case: approximately 8% of the rules extracted in the "full-long" configuration from Table 3 are headed by a virtual–virtual alignment, and a similar number have a virtual–virtual alignment on their right-hand sides.

All four of the extracted rule sets show Zipfian distributions over rule frequency counts. In the xfer-orig, full-short, and full-long configurations, between 82% and 86% of the extracted phrase pair rules, and between 88% and 92% of the extracted hierarchical rules, were observed only once. These

Rule Set	Extracted Instances Phrase	Extracted Instances Hierarchical	Unique Rules Phrase	Unique Rules Hierarchical
xfer-orig	6,646,791	1,876,384	1,929,641	767,573
compatible	8,709,589	6,657,590	2,016,227	3,590,184
full-short	10,190,487	14,190,066	2,877,650	8,313,690
full-long	10,288,731	22,479,863	2,970,403	15,750,695

Table 3: The number of extracted rule instances (tokens) and unique rules (types) produced by the Stat-XFER system ("xfer-orig") and three configurations of our rule extractor.

percentages are remarkably consistent despite substantial changes in grammar size, meaning that our more exhaustive method of rule extraction does not produce a disproportionate number of singletons.[3] On the other hand, it does weaken the average count of an extracted hierarchical rule type. From Table 3, we can compute that the average phrase pair count remains at 3.5 when we move from xfer-orig to the two full configurations; however, the average hierarchical rule count drops from 2.4 to 1.7 (full-short) and finally 1.4 (full-long). This likely again reflects the exponential increase in the number of extractable hierarchical rules compared to the quadratic increase in the phrase pairs.

4.2 Translation Results

The grammars obtained from our rule extractor can be filtered and formatted for use with a variety of SCFG-based decoders and rule formats. We carried out end-to-end translation experiments with the various extracted rule sets from the FBIS corpus using the open-source decoder Joshua (Li et al., 2009). Given a source-language string, Joshua translates by producing a synchronous parse of it according to a scored SCFG and a target-side language model. A significant engineering challenge in building a real MT system of this type is selecting a more moderate-sized subset of all extracted rules to retain in the final translation model. This is an especially important consideration when dealing with expanded rule sets derived from virtual nodes and multiple decompositions in each input tree.

In our experiments, we pass all grammars through two preprocessing steps before any translation model scoring. First, we noticed that English cardinal numbers and punctuation marks in many languages tend to receive incorrect nonterminal labels during parsing, despite being closed-class items with clearly defined tags. Therefore, before rule extraction, we globally correct the nodel labels of all-numeral terminals in English and certain punctuation marks in both English and Chinese. Second, we attempt to reduce derivational ambiguity in cases where the same SCFG right-hand side appears in the grammar after extraction with a large number of possible left-hand-side labels. To this end, we sort the possible left-hand sides by frequency for each unique right-hand side, and we remove the least frequent 10 percent of the label distribution.

Our translation model scoring is based on the feature set of Hanneman et al. (2010). This includes the standard bidirectional conditional maximum-likelihood scores at both the word and phrase level on the right-hand side of rules. We also include maximum-likelihood scores for the left-hand-side label given all or part of the right-hand side. Using statistics local to each rule, we set binary indicator features for rules whose frequencies are ≤ 3, plus five additional indicator features according to the format of the rule's right-hand side, such as whether it is fully abstract. Since the system in this paper is not constructed using any non-syntactic rules, we do not include the Hanneman et al. (2010) "not labelable" maximum-likelihood features or the indicator features related to non-syntactic labels.

Beyond the above preprocessing and scoring common to all grammars, we experiment with three different solutions to the more difficult problem of selecting a final translation grammar. In any case, we separate phrase pair rules from hierarchical rules

[3]The compatible configuration is somewhat of an outlier. It has proportionally fewer singleton phrase pairs (80%) than the other variants, likely because it allows multiple alignments and multiple decompositions without allowing virtual nodes.

Rule Set	Filter	BLEU	TER	MET
xfer-orig	10k	24.39	68.01	54.35
xfer-orig	5k+100k	25.95	66.27	54.77
compatible	10k	24.28	65.30	53.58
full-short	10k	25.16	66.25	54.33
full-short	100k	25.51	65.56	54.15
full-short	5k+100k	26.08	64.32	54.58
full-long	10k	25.74	65.52	54.55
full-long	100k	25.53	66.24	53.68
full-long	5k+100k	25.83	64.55	54.35

Table 4: Automatic metric results using different rule sets, as well as different grammar filtering methods.

and include in the grammar all phrase pair rules matching a given tuning or testing set. Any improvement in phrase pair coverage during the extraction stage is thus directly passed along to decoding. For hierarchical rules, we experiment with retaining the 10,000 or 100,000 most frequently extracted unique rules. We also separate fully abstract hierarchical rules from partially lexicalized hierarchical rules, and in a further selection technique we retain the 5,000 most frequent abstract and 100,000 most frequent partially lexicalized rules.

Given these final rule sets, we tune our MT systems on the NIST MT 2006 data set using the minimum error-rate training package Z-MERT (Zaidan, 2009), and we test on NIST MT 2003. Both sets have four reference translations. Table 4 presents case-insensitive evaluation results on the test set according to the automatic metrics BLEU (Papineni et al., 2002), TER (Snover et al., 2006), and METEOR (Lavie and Denkowski, 2009).[4] The trend in the results is that including a larger grammar is generally better for performance, but filtering techniques also play a substantial role in determining how well a given grammar will perform at run time.

We first compare the results in Table 4 for different rule sets all filtered the same way at decoding time. With only 10,000 hierarchical rules in use ("10k"), the improvements in scores indicate that an important contribution is being made by the additional phrase pair coverage provided by each successive rule set. The original Stat-XFER rule extraction provides 244,988 phrase pairs that match the MT 2003 test set. This is already increased to 520,995 in the compatible system using multiple decompositions. With virtual nodes enabled, the full system produces 766,379 matching phrase pairs up to length 5 or 776,707 up to length 7. These systems both score significantly higher than the Stat-XFER baseline according to BLEU and TER, and the METEOR scores are likely statistically equivalent.

Across all configurations, we find that changing the grammar filtering technique — possibly combined with retuned decoder feature weights — also has a large influence on automatic metric scores. Larger hierarchical grammars tend to score better, in some cases to the point of erasing the score differences between rule sets. From this we conclude that making effective use of the extracted grammar, no matter its size, with intelligent filtering techniques is at least as important as the number and type of rules extracted overall. Though the filtering results in Table 4 are still somewhat inconclusive, the relative success of the "5k+100k" setting shows that filtering fully abstract and partially lexicalized rules separately is a reasonable starting approach. While fully abstract rules do tend to be more frequently observed in grammar extraction, and thus more reliably scored in the translation model, they also have the ability to overapply at decoding time because their use is not restricted to any particular lexical context.

5 Conclusions and Future Work

We demonstrated in Section 4.1 that the general SCFG extraction algorithm described in this paper is capable of producing very large linguistically motivated rule sets. These rule sets can improve automatic metric scores at decoding time. At the same time, we see the results in Section 4.2 as a springboard to more advanced and more intelligent methods of grammar filtering. Our major research question for future work is to determine how to make the best runtime use of the grammars we can extract.

As we saw in Section 2, multiple decompositions of a single parse tree allow the same constituent to be built in a variety of ways. This is generally good for coverage, but its downside at run time is that the decoder must manage a larger number of competing

[4]For METEOR scoring we use version 1.0 of the metric, tuned to HTER with the exact, stemming, and synonymy modules enabled.

derivations that, in the end, produce the same output string. Grammar filtering that explicitly attempts to limit the derivational ambiguity of the retained rules may prevent the translation model probabilities of correct outputs from getting fragmented into redundant derivations. So far we have only approximated this by using fully abstract rules as a proxy for the most derivationally ambiguous rules.

Filtering based on the content of virtual nodes may also be a reasonable strategy for selecting useful grammar rules and discarding those whose contributions are less necessary. For example, we find in our current output many applications of rules involving virtual nodes that consist of an open-class category and a mark of punctuation, such as VBD+COMMA and NN+PU. While there is nothing technically wrong with these rules, they may not be as helpful in translation as rules for nouns and adjectives such as JJ+NNP+NN or NNP+NNP in flat noun phrase structures such as *former U.S. president Bill Clinton*.

A final concern in making use of our large extracted grammars is the effect virtual nodes have on the size of the nonterminal set. The Stat-XFER baseline grammar from our "xfer-orig" configuration uses a nonterminal set of 1,577 unique labels. In our rule extractor so far, we have adopted the convention of naming virtual nodes with a concatenation of their component sibling labels, separated by "+"s. With the large number of virtual node labels that may be created, this gives our "full-short" and "full-long" extracted grammars nonterminal sets of around 73,000 unique labels. An undesirable consequence of such a large label set is that a particular SCFG right-hand side may acquire a large variety of left-hand-side labels, further contributing to the derivational ambiguity problems discussed above. In future work, the problem could be addressed by reconsidering our naming scheme for virtual nodes, by allowing fuzzy matching of labels at translation time (Chiang, 2010), or by other techniques aimed at reducing the size of the overall nonterminal set.

Acknowledgments

This research was supported in part by U.S. National Science Foundation grants IIS-0713402 and IIS-0915327 and the DARPA GALE program. We thank Vamshi Ambati and Jon Clark for helpful discussions regarding implementation details of the grammar extraction algorithm. Thanks to Chris Dyer for providing the word-aligned and preprocessed FBIS corpus. Finally, we thank Yahoo! for the use of the M45 research computing cluster, where we ran many steps of our experimental pipeline.

References

Vamshi Ambati, Alon Lavie, and Jaime Carbonell. 2009. Extraction of syntactic translation models from parallel data using syntax from source and target languages. In *Proceedings of the 12th Machine Translation Summit*, pages 190–197, Ottawa, Canada, August.

David Chiang. 2005. A hierarchical phrase-based model for statistical machine translation. In *Proceedings of the 43rd Annual Meeting of the ACL*, pages 263–270, Ann Arbor, MI, June.

David Chiang. 2010. Learning to translate with source and target syntax. In *Proceedings of the 48th Annual Meeting of the Association for Computational Linguistics*, pages 1443–1452, Uppsala, Sweden, July.

Michel Galley, Mark Hopkins, Kevin Knight, and Daniel Marcu. 2004. What's in a translation rule? In *HLT-NAACL 2004: Main Proceedings*, pages 273–280, Boston, MA, May.

Michel Galley, Jonathan Graehl, Kevin Knight, Daniel Marcu, Steve DeNeefe, Wei Wang, and Ignacio Thayer. 2006. Scalable inference and training of context-rich syntactic translation models. In *Proceedings of the 21st International Conference on Computational Linguistics and 44th Annual Meeting of the ACL*, pages 961–968, Sydney, Australia, July.

Greg Hanneman, Jonathan Clark, and Alon Lavie. 2010. Improved features and grammar selection for syntax-based MT. In *Proceedings of the Joint Fifth Workshop on Statistical Machine Translation and MetricsMATR*, pages 82–87, Uppsala, Sweden, July.

Philipp Koehn, Franz Josef Och, and Daniel Marcu. 2003. Statistical phrase-based translation. In *Proceedings of HLT-NAACL 2003*, pages 48–54, Edmonton, Alberta, May–June.

Alon Lavie and Michael J. Denkowski. 2009. The METEOR metric for automatic evaluation of machine translation. *Machine Translation*, 23(2–3):105–115.

Alon Lavie, Alok Parlikar, and Vamshi Ambati. 2008. Syntax-driven learning of sub-sentential translation equivalents and translation rules from parsed parallel corpora. In *Proceedings of the Second ACL Workshop on Syntax and Structure in Statistical Translation*, pages 87–95, Columbus, OH, June.

Zhifei Li, Chris Callison-Burch, Chris Dyer, Juri Ganitkevitch, Sanjeev Khudanpur, Lane Schwartz, Wren N.G. Thornton, Jonathan Weese, and Omar F. Zaidan. 2009. Joshua: An open source toolkit for parsing-based machine translation. In *Proceedings of the Fourth Workshop on Statistical Machine Translation*, pages 135–139, Athens, Greece, March.

Franz Josef Och and Hermann Ney. 2003. A systematic comparison of various statistical alignment models. *Computational Linguistics*, 29(1):19–51.

Kishore Papineni, Salim Roukos, Todd Ward, and Wei-Jing Zhu. 2002. BLEU: A method for automatic evalution of machine translation. In *Proceedings of the 40th Annual Meeting of the Association for Computational Linguistics*, pages 311–318, Philadelphia, PA, July.

Slav Petrov and Dan Klein. 2007. Improved inference for unlexicalized parsing. In *Proceedings of NAACL HLT 2007*, pages 404–411, Rochester, NY, April.

Matthew Snover, Bonnie Dorr, Richard Schwartz, Linnea Micciulla, and John Makhoul. 2006. A study of translation edit rate with targeted human annotation. In *Proceedings of the Seventh Conference of the Association for Machine Translation in the Americas*, pages 223–231, Cambridge, MA, August.

Omar F. Zaidan. 2009. Z-MERT: A fully configurable open source tool for minimum error rate training of machine translation systems. *The Prague Bulletin of Mathematical Linguistics*, 91:79–88.

Ventsislav Zhechev and Andy Way. 2008. Automatic generation of parallel treebanks. In *Proceedings of the 22nd International Conference on Computational Linguistics*, pages 1105–1112, Manchester, England, August.

Andreas Zollmann and Ashish Venugopal. 2006. Syntax augmented machine translation via chart parsing. In *Proceedings of the Workshop on Statistical Machine Translation*, pages 138–141, New York, NY, June.

Author Index